The
Campaign for Atlanta

&

Sherman's March to the Sea

Volume II

The
Campaign for Atlanta

&

Sherman's March to the Sea

———

Volume II

Essays on the
American Civil War In Georgia, 1864

series editors

Theodore P. Savas   &   David A. Woodbury

series editors
Theodore P. Savas & David A. Woodbury

*The Campaign for Atlanta
& Sherman's March to the Sea, volume II*

Includes bibliographical references and index

Copyright 1994 by Savas Woodbury Publishers
1475 S. Bascom Avenue, Suite 204, Campbell, California 95008

Maps copyright 1994
by Theodore P. Savas, David A. Woodbury,
and William R. Scaife

Printing Number
10 9 8 7 6 5 4 3 2 1

ISBN 1-882810-27-9
(first paperback edition)

This book is printed on sixty-pound
Glatfelter acid-free stock.

The paper in this book meets or exceeds the guidelines for permanence
and durability of the Committee on Production Guidelines for Book
Longevity of the Council on Library Resources

TABLE OF CONTENTS

Volume Two

List of Maps Volume Two

List of Illustrations Volume Two

List of Illustrations (continued)   Volume Two

Tables

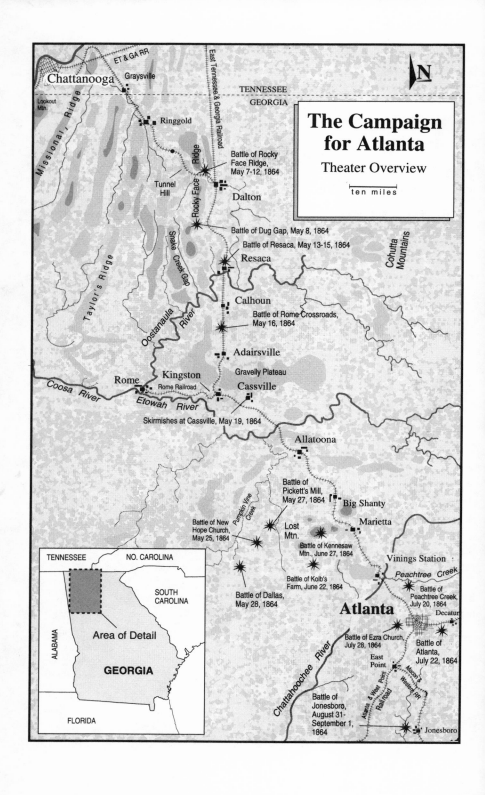

The Campaign for Atlanta

Theater Overview

ten miles

Chattanooga
Graysville
ET & GA RR
Lookout Mtn.
Missionary Ridge
East Tennessee & Georgia Railroad
TENNESSEE
GEORGIA
Ringgold
Tunnel Hill
Rocky Face Ridge
Battle of Rocky Face Ridge, May 7-12, 1864
Dalton
Cohutta Mountains
Snake Creek Gap
Taylor's Ridge
Battle of Dug Gap, May 8, 1864
Battle of Resaca, May 13-15, 1864
Resaca
Oostanaula River
Calhoun
Battle of Rome Crossroads, May 16, 1864
Adairsville
Rome
Kingston
Rome Railroad
Coosa River
Etowah River
Gravelly Plateau
Cassville
Skirmishes at Cassville, May 19, 1864
Allatoona
Battle of Pickett's Mill, May 27, 1864
Big Shanty
Pumpkin Vine Creek
Battle of New Hope Church, May 25, 1864
Lost Mtn.
Marietta
Battle of Kennesaw Mtn., June 27, 1864
Vinings Station
Peachtree Creek
Battle of Kolb's Farm, June 22, 1864
Battle of Dallas, May 28, 1864
Battle of Peachtree Creek, July 20, 1864
Atlanta
Decatur
Battle of Ezra Church, July 28, 1864
Battle of Atlanta, July 22, 1864
East Point
Chattahoochee River
Atlanta & West Point Railroad
Macon & Western RR
Battle of Jonesboro, August 31-September 1, 1864
Jonesboro

TENNESSEE
NO. CAROLINA
SOUTH CAROLINA
ALABAMA
Area of Detail
GEORGIA
FLORIDA

Editor's Preface

T*he Campaign for Atlanta & Sherman's March to the Sea,* volume
two, is a collection of original essays, the second in a series of
volumes which will comprehensively examine the Atlanta Campaign
and William T. Sherman's subsequent and devastating trek across Georgia. The scope of this project is not limited to the complicated series of
maneuvers and engagements which generally followed the Western &
Atlantic Railroad south from Chattanooga across the Chattahoochee
River into the city of Atlanta; nor does it encompass simply the cele-
brated march southeastward to Savannah. Important, but often ignored
events which took place on the periphery of the main drama—the opening stages of John Bell Hood's Tennessee Campaign, for example—will
be included in this series in order to better understand their relevance and
importance within the overall context of the Campaign for Atlanta, its
immediate aftermath, and the March to the Sea.

The eight monographs in this volume offer readers a chance to
sample the product of some of the finest modern research available on
the 1864 war in Georgia. These articles span a wide range of topics.
Three of these essays directly treat high-level command and leadership
issues in the campaign. Often argumentative, occasionally speculative,
and always provocative, readers will quickly discern that these treat-
ments of army commanders and their accomplishments (or lack thereof)
often disagree with accepted dogma on the subject. Readers who enjoy
discussions of tactics will find a detailed battle account included within
these pages which focuses on one encounter between the armies in late
May 1864. Army logistics and support services, although frequently

overlooked, must be appreciated in order to understand the evolution of any military campaign. This volume boasts two such essays, one dealing with issues of supply and the impact the Western & Atlantic Railroad had on the evolution of the campaign for Atlanta, and the second with Sherman's Pioneer Corps. The final two articles present a photographic essay on the early stages of the campaign, and a set of previously-unpublished Confederate regimental battle reports on the July 22, 1864 Battle for Atlanta. Each of these contributions deserves to be surveyed in greater detail.

Historian Richard McMurry leads off this volume of essays with an incisive disquisition of Joseph E. Johnston's Atlanta Campaign. As McMurry points out, Johnston was one of the most controversial generals of the Civil War, primarily because of his role in Georgia during the last full year of the conflict. McMurry, author of the award-winning *General John Bell Hood and the War for Southern Independence* (Knoxville, 1982), has written extensively on the Georgia campaign. His encyclopedic knowledge of this overlooked theater of operations is evident in *A Policy So Disastrous: Joseph E. Johnston's Atlanta Campaign*, which raises and critically examines a number of controversial issues surrounding Johnston's command tenure in Georgia. Was Johnston really as badly outnumbered during that summer of 1864 as he claimed in his postwar *Narrative of Military Operations*? Why has Johnston enjoyed such a high reputation among historians and military critics for more than a century after the end of the war? Did "Old Joe's" campaign across Georgia represent the work of a master military strategist, or did it reveal an incompetent, weak-willed general who was simply unwilling or unable to employ his army to full advantage? McMurry confronts his subject head-on, raising critical and often overlooked facts and issues with the skill and discrimination of a courtroom prosecutor. His lawyer-like consideration of Johnston's Atlanta Campaign is as convincing in its conclusions as it is artful in its presentation. It is sure to raise the ire of Johnston's supporters, though they will be hard-pressed to convincingly dispute McMurry's sound conclusions.

As its title implies, Philip Shiman's essay *Sherman's Pioneers in the Campaign to Atlanta*, illustrates the role of those intrepid Federal soldiers who were as adept with picks and shovels as with muskets and rifles. An admittedly esoteric area of study, Sherman's pioneers played a crucial role in the steady acquisition of Georgia real estate. Shiman, a graduate of Duke University with a taste for the obscure, explains how the pioneers were organized in each of Sherman's armies—and in many cases, they were not well-organized at all—and extolls their battlefield "victories" won with implements of a less lethal variety. Their ability to fortify hillsides, build bridges, and lay roads under the most trying of circumstances—and in many cases, under fire—was nothing short of amazing.

William R. Scaife, a veteran author of a number of Western Theater campaign studies, melds his historical avocation and considerable architectural talents in *Waltz Between the Rivers: An Overview of the Atlanta Campaign From the Oostanaula to the Etowah*. Scaife, an Atlanta native and a lifelong student of the Georgia campaigns, takes delight in pointing out that some very significant fighting and chess-like maneuvering took place south of the Oostanaula and north of the Etowah rivers. As he explains it, the important events that unfolded between the two crooked and meandering steams which eventually meet to form the Coosa River have been "all but lost to history." After Sherman moved south of the Oostanaula, the sizeable engagement that followed at Rome Crossroads prevented one of Sherman's armies from sweeping around the Confederate left and destroying its retreating train of supply wagons. Another spirited action north of Adairsville—this time under the command of hard-hitting and harder-drinking Confederate Maj. Gen. Benjamin F. Cheatham—purchased precious hours needed by Johnston to set a large-scale ambush at Cassville, which according to Scaife, "may have been [Johnston's] best opportunity of the campaign to strike an effective counter blow against Sherman." The tendency of many students of the conflict is to skip over this phase of the campaign altogether, a trend perhaps best explained by the fact that these events followed the potentially decisive face-to-face encounter between Sherman and Johnston around Resaca, and preceded the bitter and generally more interesting fighting along the Dallas-New Hope Church-Pickett's Mill line later in the month. Scaife weaves his article with threads taken from a variety of firsthand accounts, including after-action reports and memoirs. His mastery of the subject matter and thorough appreciation of the terrain between the rivers is reflected in both his insightful prose and his incomparable cartographic abilities, both of which grace the pages herein.

Dalton to Cartersville: Images of the Georgia Campaign, A Photographic Essay is an exciting addition to this second volume of *The Campaign for Atlanta.* Included are eleven contemporary photographs—most of which are previously unpublished—provided to us by Atlanta historian William E. Erquitt. Erquitt, who co-authored *The Chattahoochee River Line, An American Maginot* (Atlanta, 1991) with William R. Scaife, selected rare photos depicting scenes along the northern tier of the campaign. This selection provides us with a unique opportunity for some exceedingly uncommon views of the past, windows into the war-torn landscape of 1864 Georgia. Photos of a number of substantial structures in the town of Dalton, taken during the Federal occupation, dispel the image of that important center as a sleepy, backwoods railstop. Other highlights of the collection include both previously unpublished and seldom seen views of the battlefield at Resaca, and a rare view of the city of Rome, Georgia.

From Chattanooga to Atlanta, the two armies necessarily centered their movements on what one fellow termed the "crookedest road under the sun." In *The Western & Atlantic Railroad in the Campaign for Atlanta,* retired colonel James G. Bogle expounds on a railroad which was a logistical lifeline for both armies. The W&A funnelled troops and materiél to both sides of the northern Georgia battle lines and played an integral part in the strategic and tactical plans of generals Johnston, Sherman, and later, John Bell Hood. Colonel Bogle succinctly outlines the development and management of the railroad from its creation in 1836 to modern times, while examining in detail the critical role of the line in the 1864 campaign. No one, Bogle tells us, understood the importance of the railroad more than Sherman, who wrote after the war that "the Atlanta Campaign of 1864 would have been impossible without this road," and that "by reason of its existence, the Union was saved."

In *The Forgotten "Hell Hole": The Battle of Pickett's Mill, May 27, 1864,* former Pickett's Mill State Historic Site manager Jeff Dean presents a tactical close-up of one of the most horrific, but least known, battles of the campaign. In late May, Sherman—in a rare departure from the Western & Atlantic—left that railroad to bypass the strong Confederate position at Allatoona Pass. General Johnston moved his army to intercept and the result was a series of bloody and confused battles along what came to be called the "Dallas Line." Stopped cold at New Hope Church on May 25, Sherman sent a 14,000-man force under Maj. Gen. Oliver O. Howard through the thick woods in search of the Confederate right. Where Howard expected to meet the enemy flank, he found instead the redeployed division of the indomitable Patrick Cleburne, the best division commander in the Army of Tennessee. Dean skillfully relates a moment-by-moment account of the resulting clash, a battle that Federal Brig. Gen. William B. Hazen called "the most fierce, bloody, and persistent assault by our troops in the Atlanta Campaign." Relying heavily on official reports and participant's reminiscences—including the inimitable prose of Lt. Ambrose Bierce who, as a member of Hazen's staff, flatly pronounced the Federal assault "a criminal blunder"—Dean brings forth the horror and confusion of this savage encounter in a compelling narrative. Along with a command of the available sources, Dean brings to the article an indispensable familiarity with the lay of the land, essential to any meaningful understanding of events as chaotic as the combat at Pickett's Mill. The four "phase" maps accompanying Dean's article help to illuminate the unfolding Union debacle. By the time the fighting at Pickett's Mill was over, three Federal brigades were badly mauled in a brutal, lopsided fight that, oddly enough, goes without mention in either Sherman's official report or his memoirs. With this article, Jeff Dean takes pains to mention what General Sherman failed to tell us.

Dean's tactically-insightful essay is followed by Charles Edmund Vetter's wholly dissimilar but equally interesting monograph *From Atlanta to Savannah: A Sociological Perspective of William T. Sherman's March Through Georgia*. Vetter, a professor of sociology at Centenary College in Shreveport, Louisiana, examines Sherman's motives for crossing Georgia to the Atlantic coast and the consequent sociological results of that devastating raid. "One of the overlooked effects of Sherman's March was that it contributed to the creation of a social revolution in the South," concludes Vetter, since "Secession and the War had made it impossible to go back to the way things were." The March completely disrupted thousands of Southern families, left entire communities destroyed or in disarray, and cast their inhabitants adrift in the cauldron of war. Vetter, author of the acclaimed and controversial *Sherman: Merchant of Terror, Advocate of Peace* (Pelican, 1992), holds that the sociological impact of Sherman's March has been either largely ignored or simply assumed, since emphasis has been heavily placed on the economic and psychological results of his expedition from Atlanta to Savannah. Although many students of the Civil War consider Sherman a barbarian, Vetter, with considerable thoughtfulness, concludes otherwise. As with Richard McMurry's scathing indictment of Joseph E. Johnston, only the most apathetic readers will register indifference after digesting Vetter's essay.

Students of the Atlanta Campaign have long lamented the absence of scores of Confederate battle reports from the *Official Records*. In many cases, these reports were either never written or were destroyed during the war's final days. Some reports survived the conflict but, for various reasons, failed to surface during the efforts to compile the *Offical Records*. Closing out this assemblage of essays is *Lines of Battle: The Unpublished Reports of Confederate Brig. Gen. James Holtzclaw's Brigade*, edited by Zack Waters. This collection contains four after-action accounts of the ignored and all-but-forgotten advance and bloody repulse of Holtzclaw's regiments just north of the scene of Arthur Manigault's spectacular capture of Francis De Gress' Union guns during the July 22 Battle of Atlanta. These reports, penned by Col. Bush Jones (who commanded the brigade during Holtzclaw's unexplained absence) and three subordinate regimental commanders, shed considerable light on why the Confederate assault above the Georgia Railroad failed that afternoon. Waters, who teaches school in Rome, Georgia, presents an enriching introduction to these reports by offering readers a thoughtful and informative prologue to the personalities and commands that suffered so heavily during John Bell Hood's second Atlanta sortie. In a text paced for maximum effect and accompanied by the first map ever published detailing the advance of Holtzclaw's Brigade, Waters follows the careers of the men and regiments up to the moment they step off from the safety of the woods into the open, swampy land in their front. After that, the reports speak for themselves.

*   *   *

ACKNOWLEDGMENTS: As with every full-length work, this one could not have been put together without the assistance of many people. It was a pleasure working with the authors appearing in these pages, all of whom are making (or have already made) lasting contributions to our understanding of the war in the West.

Although it is virtually impossible to mention the names of everyone that had a hand in the creation of *The Campaign for Atlanta* (you know who you are), we would be negligent if we did not mention those that assisted with various aspects of this lengthy project on a regular basis: the always cheerful and cooperative David Lang of Sunnyvale, California who, in addition to assisting with portions of the design of this book, exorcised more than a few computer demons during the early morning hours for two editors often at their wit's end; Michael L. DeVivo, San Jose, California, for his willingness to check citations and index this behemoth; and Lee Merideth, of Sunnyvale, California, whose unyielding optimism, even in the face of significant opposition, makes all goals seem attainable. We would also like to thank Edwin C. Bearss, chief historian for the National Park Service, for taking the time to read over the manuscripts and make valuable suggestions which substantially improved this collection. His knowledge of the Civil War is unparalleled.

We would, of course, be remiss—and undoubtedly in serious trouble—if we concluded this acknowledgement without mentioning the unselfish attitudes of our respective wives when it came time to part with their husbands virtually every weekend in the name of furthering the study of the Civil War, and for their (usually) cheerful encouragement during the long and slow birth of this book.

Theodore P. Savas

David A. Woodbury

A Policy So Disastrous
Joseph E. Johnston's Atlanta Campaign

Richard M. McMurry

In December 1863 Jefferson Davis made one of the most fateful deci-
sions of his four-year stint as president of the Confederate States of
America. Acting with great reluctance, Davis selected Gen. Joseph Eg-
gleston Johnston to command the Army of Tennessee. This ill-starred
choice put Johnston at the head of the Confederacy's most important
field army during the crucial early months of the 1864 military operations that were to decide the fate of the Southern nation.

Davis' reluctance to appoint Johnston the Army of Tennessee's new
commander stemmed from personal, political, and professional factors.
In 1861 the two men had fallen into a bitter quarrel over Johnston's rank
in the Southern army. The general interpreted Confederate law to mean
that he was the highest-ranking Rebel military officer. Davis, however,
placed Johnston fourth in rank. To the thin-skinned Johnston the president's action was a personal insult, and he responded with a carping,
childish, belligerent protest. Davis, whose epidermis was no thicker than
Johnston's, replied in kind. The quarrel over rank was soon exacerbated
by differences over army organization, supplies, military transportation,

and strategy. Not very important in themselves, these differences served as irritants and made an unhappy relationship even more troubled.

Gen. Joseph E. Johnston

In 1862 while recuperating from a wound, Johnston had openly befriended and allied himself with Louis T. Wigfall, a senator from Texas and the Davis Administration's most hostile and intransigent political critic. In the following year Davis had sent Johnston to Mississippi to direct the attempt to save Vicksburg. The failure of that effort and the bitter recriminations that followed sent relations between the president and the general plummeting to new lows.

By the late summer of 1863 Davis had become convinced that Johnston was a timid, over-cautious general who would not fight. Rather than take action that might put his reputation at risk, Johnston would allow the Confederacy to be destroyed. On the other hand, Johnston had come to see himself as a martyr who was to be sacrificed on the altar of the president's hatred and incompetence. The general and his coterie believed that Davis and his sycophants were pursuing a misguided policy that inevitably would lead to Confederate defeat. To satisfy their hatred and protect their own reputations, Davis and his lackeys were scheming to blame the defeat on Johnston and even to bring about the general's disgrace on the battlefield. To that end, they denied Johnston adequate manpower and sought to push him into unwise and even foolish operations. So far did this feeling extend that Johnston, in fact, was at least mildly paranoid about his relations with the government.[1]

In December 1863 Davis had to select a new commander for the Army of Tennessee. Under its former chief, Gen. Braxton Bragg, the army had degenerated into squabbling pro-Bragg and anti-Bragg factions. In November 1863 the divided and demoralized army had been routed at Missionary Ridge and driven away from Chattanooga. Bragg gave up the command, and Davis began the search for his replacement.[2]

The president faced a bleak situation. The Confederacy's shortage of men competent to command large bodies of troops was painfully obvious. In all of Rebeldom there were only four officers of appropriate grade to replace Bragg and head a major army, and only one of them— Gen. Robert E. Lee—had ever demonstrated either much ability as an army commander or a willingness to cooperate with the government. Even had Davis desired to dip into the large pool of lower-ranking officers, there were none who had demonstrated, and but few who had even given much inkling of, an aptitude for high level, independent command. Johnston, however, was a brave man and an experienced officer who was widely regarded as a well-qualified general despite his lack of accomplishment as a field commander. From all directions came a demand that he be named to replace Bragg. Because he felt he had no

---

[1] For the Davis-Johnston feud, see Richard M. McMurry, "'The Enemy at Richmond': Joseph E. Johnston and the Confederate Government," *Civil War History*, 27 (1981), pp. 5-31. The most recent biographers of the two principals deal with the quarrel in Craig L. Symonds, *Joseph E. Johnston: A Civil War Biography* (New York, 1992), pp. 125-139, 191-226, and passim; and William C. Davis, *Jefferson Davis: The Man and his Hour: A Biography* (New York, 1991), pp. 356-361, 501-504, 509-514, and *passim*. There are other very perceptive comments on the squabble in Steven E. Woodworth, *Jefferson Davis and His Generals: The Failure of Confederate Command in the West* (Lawrence, 1990), pp. 173-185 and 196-221, and throughout Jeffrey N. Lash, *Destroyer of the Iron Horse: General Joseph E. Johnston and Confederate Rail Transport, 1861-1865* (Kent, 1991).

[2] For excellent coverage of the sorry command situation that existed in the Rebels' chief Western army see Thomas Lawrence Connelly, *Army of the Heartland: The Army of Tennessee, 1861-1862*, and *Autumn of Glory: The Army of Tennessee, 1862-1865* (Baton Rouge, 1967, 1971).

other real choice, Davis eventually yielded to the clamor and on December 16 ordered Johnston from his post in Mississippi to Dalton, Georgia, to take command of the Army of Tennessee.[3]

Johnston arrived in Dalton late on December 26, and on the following day he took up his new duties. He found his command to be an army broken in spirit, weakened in both numbers and equipment, and suffering from shortages of food, shoes, blankets, and clothing. As soldiers, the men of the army had known nothing but defeat. In the war's first three years they had been driven from Missouri and Kentucky and chased across Mississippi and Tennessee into northern Georgia. In December 1863 they were huddled in their winter camps about Dalton. During the next four months Johnston did a remarkable job. He rebuilt the army's morale and secured for it additional supplies, uniforms, weapons, and other equipment. By almost all accounts his labors won for him the affection and even the devotion of his troops. "Old Joe," they came to believe, would provide and care for them. When the campaign opened in the spring of 1864, most of them had concluded that in Johnston they at long last had a general who would lead them to victory.[4]

Through May, June, and the first half of July, however, Johnston fell back into Georgia before the advancing Yankee force of Maj. Gen. William T. Sherman. Johnston maintained—then and later—that he was so outnumbered that Sherman was always able to pin him in position with a force as large as the Army of Tennessee and swing an equally large body of troops around to the east or west to threaten the Confederates' line of supply. Unable to detach sufficient men to defeat these flanking movements, Johnston claimed, he then had no choice but to retreat. By mid-

[3] Davis' decision is discussed in Symonds, *Johnston*, p. 248; Davis, *Jefferson Davis*, pp. 528-531; and Albert Castel, *Decision in the West:The Atlanta Campaian of 1864* (Lawrence, 1992), pp. 28-30. Steven E. Woodworth in "A Reassessment of Confederate Command Options During the Winter of 1863-1864"—a part of this collection—argues that Davis had several other choices. In the sense that he had the authority to name someone else he, of course, did, but I question how realistic those options were. I hope to explore the matter in a future essay.

[4] For Johnston's efforts to rebuild the army, see Symonds, *Johnston*, pp. 249-268; and Larry J. Daniel, *Soldiering in the Army of Tennessee: A Portrait of Life in a Confederate Army* (Chapel Hill, 1991), passim.

summer Johnston had fallen back to the outskirts of Atlanta. On July 17 Davis removed him from command of the army and named newly-promoted Gen. John Bell Hood as his replacement. In the first two weeks of his command Hood lashed out at Sherman, suffering battlefield reverses and sizable losses but also slowing the hitherto inexorable Yankee advance. In late August, however, Sherman managed to cut the last railroads into Atlanta, and Hood was compelled to give up the city.[5]

Johnston was by all odds the most controversial of the Confederacy's high-ranking military figures. He has been portrayed as everything from the most brilliant and far-sighted of Rebel generals to a timid poltroon more concerned about his personal reputation than with his country's cause. His status among Confederate commanders, as Craig Symonds, his most recent biographer points out, is based "primarily on his conduct of the campaign in northern Georgia during the spring and summer of 1864."[6] Evaluating Johnston's conduct of that campaign, however, is not a simple task. For a century after the Civil War, Johnston enjoyed a high reputation among historians and military critics. This elevated standing was based mainly on four (for Johnston, fortuitous) circumstances that, in fact, had nothing to do with the general's 1864 military operations. For one thing, Johnston was extremely lucky in the fact that he succeeded Bragg and preceded Hood in command of the Army of Tennessee. Those two officers were among the less competent generals tossed up by the war. Bragg was also burdened with a thoroughly wretched personality. He and Hood suffered spectacular defeats in the Perryville, Stones River, Chattanooga, Atlanta, and Franklin and Nashville campaigns. Their failures were so visible that even historians were able to spot them. Johnston, bracketed by Bragg and Hood, took on the appearance of a competent general. A man who is five feet, five inches tall is a giant among pygmies.

---

[5] The best account of the campaign—by far—is Castel's *Decision In the West*. Johnston's view of events is in his official report, dated October 20, 1864, in U. S. War Department, *The War of the Rebellion: A Compilation of the Official Records of the Union and Confederate Armies*, 128 vols. (Washington, 1880-1901), series I, volume 38, pt. 3, pp. 612-621. Hereinafter cited as *OR*. All references are to series I. See also, Joseph E. Johnston, *Narrative of Military Operations Directed During the Late War Between the States* (Bloomington, 1959), pp. 262-370.

[6] Symonds, *Johnston*, p. 269.

The second factor that for many decades helped to prop up Johnston's reputation was the relative neglect by students of the war of the western generals, armies, battles, and campaigns. Until the late 1960s most of those writing Civil War military history tended to devote the bulk of their time and energy to the operations in Virginia. They told and retold in minute detail the story of the 1862 Shenandoah Valley Campaign and produced massive books recounting the hour-by-hour movements of every regiment, battalion, and battery that was engaged at Chancellorsville, or Gettysburg, or any of the other great battles in the East. In such an environment western battles and campaigns usually received superficial treatment, and the generals' conduct of operations was not subjected to critical study. The Rebels had suffered no obvious and visible major defeat during Johnston's 1864 tenure. His reputation flourished in this climate of relative neglect.

The third factor that once worked to elevate Johnston's reputation was the fact that for a century and more after 1865 the military history of the war in general and that of the western campaigns in particular was based almost exclusively on three sources—the unreliable, self-serving official after-action reports submitted by the generals; the equally unreliable and self-serving postwar memoirs written by those same generals; and the romanticized, untrustworthy reminiscences penned by old veterans. These published sources were easily available, and lazy historians found it more convenient to use them than to traipse across the country in search of more reliable, but widely-scattered contemporary letters, telegrams, and diaries.

Scholars who confine their research to the writings of a particular general will quickly conclude that that general was a brilliant commander and that any defeats he may have suffered were the faults of others. The result is even more complete when the research is limited to the general's after-the-fact accounts. Postwar writings by enlisted men are no better. The old veterans often remembered things that never happened, penned exaggerated and romanticized accounts of many of those that had, wrote even the valid parts of their memoirs with the benefit of hindsight, and generally produced works of very limited value. No Civil War general's reputation benefited more from the use of these unreliable sources than did that of Joseph E. Johnston.

Finally, and ironically, Johnston's reputation soared because of an action taken by his archenemy Jefferson Davis. The president removed Johnston from command of the army before the results of the general's campaign had become obvious. The fact that Hood lost Atlanta while following a policy different from that pursued by Johnston served to solidify the latter's reputation. In this atmosphere those who believe Johnston to have been a great general can dogmatically assert that he would never have lost Atlanta, and no one can prove that they are wrong. With a faith equaled only by that of Islamic zealots, they maintain that Davis removed their hero from the head of the army just as he was about to smite the Yankees hip and thigh. Had Johnston remained in command of the Army of Tennessee, they pontificate, he would have defeated Sherman, smashed the Federal army, chased the Unionists out of Georgia, driven them into Hudson Bay, and won victory and independence for the Confederacy. It is this simple, religious-like faith that makes many of Johnston's adherents so uncompromising in their beliefs. Calvin Coolidge and Ronald Reagan dodged blame for the economic troubles that beset their successors Herbert Hoover and George Bush. In like manner Johnston escaped responsibility for the fall of Atlanta which occurred while Hood commanded the army. Hood's fiancee, Sally Buchanan Campbell Preston, put it best. When she heard of the change of commanders at Atlanta she said, "Things are so bad out there. They cannot be worse. . . .And so they have saved Johnston from the responsibility of his own blunders—and put. . .[Hood] in. Poor . . .[Hood]!"[7]

The second and third factors listed above—the relative neglect of the West and an over-reliance on postwar accounts—are the more important reasons for the high standing that Johnston has enjoyed among many students of the Civil War. A few examples will illustrate how Johnston

---

[7] The "traditional" view of Johnston's campaign is to be found in his own writings (see note 5) and—in full-blown form in Allen Phelps Julian, "From Dalton to Atlanta—Sherman vs. Johnston," *Civil War Times Illustrated*, Vol. 3, No. 4 (July 1964), pp. 4-7, 34-39; and Gilbert E. Govan and James W. Livingood, *A Different Valor: The Story of General Joseph E. Johnston, C. S. A.* (Indianapolis, 1956), pp. 240-322. Symonds, in *Johnston*, pp. 249-335, is much less hagiographical, but he too accepts many of Johnston's self-serving statements at something approaching face value. Buck Preston's comment is in Mary Boykin Chesnut, *Mary Chesnut's Civil War,* edited by C. Vann Woodward (New Haven, 1981), p. 622. Preston used Hood's nickname "Sam," and not his last name.

has benefited from the willingness of historians to accept uncritically the unsubstantiated assertions found in after-the-fact writings. In his memoirs, *Narrative of Military Operations Directed During the Late War Between the States*, published in 1874, Johnston made certain claims about the strength and losses of his army and those of the Federals and about the morale of his own troops as he fell back across northern Georgia in May, June, and July 1864.

In his *Narrative*, Johnston asserted that his "entire strength. . .'at and near Dalton'" (which he also called his "effective Strength") on May 1 was 42,854. (See Table One on facing page.) Many of Johnston's disciples have uncritically accepted this number and used it as the Confederate strength for the campaign. In early May 1864, Johnston claimed, Sherman's force outnumberd his army by "almost three to one."[8]

If one reads carefully through Johnston's text, however, one learns that more Confederate troops soon joined the Army of Tennessee. In fact, many of them were with it on May 1 and were not included in Johnston's count. As Table One indicates, Johnston himself admitted to—but nowhere clearly stated that he had—a total "effective strength" of 63,059 in the campaign. Even this number, however, is too low, for as Johnston confessed, it does not included the brigade of Brig. Gen. Hugh W. Mercer that joined the army in early May. The total also excludes the Georgia state forces that reinforced the Army of Tennessee during the campaign. Those two commands probably totaled at least 4,500 men.

In truth, Johnston's army was considerably larger than he ever admitted and than most historians have acknowledged. Use of the "effective strength" figure is misleading. It is a minimum number. It excludes all officers and all enlisted men who were not physically present with their regiments or batteries and equipped for service at the time the report was compiled. A cavalryman temporarily without a mount because his horse had thrown a shoe was not considered to be "effective." An artilleryman who had gone on sick call to receive treatment for a minor injury was not counted as "effective." An infantryman detailed for a day or two as a headquarters guard or as a hospital orderly was also ex-

---

[8] Johnston, *Narrative*, pp. 302, 315.

TABLE ONE		
Confederate Strength in the Atlanta Campaign as Presented in General Joseph E. Johnston's Memoirs		
Date Joined	**Force/Command**	**"Effective Strength"** [a]
May 1, 1864	The army "at and near Dalton"	42,854[b]
May 7, 1864	Brig. Gen. James Cantey's Division	1,605[c]
May 9, 1864	Maj. Gen. W. T. Martin's Cavalry Division	3,500[d]
May 11, 1864	Maj. Gen. William W. Loring's Division	5,000[e]
May 17, 1864	Brig. Gen. W. H. Jackson's Cavalry Division	3,900[f]
May 18, 1864	Maj. Gen. Samuel G. French's Division	4,000[g]
May 26, 1864	Brig. Gen. William A. Quarles' Brigade	2,200[h]
Total "effective strength" as admitted by General Johnston		63,059[i]

[a] Johnston, *Narrative*, p. 302. Johnston chose to present the "effective strength" of his forces. "Effective strength" consisted of enlisted men, present for duty, equipped. It excluded officers, men detailed as couriers or headquarters guards, men who had lost their weapons, and men who had gone on sick call on the date of the report. The result of using the "effective strength" figure was to give the lowest possible strength for the Rebel forces.

[b] Johnston, *Narrative*, p. 302. Johnston gave two figures for his "effective" cavalry on May 1: 2,392 (pp. 302, 352) and 2,390 (p. 354). I have used the lower number.

[c] Johnston maintained (*Narrative*, p. 302) that 1,395 men of Cantey's command were included in the 42,854 total. The document on which Johnston relied for his data indicates that Cantey's Division had some 3,000 "effectives." Ibid., p. 574.

[d] Johnston, *Narrative*, p. 352.

[e] Ibid., pp. 308, 352.

[f] Ibid., p. 353.

[g] Ibid., pp. 321, 352.

[h] Ibid., p. 352.

[i] The total omits the brigade of Brig. Gen. H. W. Mercer (ibid., p. 302) and the Georgia State forces that Johnston admits joined his army but for which he gives no strength figures. (ibid., pp. 332, 344).

cluded. All such men, however, were "present for duty" with the army
and could have been used to meet an enemy threat.

Even Johnston's "effective total" is highly suspect. What did he
mean by the qualification "at and near Dalton?" Even if he excluded
units posted ten or twenty miles away, those troops were under his
command and could have been moved to Dalton or to any other point
where he thought they were needed. At the opening of the campaign, for
example, he had two infantry regiments stationed at Dug Gap a short
distance southwest of Dalton. Are those units included in his total? We
do not know. Compare the data from Johnston's 1874 *Narrative* with
those from his April 30, 1864 strength report shown in Table Two (note
that the "effective" total in Tables Two and Three is always lower than
the number of enlisted men who were present and performing duty).

The April 30 report excluded Maj. Gen. W. T. Martin's Cavalry
Division, two additional brigades of cavalry, and more than three batteries of artillery for which no reports had been received. If these un-
counted units had an "effective" strength of only 5,000 men—Johnston
put that of the missing cavalry division alone at 3,500—see Table One—
then the April 30 "effective" total was 50,101. Adding these same 5,000
"effectives" to the reported "present for duty" strength raises the total to
59,500. It is impossible to escape the conclusion that Johnston on April
30, 1864 had some 60,000 officers and men present, subject to his orders, able to perform duty, and available for combat.

If Johnston was able to muster only 42,854 of these soldiers for
battle on May 1, what does it mean? What happened to the 2,247 men
who were "effective" on April 30 but not on May 1? Was there some
hitherto unknown engagement during the night of April 30-May 1 in
which the Army of Tennessee suffered 2,247 casualties? (More likely the
missing men are explained by the error referred to in note f, Table Two,
on page 227.)

If Johnston could get only 71.4 percent of his force to be "effective,"
can he be called an effective—or efficient—commander? Or did
Johnston simply use the 42,854 figure to make his force seem as small as
possible so as to excuse his failure to accomplish anything with it?
Students of the campaign must answer these questions for themselves,
but even Johnston's most fanatical disciples must answer them. We can

TABLE TWO			
Strength of General Johnston's Army as Reported on April 30, 1864[a]			
	Present for Duty		
Command	Officers	Enlisted Men	"Effective"
Army Headquarters	42	599	596
Lt. Gen. William J. Hardee's Corps	2,066	19, 881	19,311
Lt. Gen. John B. Hood's Corps	1,633	19,677	19,201
Cavalry Corps[b]	735[b]	7,327[b]	2,419[b]
Cantey's Brigade[c]	65	1,578	1,543
37th Mississippi Regiment[d]			400[d]
Artillery Reserves	48	849	817
63rd Georgia Regiment[e]		814	
TOTALS:	4,589	49,911	45,101[f]
Total "Present for Duty": 54,500			

[a] *OR* 38, pt. 3, pp. 675-676.

[b] Does not include Martin's cavalry division which was not reported. Nor do these figures include the brigades of Cols. George C. Dibrell and Thomas H. Harrison which were in the rear recruiting horses. They also exclude more than three batteries of the Cavalry Corps artillery for the same reason (Huwald's Tennessee Battery, White's Tennessee Battery, and Wiggins' Arkansas Battery, as well as all but one section of Ferrell's Georgia Battery).

[c] Joined from District of the Gulf and camped at Rome, Georgia, where Johnston was expecting a Federal attack. See Table One, note c.

[d] Of Cantey's Brigade, but excluded from above. Effective strength estimated.

[e] Joined the army soon after report compiled.

[f] In a postwar article, Johnston said that the effective total on the April 30 report had later been "corrected" to the 42,854 figure that he used in his postwar writings. See his "Opposing Sherman's Advance to Atlanta," in Robert U. Johnson and Clarence C. Buel (eds.), *Battles and Leaders of the Civil War*, 4 vols. (New York, 1956), vol. 4, p. 261. The difference is not great enough to change significantly the argument in this paper.

no longer simply accept on faith Johnston's self-serving claims as to how weak his army was. (See Table Three on facing page.)

Soon after the campaign began Johnston's army was reinforced by a massive infusion of troops taken from the Rebel forces in Mississippi and other areas. This reinforcement was the largest inter-departmental transfer of troops in Confederate history. The additional men became a third corps and an independent cavalry division in Johnston's army. The new corps was commanded by Lt. Gen. Leonidas Polk; the new cavalry division by Brig. Gen. William H. "Red" Jackson. These units are listed in Table One as Cantey's, Loring's, Jackson's, French's, and Quarles' troops.) In his *Narrative*, Johnston put these reinforcements at 18,101 "effectives." In truth, however, they numbered more than 20,000 "effectives" and more than 22,000 "present for duty." (In Table Three they are shown as Polk's Corps and Jackson's cavalry division.)

To the totals shown for these units in Table Three we must add the losses they had suffered between the time they joined the army and June 10 when the report reflected in Table Three was compiled. In his *Narrative* Johnston admitted that the infantry divisions brought from Mississippi lost 686 killed and wounded up to June 10. If Jackson's cavalry division lost 69 men killed and wounded during that time—and one of its brigades is known to have lost at least 170—then Johnston received 20,000 "effective" reinforcements from Mississippi. (This statement assumes that all men who became casualties were "effective.")[9] If we add Johnston's admitted killed and wounded in his infantry and artillery up to June 10, and the killed and wounded that he acknowledged in part of his cavalry in May—a figure that he put at 5,807—to his "effective total" on June 10, we arrive at a total "effective strength" of 66,371.[10] If we add Johnston's admitted killed and wounded to the June 10 "present for duty" strength, the total is 75,753. To these totals we must also add the killed and wounded in Jackson's cavalry division up to June 10 and in the Cavalry Corps in the first ten days of June as well as the men who were captured at Rocky Face Ridge, Dalton, Resaca, on the retreat from

---

[9] Ibid., pp. 325, 335; Jackson's casualty faigures (one brigade) in *Memphis Daily Appeal* (published in Atlanta), June 2, 1864.

[10] Johnston, *Narrative*, pp. 325, 335.

TABLE THREE			
Strength of Johnston's Army As Reported June 10 1864[a]			
	Present for Duty		
Command	**Officers**	**Enlisted Men**	**"Effective"**
Army Headquarters	44	611	608
Lt. Gen. William J. Hardee's Corps	2,142	18,599	18,035
Lt. Gen. John B. Hood's Corps	1,582	15,797	15,332
Lt. Gen. Leonidas Polk's Corps[b]	1,486	15,052	14,708
Cavalry Corps	776	7,700	6,366
Brig. Gen. William H. Jackson's Cavalry Division[b]	442	4,628	4,537
Artillery Reserve	66	1,021	978
Total:	6,538	63,408	60,564
Total Present for Duty:	**69,946**		

[a] *OR* 38, pt. 3, pp. 676-677.

[b] Polk's Corps and Jackson's cavalry division were sometimes lumped together as the "Army of Mississippi." Another report (ibid., p. 677) gives slightly different totals for them: 1,917 officers and 19,630 enlisted men "present for duty"; 19,244 "effectives."

the Oostanaula to the Etowah, and in the fighting near New Hope Church. Incomplete Federal reports show that 1,829 Rebel prisoners of war were processed through June 4.[11] Adding that number to the above totals gives us Johnston's strength as 68,200 "effectives"; 77,582 "present for duty." These numbers still exclude most of the killed and wounded in Jackson's cavalry division and all men who deserted as well as the prisoners captured between the 5th and 10th of June. In summary, it is clear that Johnston had close to 70,000 "effectives" without counting the state troops who joined him in late June. The far more meaningful "present for duty" strength of his army approached, if it did not exceed, 80,000. His force in the Atlanta Campaign was the second or third largest army that the Confederacy put into the field. It was exceeded in numerical strength only by Robert E. Lee's army of 85,000 in the Seven Days Battles and possibly by Lee's force of about 80,000 at Fredericksburg.[12]

Sherman's force in Johnston's front numbered 110,123 officers and men on April 30, 1864.[13] Johnston's "effective total" on April 30 was 41 percent of the Yankee force in his front. His more meaningful "present for duty" strength was 49.5 percent of Sherman's. Johnston's June 10 "effective strength" was 53.7 percent of Sherman's May 31 force. Rebel "present for duty" strength on June 10 was 62 percent of Sherman's May 31 strength. Johnston was outnumbered—but never by the almost three-to-one margin that he claimed in his *Narrative*. Sherman's force on May 31 was 1.61 times as large as Johnston's "present for duty" strength on June 10 and about 1.86 times larger than the Confederate "effective total" on that date. The strength of Johnston's force relative to that of the enemy in its front was typical for a Confederate army. At the beginning of the 1864 campaign the Rebel army in Virginia, some 60,000 men under Robert E. Lee, opposed a 120,000-man Union army. Whatever his

---

[11] *OR* 38, pt. 1, p. 147.

[12] For an early (and usually ignored) discussion of Johnston's strength see E. C. Dawes, "The Confederate Strength in the Atlanta Campaign," *Battles and Leaders of the Civil War*, 4, pp. 281-283. Dawes concluded that Johnston had a total strength of "at least" 84,328 men.

[13] *OR* 38, pt. 1, pp. 115, 117.

personal feelings toward Johnston, it is clear that Jefferson Davis did not stint in furnishing his western commander with troops.

Johnston's claims regarding casualties in the campaign are as unreliable as those he made about his army's strength. Under his command, Johnston asserted, the Army of Tennessee waged a defensive campaign and lost only 9,972 men killed and wounded. This figure, however, is only for the three infantry corps of the army (which included most of the artillery). The number excludes all losses in the cavalry and state forces and all prisoners lost by the army. (At another point in his *Narrative*, Johnston admitted the loss of about 250 prisoners—"the only prisoners taken from us during this campaign that I heard of.") Sherman's forces, Johnston claimed, lost 60,000 men killed and wounded during the period up to the night of July 17.[14] In truth, Johnston's army suffered considerably more casualties than he acknowledged. We must add these additional losses to his admitted 9,972 killed and wounded in his infantry and artillery to get a true figure. The cavalry's losses can be estimated at at least 1,200.[15] Federal reports indicate that the Federals processed 4,278 Confederate prisoners and deserters in May and June.[16] These very conservative estimates, it should be noted, exclude large numbers of deserters who went home rather than to the enemy.

Johnston's total losses—killed, wounded, and missing—thus come to at least 15,450. This total excludes the many prisoners and deserters lost in early July when Johnston abandoned three strong positions at Kennesaw Mountain, Smyrna Campground, and along the Chattahoochee River, as well as all losses in the Confederate cavalry in the first two and one half weeks of July. Sherman's casualties were reported in such a way as to make direct comparison with those of the Rebels impossible. For the entire campaign (May through August) the Yankees

[14] Johnston, *Narrative*, pp. 354, 356-357.

[15] General Joseph Wheeler, commanding Johnston's Cavalry Corps, wrote to Gen. Braxton Bragg on July 1 that he had lost 1,000 men up to that time; the adjutant of one brigade of Jackson's Division (not part of Wheeler's command) reported on May 30 that his brigade had lost 170. Wheeler letter in Bragg Papers, Western Reserve Historical Society; other casualties in *Memphis Daily Appeal*, June 2, 1864.

[16] *OR* 38, pt. 1, pp. 147, 153.

lost 34,523 killed, wounded, and captured.[17] If Sherman lost 20,000 of those men during the time that Johnston commanded the Confederates, he lost 18 percent of the force he had on April 30. Johnston's 15,450 casualties constituted 36 percent of his claimed "effective total at and near Dalton" on May 1; 34.3 percent of the "effective total" he reported on April 30; 24.5 percent of Johnston's admitted "effective strength" for the campaign; 25.5 percent of his "effectives" reported on June 10; and 22.1 percent of his "present for duty" strength on June 10. Even if one thinks Johnston's army to have totaled 80,000 men, his known losses come to more than 19.3 percent of his force. The conclusion is inescapable. No matter which number one accepts for Confederate strength, the Rebel army suffered proportionally more losses than did Sherman's force during the period that Johnston commanded the Southerners.

The second example concerns the morale of Johnston's army. Were his men demoralized by the long retreat from Dalton to Atlanta? Both logic and experience would seem to indicate that the soldiers would have suffered demoralization as the army continually fell back. In his *Narrative*, Johnston asserted that at the time he was removed from command the troops were "full of devotion to him who had commanded them, and belief in ultimate success in the campaign" and were "more confident and high-spirited" than they had been in early May at the beginning of the spring's operations. The men, he maintained, realized that they faced overwhelming numbers and therefore understood the necessity for the constant retreats. They believed that when the time came Johnston would turn upon Sherman and annihilate his army. To substantiate this claim, Johnston quoted postwar letters from two of his former corps commanders.[18]

For decades most of those who wrote about the campaign accepted Johnston's assertions without question, sometimes buttressing their position with quotations from the postwar accounts of one or two enlisted men—accounts, of course, written with full knowledge of the disasters that befell the Rebels after Johnston left the army. From time to time

---

[17] Ibid., p. 85. Federal casualties were reported by the month. Thousands more men in both armies were lost to sickness. They are not included in any of these figures.

[18] Johnston, *Narrative*, pp. 351, 365-369.

some diligent scholar would unearth a quotation from a contemporary letter or diary that supported Johnston's position.[19]

Not until 1970 did any historian publish the results of a systematic study of Confederate morale in the Atlanta Campaign. After an extensive survey of letters and diaries written during the campaign, he found overwhelming evidence that a substantial—but indeterminable—percentage of Rebel soldiers lost faith in Johnston and became demoralized as the campaign went on and the army continued its long retreat.

A 1991 survey by the historian Larry Daniel led to the same conclusion. Daniel writes of Johnston's men that "a significant minority questioned his strategy as the month [May] wore on and he fell back from one position to another." By July, states Daniel, "there was a noticeable decline in confidence in Johnston's leadership" and "many were questioning or opposing Johnston's leadership." These two studies make it clear that Johnston's constant retreats sapped the morale of many of his soldiers. Some of these men were among those who deserted and went home or to the Federals. Others allowed themselves to be captured. In writing of the battle of Resaca (May 13-15), one Northern soldier observed, "In this battle for the first time in my experience, Confederate soldiers who might have escaped came in and gave themselves up as prisoners." Still other dispirited men remained with the army and confided their opinions to their letters and diaries.

After the war, however, virtually all of those who published memoirs of their military service claimed that Johnston's retreat to Atlanta had not impaired morale. For many men, of course, it had not, but it is obvious that for many others it did. "Clearly," concluded Daniel, "those who claim that Johnston's retreats did not adversely affect morale do so in the face of significant evidence to the contrary. . . ."[20]

---

[19] See, for example, Bell I. Wiley's classic *Johnny Reb: The Common Soldier of the Confederacy* (New York, 1943), pp. 240-241. Note, however, that Wiley cites no specific source. Larry Daniel has pointed out that Wiley used very few Army of Tennessee soldiers in his study (*Soldiering in the Army of Tennessee*, p. xi). Symonds, *Johnston*, pp. 317, 331, maintains that the army did not lose confidence in Johnston. He cites only two sources—one by a general who was unlikely to know what enlisted men were thinking. It should be noted that lack of confidence in Hood after the change of commanders was not the same thing as confidence in Johnston before the change.

[20] Richard M. McMurry, "Confederate Morale in the Atlanta Campaign of 1864," *Georgia*

Johnston's general conduct of the campaign does not stand up under close scrutiny any better than do his assertions about numbers, casualties, and morale. During the winter Johnston carried on a long, arid, and sometimes acrid debate by mail and telegraph with Confederate authorities in Richmond. The government wanted Johnston to seize the initiative and move to re-establish Rebel control of Tennessee. Johnston, on the other hand, maintained that his army could not possibly be ready to advance before the Federals launched their spring campaign, and, in any case, he thought, his army was not strong enough to undertake an offensive. Far better, he argued, to stand on the defensive, await the Yankees' onslaught, defeat it, and then move into Tennessee. This difference was never resolved. Johnston simply refused to act as the government wished and proceeded to conduct the campaign in his own fashion without telling his government what he was attempting to do or even keeping his superiors adequately informed as to what had happened. His objective was "to beat the enemy when he advances and then move forward."[21]

There was one fundamental, glaring weakness in Johnston's strategy: he could never beat the enemy. In fact, he could (or would) never even make a serious effort to do so. Something always arose to make it impossible for him to defeat—or even to fight a major battle against—Sherman's forces. He could not hold a position; often he was unable to anticipate, and he was never able to block, Sherman's flanking movements; he could not even inflict significant losses on the Federals. Johnston, therefore, fell back from Dalton to Resaca, to Adairsville, to Cassville, to Kennesaw Mountain, and on to Atlanta.

As he retreated, however, Johnston developed a corollary to his original strategy. Sherman's army, he reasoned, was dependent for supplies on a railroad that ran back through Chattanooga to Nashville. If the Rebels could break that railroad, he thought, Sherman would either have

Historical Quarterly, 54 (1970), pp. 226-243; Daniel, *Soldiering in the Army of Tennessee,* pp. 140-146. For a different view of a different but related topic, see William J. McNeill, "A Survey of Confederate Soldier Morale During Sherman's Campaign Through Georgia and the Carolinas," *Georgia Historical Quarterly,* 45 (1971), p. 125.

[21] Johnston, *Narrative,* p. 275; Symonds, *Johnston,* pp. 261-263.

to retreat or abandon his flanking movements and assault one of the Confederates' strongly fortified positions in a desperate effort to win a victory before a shortage of supplies forced him to give up the invasion of Georgia.

There were two fatal flaws with this scheme. One was that Johnston was unable to find a force of Rebel horsemen to strike at Sherman's rail line. There were only two possibilities—the cavalry of his own army or the mounted troops in Mississippi under the command of Maj. Gen. Nathan Bedford Forrest. To Johnston it seemed logical to order Forrest into Middle Tennessee or northern Georgia to tear up Sherman's railroad. The Army of Tennesee's own cavalry would, meanwhile, continue to guard the flanks of that army.

Forrest, however, was not subject to Johnston's orders. Unless the government changed his assignment, he would remain in Mississippi. Rebel authorities were willing to send Forrest after Sherman's line of supply if doing so did not endanger the territory for which Forrest was responsible. Fearing for his supply line, Sherman continually sent raiding expeditions into Mississippi, and Forrest had to deal with them. The fact that the government overruled him and refused to abandon Mississippi did not dissuade Johnston from continuing to urge his idea. In early July he told a visiting Confederate senator that only Forrest's cavalry could stop Sherman. With 5,000 men, Johnston declared, Forrest in one day could do enough damage to the railroad to compel Sherman to retreat. Then and for years after the war Johnston claimed that only the refusal of the Davis Administration to use Forrest against Sherman's line of supply saved the Yankees from defeat.[22]

The authorities in Richmond pointed out that Johnston already had with his own army virtually all of the troops who had originally been assigned to defend Mississippi. To strip the Magnolia State of Forrest's men would, in fact, be to abandon it and open all of west and central Alabama to devastation. Citizens, soldiers, and politicians from Mississippi and Alabama were unlikely to take kindly to the abandoning of their states. Besides, the authorities pointed out, Johnston's own cavalry

---

[22] Johnston, *Narrative*, pp. 358-360.

numbered 13,546 officers and men "present for duty" on June 10 (10,903 "effectives," see Table Three) and those horsemen were much closer to Sherman's railroad than was Forrest. Would it not be more practicable to send 5,000 of these men from the Army of Tennessee to attack the railroad? Sherman's mounted arm was weak, inept, and poorly-led. Under the circumstances, surely one-third or even one-half of Johnston's troopers could reach and wreck the railroad far more easily and quickly than could Forrest's men riding from Mississippi. To be sure there would be some risk, but the cavalrymen would be gone only a few days, and—all things considered—the danger was not great. Johnston refused to do more than send out a few small, ineffectual raiding parties. As a result of this gridlock of opinion the Rebels never made a serious effort against Sherman's line of supply.

The other flaw in Johnston's proposal was that even if Confederate horsemen had gotten to Sherman's railroad they almost certainly could not have forced the Federals to abandon their campaign into Georgia. An attack on the Yankee supply line was such an obvious riposte that Sherman had taken more than adequate steps to deal with it. He left large numbers of troops in Middle Tennessee, northern Alabama, and northern Georgia to protect his rail line, and he organized a large, highly-trained, well-equipped engineer force which had as its sole mission the quick repair of any damage that might be done to the track and bridges. Sherman had a massive supply base at Nashville where his warehouses bulged with everything that his army might need. Any damage to the railroad north of Nashville would have no effect on his army. From Nashville to within thirty miles of Chattanooga and from Chattanooga to Dalton, Sherman had two railroads to supply his men. Rebel horsemen were unlikely to be able to cut both. Like Nashville, Chattanooga housed enormous quantities of supplies, and as Sherman moved into Georgia, he established advanced bases at Dalton, Resaca, Kingston, Allatoona, and Marietta.

Had the railroad been cut, Sherman could simply have fortified some strong position, drawn supplies from his advanced bases, and hunkered down until the damage was repaired and the flow of supplies was resumed. It is about as certain as any such speculation can ever be that Johnston's hope of defeating Sherman's campaign by attacking his rail line would have proved no more successful than his plan to "beat the enemy when he advances."[23]

As the examples of numbers, morale, and strategy all indicate, Johnston's version of the 1864 Georgia Campaign does not hold up under examination. Over the past two or three decades historians, at long last, have begun to lavish upon the great struggle for Atlanta the attention that it deserves. Such writers as Albert Castel, Thomas Lawrence Connelly, Larry Daniel, Jeffrey Lash, Steven E. Woodworth, and others have given particular attention to Johnston's stint as commander of the Army of Tennessee. Under their scrutiny, Johnston's reputation has all but collapsed.[24]

Perhaps the best way to summarize recent research—and thus Johnston's current standing—is to consider the different levels on which his campaign must be judged. No military operation takes place in a vacuum, and commanders at the level Johnston occupied in 1864 must take into consideration far more than simple military factors. It therefore seems appropriate to evaluate Johnston's performance on four separate but related levels. These are his day-to-day military operations, his overall campaign, his campaign as part of Confederate grand strategy for 1864, and his campaign's place in the Rebels' overall military-geopolitical approach to the war.

Day-to-Day Operations: Johnston made one major blunder at the beginning of the campaign when he left Snake Creek Gap through the south end of Rocky Face Ridge unguarded. It was through Snake Creek Gap that some 20,000 of Sherman's men marched on May 8-9 to threaten the railroad that supplied Johnston's army at Dalton some fifteen miles to the north. Only an over cautious Yankee commander (Maj. Gen. James B. McPherson) saved Johnston from an embarrassing, if not

---

[23] Castel, *Decision in the West*, pp. 301-302, 328-329. See also Philip L. Shiman, *Engineering Sherman's March: Army Engineers and the Management of Modern War, 1862-1865*, Ph.D. dissertation, Duke University, 1991.

[24] In addition to the works by the authors cited in the text, see Richard M. McMurry, "The Atlanta Campaign of 1864: A New Look," *Civil War History*, 22 (1976), pp. 5-15.

fatal, defeat at the very outset of the campaign. The Confederate commander made no other mistake of so serious a nature, but he frequently failed to spot and take advantage of opportunities presented by Federal miscues. Some of these failures were the immediate fault of subordinate generals, but Johnston as the commander must bear the overall responsibility. At least twice during the campaign Johnston made the serious error of assuming that he knew what Sherman was going to do and of being, therefore, largely oblivious to rapidly accumulating evidence that the Yankee commander was, in fact, doing something else. In the first few days of the campaign Johnston deployed far too much of his strength on the right of his line north of Dalton because he had convinced himself that Sherman would make his major effort there. South of the Chattahoochee River, not long before he was removed from command, Johnston concentrated far too much of his strength along the river below Atlanta because he believed the Yankees would try to cross in that area. At Dalton Sherman struck through the unguarded Snake Creek Gap on Johnston's far left; at the Chattahoochee he easily crossed against the weak Rebel right some distance above Atlanta.[25] Johnston's grade on his day-to-day operations in the campaign: *C-*.

Overall Campaign: One of Johnston's basic problems in 1864 was that he thought almost exclusively on the level of day-to-day operations. He seems only rarely to have concerned himself with how his daily activities fit into the larger scheme of the struggle for northern Georgia. For this reason Johnston could believe that he had preserved his army by a masterly campaign of Fabian tactics simply because he had suffered no obvious major battlefield defeat. In truth, Johnston's 1864 campaign was, for the Confederacy, a strategic, political, economic, and logistical disaster of the first magnitude. Without fighting a major battle or even inflicting heavy losses on the enemy, Johnston fell back into the heart of the Confederacy. He abandoned the important industrial town of Rome in northwestern Georgia, and his early July retreat across the Chattahoochee River gave the Yankees uncontested control of the entire right

---

[25] See Richard M. McMurry, "The Opening Phase of the 1864 Campaign in the West," *Atlanta Historical Journal*, 28 (1983), pp. 5-24; and Castel, *Decision in the West*, p. 340.

bank of that stream. Loss of the Chattahoochee's right bank was potentially an especially severe blow to the Rebels because it opened to possible Federal occupation crucial areas of Alabama—including Mobile, the South's last stronghold on the Gulf of Mexico; Montgomery, the first capital of the Confederacy; valuable agricultural areas whence came many of the foodstuffs for Johnston's own army; and the great munitions complex at Selma. Fortunately for the Confederates, Sherman chose not to exercise the option that Johnston had granted him at so little cost.[26]

Johnston's overall failure stands in glaring contrast to the 1864 operations in Virginia. There Lee pursued a vigorous policy of opposition to the Yankee advance. By fighting back when he was threatened, Lee, in effect, kept his enemy on the circumference of a strategic circle which had Richmond as its center. Lee also inflicted massive casualties on the Federals. By mid-June when the Unionists drew back from the first unsuccessful efforts to take Petersburg, the Yankee army in Virginia had lost some 65,000 men—more men than Lee had had at the beginning of the campaign and almost twice as many casualties as Sherman was to suffer in the entire four-month Atlanta Campaign. Had the Northerners suffered similar losses in Georgia, the entire political-military equation of 1864 would have been changed. Johnston's grade on his overall campaign: *F.*

Johnston's campaign and Confederate grand strategy for 1864: Many students of the Civil War believe that by 1864 the Confederacy's best—if not its only—chance to gain its independence was to deny the Federals a victory. The hope was that, absent a tangible success for their armies, Northern voters would reject the Republican Party in the fall elections and choose a new president who would negotiate peace with the South and recognize Confederate independence. In July 1864 that prospect seemed bright everywhere but in Georgia.

In Virginia the Yankees were bogged down before the massive fortifications at Richmond and Petersburg. Lee, in fact, had even detached a sizable portion of his own army and sent it smashing northward through

---

[26] See the comments in Connelly, *Autumn of Glory*, pp. 369-371.

the Shenandoah Valley and on into Maryland. At the very time Johnston was retreating across the Chattahoochee, this force routed a Union army in the Battle of the Monocacy and struck into the outskirts of Washington itself. On the southern Atlantic Coast, Charleston stood as strong as ever, hurling defiance at the Yankees. In Mississippi, Forrest met column after column of invading Unionists, defeated them, and sent them reeling back to their base at Memphis. Even in the distant Trans-Mississippi, the Confederate forces seemed to be stirring.

Only in Georgia had the Federals as of mid-summer enjoyed any success. If Johnston evacuated Atlanta he would hand the Yankees the great triumph they had been unable to win elsewhere. Already, by early July, Davis was worried about the possibility that Sherman would herd Johnston across the Chattahoochee and then strike southwest into Alabama. On July 11, Johnston—without any explanation or elaboration—advised the Confederate government to move the Federal prisoners being held at Andersonville, some 130 miles south of Atlanta. What did that message mean? On July 16, Davis sent Johnston a direct request for information "as to present situation and your plan of operations so specific. . .as will enable me to anticipate events." The general sent a vague reply, refusing to reveal to Davis any plans that he may have had or even to say that he would make a serious effort to hold Atlanta. If Johnston would not even try to fight for Atlanta, all the Rebels' hard-won successes elsewhere would go for naught.[27]   Johnston's grade on furthering Confederate grand strategy for 1864: *F-*.

Johnston's campaign in the overall Confederate geopolitical strategy for the war: Throughout the war Johnston's whole approach to military operations was fundamentally at odds with that of his government. For military, political, logistical, economic, psychological, and diplomatic reasons the Rebel government stressed the defense of territory. The government, therefore, was willing to risk a great deal and to pay a high price to maintain its authority over as much of its area and as many of its

---

[27] Castel, *Decision in the West*, passim; James M. McPherson, "American Victory, American Defeat," in Gabor S. Boritt, ed., *Why the Confederacy Lost* (New York, 1992), pp. 15-42; *OR* 38, pt. 5, pp. 867, 876, 882-883.

people as possible. Johnston, on the other hand, thought in terms of preserving his army. Better, he reasoned, to yield a town or a region "for a time" to save the troops committed to its defense and to join those men with other Rebel forces for a decisive battle. Once the invading Yankee army had been defeated, the Confederates could easily regain what they had previously abandoned.

Jefferson Davis, however, was well aware that once the secessionists had lost an area they had never managed to regain permanent control of it. He saw that Johnston had not fought the decisive battle and gave no indication that he was going to do so. The president knew too the devastating consequences that Union occupation had on the institution of slavery—the very raison d'etre of the Confederacy—and on the morale of Rebel soldiers and civilians. Davis also recognized that there were some points so important that the Confederacy could not lose them without suffering a probably mortal wound. Richmond was obviously one such point; communication with the Trans-Mississippi had seemed, in 1863, another; Atlanta in 1864 was certainly a third.

Johnston would doubtless have been willing to abandon Atlanta if he believed the alternative was the destruction of his army.[28] Retention of Atlanta, however, was the key to the Rebels' hope of winning by not losing. Thus, Johnston would spare his men, save his army, re-elect Lincoln, and doom the Confederacy to destruction—but he would not have lost a battle. Johnston's grade on his campaign's place in the overall Confederate geopolitical strategy for the war: zero

These harsh grades on Johnston's performance in Georgia in 1864 do not mean that Davis was right and that Johnston was wrong. They do mean that Joseph E. Johnston was not suited to command an army for a government headed by Jefferson Davis. With the government following one strategy for the war and the general charged with the command of its most important army and area another, it was impossible for the Rebels to avoid defeat. During the time that it still had a chance to gain its independence, the Confederacy suffered two great military-geopolitical

---

[28] Symonds, *Johnston*, pp. 271, 327-329.

disasters—the Vicksburg Campaign and the Atlanta Campaign. It is no coincidence that Joseph E. Johnston was the chief Rebel military figure in both of them. Nor is it any coincidence that in both of these campaigns Johnston was thinking in terms of one general approach to the situation and the government for which he fought in terms of another.

The Confederacy would have been better off had Davis and Johnston admitted (or realized) that their irreconcilable differences made it impossible for them to work together and therefore counterproductive for Johnston to hold an important field command. As it was, the two men were striving to use the same limited military resources to pursue mutually-exclusive and wholly incompatible policies, although their ultimate objective—Confederate independence—was the same. From the Confederate point of view, Johnston's conduct of the Atlanta Campaign was what Jefferson Davis called it on July 18, 1864: ". . .a policy which had proved so disastrous."[29]

---

[29] *OR* 38, pt. 5, p. 888.

Sherman's Pioneers
in the Campaign to Atlanta

Philip Shiman

A ccounts of the Atlanta Campaign—indeed, of any campaign or battle of any war—naturally emphasize the combat soldiers, the men who fought with pistol, rifle and cannon. Yet there were others who waged war with different implements: the axe, the pick and the spade. These were the pioneers, who played a significant if unheralded part in winning Atlanta for William T. Sherman and the Union. Similar to engineers, the pioneers were the handymen of the army. Their tasks were to assist the army to march, and fight whenever necessary. As the name suggests, they often accompanied the vanguard of the army and sometimes performed their work under fire. Beyond that, however, it is difficult to characterize the pioneers. Army Regulations said little about them other than to remark that they should be used "to mend roads, remove obstacles, and erect defenses."[1]

---

[1] U. S. War Department, *Revised Regulations for the Army of the United States, 1861* (Philadelphia, 1861), paragraph 750.

Unlike the engineers, pioneers had no legal status; officially, they were men assigned only on an ad hoc basis to perform work as needed. Nor did the pioneers have any standard, uniform organization. Some pioneer units were made up of whole regiments and companies of infantry or cavalry; others consisted of detachments of soldiers, and still others were bodies of hired civilians (usually freed slaves). These units varied in size from a few individuals to thousands of men. Although in theory such details were only temporary, practice proved that many were more or less permanent assignments. Any military organization, from an army corps down to a regiment (and even a company), was allowed its own force of pioneers. Generally speaking, in the absence of standing orders from army headquarters on the subject—and sometimes in spite of them—commanders were free to organize their pioneers however their experience and fancy dictated.

Rarely did the men serving as pioneers receive any credit for their valuable work except for when they performed some particularly noteworthy feat. Detailed soldiers were considered to be members of their own regiments, so pioneer units rarely had much of an administrative structure. Unfortunately, the pioneers kept only the most rudimentary records on their activities—if they kept any at all. Members felt little sense of unit esprit and as a consequence left no unit histories, although pioneering efforts warranted an occasional appendix in a published regimental history. Pioneer service was, after all, considered merely incidental to the soldier's combat activities in his regiment. Information about black pioneers is even scarcer because they left no account of their activities, and the post-war reading public was little interested in the role of blacks during the war. Despite the current level of interest in the participation of blacks in the war, historians consider the manual labor that the blacks performed to have been demeaning, and they focus instead on the careers of the combat regiments. Thus the pioneers—white and black—have faded into the relative obscurity of the occasional footnote.

By the time of Maj. Gen. William T. Sherman's 1864 Atlanta Campaign, pioneers had become a ubiquitous feature of the military landscape. Pioneering assumed particular importance under Sherman because of his emphasis on mobility, and because of the nature of the

terrain over which army operations were conducted. The importance of
the terrain encountered during the Atlanta Campaign must be understood
in order to appreciate the overall role of Sherman's Pioneers.

Northern Georgia was and still is a rugged country of mountain
ranges and dense second-growth forests. The country north of the
Oostanaula River, for example, was divided by a series of parallel ridges
which channeled movement into relatively narrow valleys. The region
south of the Etowah River, which witnessed some of the most vicious
sustained fighting of the campaign, was largely a wilderness of tangled
thickets, boggy creeks, and narrow, steep ravines which could frustrate
an army's movements. The entire region was relatively lightly settled in
the 1860s, and the rough dirt tracks that broke through the forests and
ridges and connected the isolated homesteads only occasionally earned
the dignity of being labeled a road. Several sizable rivers—the
Oostanaula, the Conasauga, the Etowah, and the Chattahoochee—
flowed generally southwestwardly across the line of Sherman's advance,
and innumerable small streams (and some that were not so small)
sprawled in every direction. Sherman's three armies, more than a hundred thousand men, were forced to struggled south through this heavy
country opposed by both the rough terrain and the Confederate Army of
Tennessee.

The tactics of the campaign also gave special emphasis to the labors
of the pioneer. In what proved to be a vain attempt to hold back an
enemy with a sizable numerical advantage, Confederate Gen. Joseph E.
Johnston constructed long lines of earthwork fortifications and kept his
men under cover whenever they fought on the defensive, which was
most of the time. These defenses, which were constructed in his rear by
slaves, were available for his army to occupy when his army retreated.
Johnston's tactics made it difficult for Sherman's subordinates to catch
his army in the open, and the Federal soldiers had little choice but to dig
in and build their own fortifications—miles and miles of them. Both
sides threw up obstacles of tree branches, sharpened stakes, or chevaux-
de-frise, in front of these long lines of infantry breastworks and artillery
batteries. Skirmishers, deployed in front of the main line of entrenchments, dug rifle pits and smaller trenches for their own protection. Engagements often took on the character of a siege, with both sides

glowering at each other from behind their impenetrable defenses until the larger Federal army was able to execute a turning movement to force the Southerners back from their trenches to a new field of battle. As the long spring and summer wore on, the employment of these tactics increased the demand for the services of the pioneers.

Sherman later claimed that he provided for the organization of pioneers by authorizing each division commander to hire two hundred black laborers. According to the Federal commander, these black workers could sleep while his soldiers engaged the enemy, and dig entrenchments while the soldiers rested. During the campaign, Sherman explained to the Adjutant General "I have used [blacks] with great success as pioneer companies attached to Divisions, and I think it would be well if a law would sanction such an organization one hundred to each division of four thousand men. . . ."[2]

If he ever gave such an order, however, there is no record of it. On the contrary, the evidence suggests that Sherman himself played very little role in organizing the pioneers of his army. That specific responsibility was left to the commanders of the separate armies, corps, divisions, brigades, and even regiments. On the whole, Sherman's pioneer organization followed no logical system whatsoever.

The best organized and most effective pioneer organization to serve with Sherman—or any other Union commander—belonged to James Birdseye McPherson's Army of the Tennessee. A large, well-equipped pioneer company was attached to each division of McPherson's army. These pioneer companies were formed at the end of 1862 by Maj. Gen. Ulysses S. Grant, who ordered his division commanders to detail skilled mechanics and artisans for the duty. In 1863, Grant set the details at 146 men, organized as follows: four officers (a captain and three lieutenants), 20 non-commissioned officers, 120 men, and two musicians. That same year, he added 300 blacks to each pioneer company, ex-slaves recruited from the local plantations and the army's refugee camps.

---

[2] William T. Sherman, *Memoirs of Gen. W. T. Sherman, by Himself,* 2 vols. (New York, 1891), vol. 2, p. 55; Sherman to Lorenzo Thomas, June 26, 1864, U.S. Adjutant General's Office, *The Negro in the Military Service of the United States, 1639-1886,* National Archives and Records Administration, Washington, D.C., microfilm publication M858, roll 3, fr. 2645-2646. Hereinafter cited as NA.

These men were fed, clothed, and paid 10 dollars per month (the amount permitted by law), of which three dollars could be deducted for clothing. They were organized into squads of 30 men each under the direction of a white enlisted man. Thus, on paper at least, each pioneer company numbered 450 men.[3]

In reality, the size and organization of these pioneer companies varied greatly. In the Army of the Tennessee's XV Corps, for example, Peter Osterhaus' First Division showed 111 officers and enlisted men and 128 blacks on its pioneer rolls in February 1864. Out of those totals, only 92 of the former, and 88 of the latter, were actually present for duty. The pioneer company of William B. Hazen's Second Division reported approximately 100 each of whites and blacks in November.[4] In the XVII Corps, which was reorganized from furloughed veterans in the spring of 1864, the pioneer company of Mortimer Leggett's Third Division apparently had no black pioneers. These men had been released in April for enrollment into Federal service as United States Colored Troops.[5]

The XVI Corps, under Maj. Gen. Grenville Dodge, had a large and efficient body of white pioneers. These men, said to number 1,500, were commanded by an enlisted man who was respectfully addressed as "Major." This force was supplemented by a scattering of companies of blacks who were nominally enrolled and mustered as soldiers. Three companies of the 110th U.S. Colored Troops (originally the 4th Alabama) were attached as pioneers to Brig. Gen. Thomas Sweeny's Second Division, while two companies of the 106th U.S. Colored Troops (origi-

---

[3] Special Field Orders No. 22, HQ XIII Corps, Dept. of the Tennessee, Dec. 13, 1864, in NA Adjutant General's Office, Orders and Circulars, 1797-1910: Special Orders, Dept. of the Tennessee, Record Group 94, entry 44, NA; General Orders No. 47, HQ Dept. of the Tennessee, July 24, 1863, in NA RG 393, pt. 1, entry 4724, NA; Special Orders No. 66, HQ Dept. of the Tennessee, March 7, 1863, copy enclosed in letter Capt. Frederick Prime to Brig. Gen. Joseph Totten, March 11, 1863, P1297, NA RG 77, entry 18, NA.

[4] Report of Pioneer Corps, First Division, XV Army Corps, Feb. 19, 1864, in NA RG 393, pt. 2, entry 5886; pioneer report, Second Division, XV Army Corps, Nov. 8, 1864, in U.S. Army Archives, Army of the Tennessee Papers, Manuscripts Reading Room, Special Collections Department, Duke University Library, Durham, NC. Hazen, who had previously commanded the Second Brigade, Third Division, IV Corps in the Army of the Cumberland, was transferred from the IV Corps to the Army of the Tennessee and took command of the Second Division on August 17, 1864.

[5] Special Order No. 89, XVII Corps, April 2, 1864, in NA RG 393, pt. 2, entry 6308.

nally the 2nd Alabama) were employed constructing fortifications for the XVI Corps.[6]

Whatever the specific organization of the respective pioneer companies, the essential feature of the Army of the Tennessee's system was that these companies were relatively large units assigned to, and controlled by, division headquarters. The attachment of the pioneers to the divisions—as opposed to the corps, brigades, or regiments—proved an effective arrangement, providing the proper blend of centralization, mass effort, and tactical flexibility. The work of the pioneers was coordinated with the activities of the combat troops, and the pioneers always acted in direct support of, and were never far from, their own friends in the line. Finally, they were never called upon to fight as combatants in battle, so they could often sleep while the soldiers fought during the day, and were thus fresh for work during the night hours.

By contrast, the pioneer organization of Sherman's largest army, Maj. Gen. George Thomas' Army of the Cumberland, was smaller and less effective than its counterpart in the Army of the Tennessee. This is ironic, because Thomas' army did have a large and well-organized Pioneer Brigade. Numbering up to 5,000 men at its peak, this brigade had been formed at the end of 1862 by massing the pioneer details of every regiment in the army. The original purpose of the Pioneer Brigade was to assist the army to advance through the rugged countryside of Middle and East Tennessee. However, because of their valuable skills, these pioneers were diverted into traditional engineering work, so that by 1864, the brigade's activities were almost wholly confined to the construction of fortifications and similar tasks in Tennessee.

Only the Army of the Cumberland's XX Corps had its own pioneers available for duty in the field in the spring of 1864. This corps, under the command of Maj. Gen. Joseph Hooker, was composed of troops sent west from the Army of the Potomac during the previous fall, and thus

---

[6] Grenville Dodge, "Reminiscences of Engineering Work on the Pacific Railways and in the Civil War," *Engineering News,* Oct. 28, 1909, pp. 456-57; Regimental Papers, 106th, 110th Regiments of U.S. Colored Infantry, in NA RG 94, entry 55. During the summer, two other companies of the 110th U.S. Colored Infantry were ordered to the front for pioneer duty with the Fourth Division, XVII Corps, but it is unclear if they ever served in that capacity.

had no troops assigned to the already-existing Pioneer Brigade. Hooker's Easterners had brought with them the pioneer companies they had used in Virginia. Each of these companies numbered approximately 100 men (20 from each regiment), and were attached to each brigade, all supervised by a captain designated the "division pioneer officer."[7]

The other two corps of the Army of the Cumberland, the IV and the XIV, had no pioneers—or, more accurately, their pioneers were performing engineering work in the rear. To rectify this situation, Major General Thomas directed them to organize additional pioneers for field service in the approaching campaign. Major General Oliver Otis Howard, commander of the IV Corps, ordered each of his regiments to detail a pioneer company of 20 men who would march and work with the regiment under the command of their colonel. The use of such decentralized regimental pioneers was tactically less efficient than concentrating the pioneers at the brigade or division level, but it was politically necessary. Howard had initially recommended the formation of divisional pioneer units, but his recommendation was not acted upon.

The army was still smarting from its unpleasant experience with the Pioneer Brigade. When called upon to organize pioneer detachments in 1862, the regiments had detailed some of their best men in the belief that the pioneers would remain close at hand. Instead, the men had been taken away for service in the Pioneer Brigade and were lost to their comrades and useless to their regiments. Regimental colonels had no desire to repeat this drain on valuable manpower, preferring instead to keep their pioneers within reach and firmly under their control. This decentralization resulted in a clumsy system, and as the campaign for Atlanta progressed, it became increasingly common for the pioneer details to be massed temporarily into larger fatigue parties. One division commander went so far as to organize his pioneers into battalions to march at the head of each brigade, but he was careful to allow the men to

---

[7] U. S. War Dept., *The War of the Rebellion: A Compilation of the Official Records of the Union and Confederate Armies* 128 vols. (Washington, 1880-1901), series I, vol 38, pt. 4, p. 179. Hereinafter cited as *OR*. All references are to series I. During the summer of 1864, the Pioneer Brigade was finally reorganized as the First U.S. Veteran Volunteer Engineer Regiment. Ibid., pp. 377, 385-386, 407.

return to their own regiments at the end of each day for what he deemed "their comfort and convenience."[8]

The XIV Corps never officially organized pioneers, or at least there is no mention of them in the corps' records. Unlike his fellow corps commanders, Maj. Gen. John M. Palmer had not been trained at West Point and gave less thought to formal organization than professional soldiers. Instead, detachments and occasionally whole regiments, were assigned to fatigue duty as needed. Some regiments, such as the 10th Michigan, detailed their own pioneer squads, but such details appear to be relatively isolated cases. On the whole, the pioneer force of the Army of the Cumberland was never adequate for the army's needs, and Thomas was forced to resort to other expedients, such as putting deserters awaiting courts martial to work digging front-line trenches.[9]

Major General John M. Schofield's Army of the Ohio, composed of a single corps (the XXIII) and one division of cavalry, relied heavily upon its Engineer Battalion. Formed during 1863 for the East Tennessee Campaign, this force combined the features of the old Pioneer Brigade of the Army of the Cumberland with the pioneer companies of the Army of the Tennessee. At full strength, the white force composing Schofield's Engineer Battalion consisted of eight officers and 300 enlisted men who were detailed from every regiment in the corps. By early 1864, however, the battalion was seriously under-strength due to the mustering out or furloughing of veterans. The Engineer Battalion also employed some 250 black men, hired during the siege of Knoxville in the fall of 1863. "Their services have been very valuable and the expense of their maintenance small," the chief engineer of the corps wrote in December 1863. "They perform, under the direction of the Battalion, the work of three times their number of soldiers," he added, "and do it in better style." Unfortunately it is not known how many black laborers— or whites soldiers, for that matter—served in the Engineer Battalion

---

[8] Circular, HQ IV Corps, April 14, 1864, and General Orders No. 7, HQ IV Army Corps, in NA, RG 393, pt. 2, Entry 4030; General Orders No. 31, HQ Third Division, IV Army Corps, May 1, 1864, in ibid, entry 4092; William B. Hazen, *A Narrative of Military Service* (Boston, 1885), pp. 405-407.

[9] *OR* 38, pt. 4, p. 594.

during the Atlanta Campaign. In addition, at least one division (Jacob Cox's Third Division), organized its own detachment of soldier pioneers to both supplement the work of the Battalion, and to ensure that the division always had ready labor available.[10]

Altogether, as many as 4,000-5,000 men may have served as engineers and pioneers during the Atlanta Campaign. Unfortunately, the dearth of primary records in this area makes it unlikely that we will ever be able to conclusively state a more exact figure. It is especially difficult to determine the number of blacks who took part in the campaign as pioneers because the Army of the Tennessee, in which most of them served, was particularly careless in its record-keeping.[11]

All of the pioneers in Sherman's three armies were generally well supplied with tools. The companies of the Army of the Tennessee were authorized 150 shovels and a like number of axes, 50 picks, and a set of blacksmith's and carpenter's tools. In September, immediately following the successful conclusion of the campaign, William Hazen's division reported the following implements on hand:

187 spades and shovels, 14 adzes, 6 squares
100 axes, 4 draw knives, 1 level
100 picks, 1 monkey wrench, 6 blocks
4 broad axes, 4 jack screws, 1 bellows
6 hatchets, 5 scratch awls, 1 anvil
3 hammers, 4 spike mauls, 20 chisels
4 crosscut saws, 1 screw plate, 400 ft. rope
4 hand saws

These tools were carried in tool wagons assigned to the pioneers or, during active operations, by the men themselves.[12]

---

[10] *OR* 30, pt. 2, p. 566; C. E. McAlester to G. W. Bascom, Jan. 16, Feb. 6, 1864, in NA, RG 393, pt. 2, entry 423; report of Capt. C. E. McAlester, Dec. 23, 1863, in ibid.; General Orders No. 15, HQ Third Division, XXIII Corps, April 26, 1864, in ibid., entry 430.

[11] The 4,000 figure includes pioneers that served in Sherman's cavalry divisions.

[12] Special Field Orders No. 34, HQ Dept. and Army of the Tennessee, June 9, 1864, in NA, RG 393, part 1, entry 4727; list of tools in Pioneer Corps, Second Division, XV Corps, Sept. 30, 1864, in U.S. Army Archives, Army of the Tennessee Papers, Duke University.

The pioneers of the other armies were usually not so well equipped, bearing only the more basic implements: spades, picks, and axes. In each pioneer company of Howard's IV Corps, Thomas' Army of the Cumberland, for instance, 10 men carried axes, five carried picks and five carried shovels. These tools were carried in wagons that rolled along with the central baggage trains, under the supervision of quarter-masters who doled out the implements to the pioneers. When not using the tools themselves, the pioneers often loaned them to the infantry and artillery. The line soldiers did not take good care of the tools and often lost or damaged them, a constant source of irritation for the pioneer officers. For their part, the pioneer officers watched for opportunities to supplement their own supply of tools with a few extra items belonging to combat units.[13]

References to the pioneers in reports, correspondence and orders indicates that they played a valuable supporting role in the success of Sherman's army, both on the march and in battle. Some of their achievements were astonishing. Late in the campaign during the march to Jonesboro, for example, the pioneers of the XV Corps cut a three-mile road so quickly that the head of the column was never delayed. According to Maj. Gen. John Logan's report of the campaign, "This road was made through dense woods by the pioneers of the First Division, under the supervision of General Osterhaus and Captain [Herman] Kloster-mann, chief engineer of the corps, and was completed so rapidly that the advance was at no time checked."[14]

Occasionally poor or muddy roads were improved by corduroying, a system of paving the roadway by laying logs or rails across the way to form a rough but serviceable wooden road. At times, the pioneers were called upon to clear obstructions thrown out by the Confederates, such as trees felled in the road, a relatively insignificant problem if the men were handy with their axes. Pioneer troops, in addition to repairing and making roads, participated in the destruction of railroad lines. Major General Howard's pioneer companies of his IV Corps, for example, helped de-

---

[13] General Orders No. 7, HQ IV Corps, April 21, 1864, in NA, RG 393, pt. 2, entry 4030.

[14] *OR* 38, pt. 3, p. 107.

stroy the Macon & Western Railroad, the last rail line supplying Atlanta during the raid on Jonesboro. This vital logistical lifeline was set upon by pioneers from Brig. Gen. August Willich's 1st Brigade, Third Division. These men, led by Maj. [Bruce] Kidder of the 89th Illinois, ripped up and destroyed two miles of trackage before moving with the rest of their comrades to Jonesboro.[15]

The pioneers also built numerous bridges during the campaign. Most were hurried affairs thrown over small streams and rivulets, but a few spanned sizable rivers. One of the largest bridges was thrown up after the fighting around Resaca in May, when the pioneers of Brig. Gen. Alpheus Williams' division of the XX Corps constructed an important bridge over the Coosa River. According to Col. Horace Boughton of the 143rd New York Infantry, his regiment ". . .and the several pioneer corps of the division were assigned to me for that purpose, and in five hours a substantial trestle bridge was finished. . . ." Boughton noted that the hastily-constructed affair ". . .was 200 feet in length and over water which was from four to six feet deep."[16]

At Roswell, the XVI Corps pioneers astonished Sherman by building a trestle bridge 710 feet long and 14 feet high over the Chattahoochee River in just three days. Lower down, the pioneers of the IV Corps helped build another bridge at the same time. The pioneers of the Army of the Cumberland also provided valuable assistance to their comrades in the crossing of Peachtree Creek. The operation was a tricky one, and occasionally required building bridges under fire. Colonel Frederick Knefler's IV Corps brigade successfully avoided a Confederate force entrenched on Peachtree Creek's opposite bank by constructing a bridge over which to cross a flanking party. According to division commander Thomas J. Wood,

> The pioneers of the brigade were each provided with a long pole, about thirty feet long, to be used as sleepers for the construction of the bridge, and the 100 picked men each took

[15] Ibid., pt. 1, pp. 404, 440.

[16] Ibid., pt. 2, p. 105.

a rail. Thus provided these parties moved quietly down the
ravine to the water's edge and quickly threw the bridge over.
The 100 men passed rapidly over, deployed, and drove back
the enemy's skirmishers.[17]

Knefler's pioneers laid the poles across the creek, and the infantry-
men laid their rails on the stringers, forming an instant bridge for the
troops to cross and flank the defenders out of their positions. "[I]t may
truly be asserted that no handsomer nor more artistic operation was
made during the campaign," the division commander reported.[18]

The pioneers performed some of their most important work during
active combat operations, primarily by helping the army to fortify a front
quickly. They constructed reserve lines of entrenchment and assisted the
infantry in digging front-line trenches and even rifle pits for skirmishers.
As was often the case, when an infantry company or regiment was
detailed for duty on the skirmish line and thus unable to build its assigned section of main-line defenses, the pioneers would perform the
work. They were particularly useful in special tasks, such as the construction of artillery batteries and the preparation of obstacles in front of
the lines. As it required exposure to enemy fire, much of this work was
performed at night.[19]

The pioneers provided whatever assistance they could during combat. At Resaca, the pioneers of Brig. Gen. Morgan L Smith's Second
Division, XV Corps, followed behind the line of battle as it charged
across Camp Creek and seized a fortified position. The colonel of the
57th Ohio Infantry, Americus V. Rice, left a detailed report of the fighting around Resaca which acknowledged the prominent services rendered
under fire by the pioneers: ". . .the fighting was severe, and the whole
heavens seemed to be split with bursting shells. . . .Mean time, the
pioneer corps of the Second Division, which had promptly followed us
with picks and spades, strengthen[ed] the line of rifle-pits facing the east

[17] Ibid., pt. 1, p. 382.

[18] OR 38, pt. 1, pp. 225, 381-82; Dodge, "Reminiscences," pp. 456-457.

[19] OR 38, pt. 1, pp. 241, 321, 411, 482, 495, 499; pt. 2, pp. 297, 301, 371; pt. 3, p. 385; pt. 4, p.
200; Hazen, *Narrative*, p. 264.

just abandoned by the enemy," wrote Rice. A bitter struggle followed the capture of the enemy's line. That night, the pioneers returned to help the infantry complete a strong line of works and to build bridges across the creek. "Immediately after the the battle the pioneer corps. . .whose work no doubt saved many casualties in the regiment, with the assistance of heavy details from my regiment. . .went to entrenching," continued Rice, "and before morning, strong works were constructed, behind which we could have defied the enemy."[20]

Sherman's pioneers continued to play an important supporting role as the fighting drove the armies deeper into Georgia. Near Kennesaw Mountain, for example, they followed the assaulting columns in order to help clear away enemy obstacles and secure whatever ground was gained. On June 21, almost a week before the assault on Kennesaw Mountain, two regiments of the IV Corps brigade of Brig. Gen. Charles Cruft (under the command of its senior colonel, Isaac Kirby), attacked and carried a commanding position. According to Kirby, the attacking regiments were supported by all of the pioneers of the brigade, which followed the attacking force up the hill. "The enemy opened a heavy artillery fire on us, but our pioneers succeeded so soon in erecting good works on the crest of the hill, that his artillery fire did comparatively little damage. My pioneers particularly deserve my thanks, and won my admiration on this occasion for their almost superhuman efforts and great gallantry displayed," Colonel Kirby noted in his after action report.[21]

The experiences of the pioneer detachment of the 59th Illinois, under Lt. Chesley Mosman, was typical of many of the pioneer units. The detachment took part in most of the actions of the regiment, marching

---

[20] *OR* 38, pt. 3, pp. 213-214.

[21] Ibid., pt. 1, p. 232; Special Field Orders No. 51, issued June 26, 1864, discussing preparations for the assault on Kennesaw Mountain the following day, stated that "The pioneer corps of the respective divisions will follow the assaulting columns, in charge of the engineer officer of the division, prepared to secure by rifle-pits, &c., any vantage ground gained." Ibid., pt. 4, p. 606. The pioneers were certainly not battle-shy. When they were attacked by the enemy's skirmish line—a relatively common event—Maj. Marshall S. Hurd ordered his XVI Corps pioneers to stand their ground. The men laid down their implements and drove back the skirmishers with their rifles. Typically, however, pioneers withdrew when faced with imminent combat. Dodge, "Reminiscences," p. 457.

and sometimes fighting as a separate company. The pioneers did not always go into combat with their tools, but sometimes took their place in the line of battle with rifles. The pioneers usually worked on fortifications at night, often near to the enemy lines and under fire. On one occasion, they worked on a bright moonlit night only 80 yards from the Confederate line. Mosman's men cut down trees a foot or two thick, sawed off logs 20-35 feet long, and then carried them with handspikes to the proper place in line. Guided by the sound of their axes and the flash of their ax blades in the moonlight, the Confederates blazed away at the workers. "Such a fusillade as we got I never [before] experienced but we worked right on all night," Mosman recorded in his diary. Fortunately no one was injured, but "the snap of those bullets as they went by will live ever in my memory," he added. A few days later, Mosman suffered a severe jolt when a spent bullet struck his pistol cartridge box as he stood on the front of a breastwork, working on an embrasure for a cannon. Mosman's pioneers usually braved infantry fire, but artillery was different. When the enemy, or for that matter, Union cannon, opened fire, Mosman noted, the men would immediately scatter and "hunt their holes."[22]

One night in early July as Sherman was establishing his bridgeheads across the Chattahoochee River, Mosman's pioneers and those of the 77th Pennsylvania took part in an unusual feint. Escorted by a company of skirmishers, the pioneers crossed to an island in the river and at a given signal, began cutting down trees as if preparing to build a bridge. As they did so, several officers, including Col. Thomas Rose of the 77th Pennsylvania, began issuing commands loudly: "Battalion, forward guide center, march! . . .Right dress!. . .On the right by file into line! Halt!. . ." While Mosman laughed at the spectacle, Southerners were fooled by the charade and blazed away at the phantom corps, making hot work for the pioneers. No one among the 35 or 40 men on the island was hit, they evacuated the next day, their mission accomplished.[23]

---

[22] Chesley A. Mosman, *The Rough Side of War: The Civil War Journal of Chesley A. Mosman,* edited by Arnold Gates (Garden City, 1987), pp. 217, 220, 224-225, 230-231.

[23] Ibid., pp. 239-240.

Lieutenant Mosman disliked pioneer service intensely and resented being assigned to command of his regiment's detachment. The labor was fatiguing and unglamorous, and keeping track of the tools was an exasperating business. "I don't like working all night and marching all day," Mosman griped to his diary, "and [I] think the pioneer service [is] not the best."[24] Mosman's discontent was shared by others, including men belonging to the 106th and 110th U.S. Colored Troops. The officers of these regiments protested their assignment to pioneer duty, arguing that they had been raised for combat and not fatigue duty. By 1865, however, no redress had yet been given, and their already low morale declined further, the soldiers deserting and the officers resigning or refusing to rejoin their companies. It was not until the end of the war that these troops were released from pioneer service.[25]

In August 1864, fully one quarter of the black laborers of William Hazen's division were reported as deserters, absent without leave, or as the report noted, "run off under fire."[26]

While pioneering was rough, dangerous work, it was still not as dangerous as serving on the battle line. While on occasion the men worked under fire, they were frequently kept out of the heaviest fighting, working at night or in the rear, so they did not often take very heavy casualties. The pioneer company of Hazen's division, for example, lost only one of its black workers to enemy action, though a number became sick and two recruits became lost on a night march prior to the fighting around Jonesboro during late August and early September, 1864.[27]

The pioneers of the XVI and XVII Corps suffered losses when they were overrun by the surprise Confederate attack on July 22 at the Battle of Atlanta. Many of the men and, in the case of the XVII Corps, all of the tools, were captured. For a few days, the two corps were forced to

---

[24] Ibid., p. 242. Mosman eventually got his wish and was relieved from pioneer duty on July 24, 1864.

[25] See correspondence in Regimental Papers, 106th and 110th Regiments of U.S. Colored Infantry, NA, RG 94, entry 55.

[26] Report of Pioneer Company, Second Division, XV Corps, August 1864, in NA, RG 92, entry 238, File no. 1453.

[27] Ibid.

utilize temporary fatigue details with tools borrowed from the XV Corps. Later, each pioneer company was required to keep a spare set of tools for such mishaps.[28]

In many ways, the work of the pioneers during the Atlanta Campaign was a trial run for the far more demanding march (in terms of the support services) through Georgia and the Carolinas. During the latter operations, the emphasis shifted almost entirely away from combat in favor of mobility. The army's ability to maneuver became critical. Lacking a steady source of supplies, the army had to advance continually in the face of sodden country and surprisingly inhospitable winter weather. Pioneer units proliferated at all levels, and the line troops themselves became so handy with tools that the army passed large swamps, overflowing rivers, and muddy roads in the middle of winter with unprecedented speed.

Yet it was the previous experiences, and particularly the Atlanta Campaign, that made these marches possible. The four-month spring and summer campaign across northern Georgia honed the skills of the pioneers, taught the commanders how best to employ them, and suggested to the army—and to Sherman—just what could be accomplished by dedicated men with the proper equipment.

---

[28] Special Orders No. 182, HQ XVII Army Corps, July 24, 1864, in NA, RG 393, pt. 2, entry 3608; Special Field Orders No. 175, HQ Dept. and Army of the Tennessee, July 23, 1864, in ibid, entry 6241; O. O. Howard, "The Battles about Atlanta," *The Atlantic Monthly*, 38 (October, 1876), p. 396.

WALTZ BETWEEN THE RIVERS

An Overview of the Atlanta Campaign from the Oostanaula to the Etowah

William R. Scaife

On the night of May 15, 1864, Confederate Gen. Joseph E. Johnston evacuated the village of Resaca in northern Georgia and retreated across the Oostanaula River. Four days later and some 26 miles to the south, near Cassville, he evacuated another position that he described as "the best I saw occupied during the war," before withdrawing across the Etowah River. Just what happened between the Oostanaula and Etowah rivers during the intervening four days has been all but lost to history. Most writers have covered the period with a few sentences, explaining that Johnston looked for suitable ground on which to make a stand, but finding none, continued to retreat southward. Others have taken the opportunity at that point in their text to editorialize on the lack of military skill demonstrated by Johnston—thus avoiding the necessity of describing military operations in any detail.

There is consequently little in the history books to indicate that a sizable battle was fought at Rome Crossroads, just west of Calhoun— which prevented James B. McPherson's Army of the Tennessee from cutting in behind the Confederate army and destroying its retreating wagon trains; that another spirited rear guard action by Benjamin F. Cheatham's Division, just north of Adairsville, allowed Johnston adequate time to set a trap at Cassville, which may have been his best opportunity of the campaign to strike an effective counter blow against Sherman; or that a sizable battle came within hours of being fought for the control of the important industrial town of Rome, Georgia. While the meeting held between Johnston and his corps commanders prior to the Confederate withdrawal from Cassville is often discussed rather superficially, little has been written about an equally dramatic and confrontational council of war which took place preceding the withdrawal from Adairsville only two days earlier.

Johnston had little choice but to withdraw from the position at Resaca on the night of May 15. John A. Logan's XV Corps of McPherson's Army of the Tennessee had pushed forward on Johnston's left flank to a point where his artillery could shell the Oostanaula River railroad bridge just south of town—while Thomas W. Sweeny's 2nd Division of Grenville Dodge's XVI Corps had crossed the Oostanaula River at Lay's Ferry, four miles to the rear of Resaca, threatening the railroad even farther to the south.

South of the Oostanaula River, the rugged and heavily wooded mountain terrain changed to more open, cultivated fields and gently rolling hills, with few naturally strong defensive positions. Calhoun was the next town on the Western & Atlantic Railroad, five miles south of Resaca, situated just east of a sweeping turn in the Oostanaula River, while Adairsville lay on the railroad, nine miles farther to the south. Oothkalooga Creek flowed northward and emptied into the Oostanaula just west of Calhoun, and the valley of Oothkalooga Creek formed a natural passageway southward toward Adairsville, through which both the rail and wagons roads passed.

*   *   *

ROME CROSSROADS:

As the retreating Confederate wagon trains made their way through Calhoun in the direction of Adairsville on May 16, Grenville Dodge's XVI Corps began advancing from the bridgehead established the day before at Lay's Ferry and approached Rome Crossroads, the intersection of the Rome-Calhoun and Sugar Valley-Adairsville Roads, only 1-1/2 miles west of Calhoun. William J. Hardee's corps was sent to meet the threat to the Confederate left flank and formed in the woods just southeast of the crossroads with its right on Oothkalooga Creek near Oothkalooga Mill, and its left extended westward, overlooking the Rome-Calhoun Road.[1]

Thomas W. Sweeny's 2nd Division led the advance of Dodge's XVI Corps, followed by James C. Veatch's 4th Division and the remainder of McPherson's Army of the Tennessee. Sweeny's division was temporarily commanded by Brig. Gen. John M. Corse, who deployed with Col. Patrick E. Burke's 2nd Brigade on the Sugar Valley-Adairsville Road, Brig. Gen. Elliott W. Rice's 1st Brigade on the left, and Col. Moses M. Bane's 3rd Brigade on the right. As they approached Rome Crossroads, Company I, 1st Missouri, with four Napoleons, and a section of Company B, 1st Michigan, with two 3-inch ordnance rifles, were posted on a hill to the right of the road, overlooking the crossroads, with the 12th Illinois Infantry Regiment in support.[2]

Corse ordered a complex series of crisscrossing maneuvers with Bane's brigade crossing to the left of the road, the 66th Illinois and 81st Ohio regiments in advance in a double line of skirmishers—while Burke's brigade moved from the center to the right and Rice's brigade continued to advance on the left, the 2nd Iowa Regiment as skirmishers.[3]

---

[1] U.S. War Department, *The War of the Rebellion: The Official Records of the Union and Confederate Armies*, 128 vols. (Washington, D.C., 1890-1901), series I, vol. 38, pt. 3, p. 763. Hereinafter referred to as *OR*. All references are to series I.

[2] Ibid., p. 402.

[3] Ibid.

Just as the advancing Federals began to overrun the critical crossroads, Hardee's Corps of Confederates burst suddenly from the woods in
an extended line of battle. Patrick Cleburne's Division was on the left,
William H. T. Walker's Division on the right, and William Bate's Division followed in reserve, while Hardee's artillery opened on the Federal
wagon trains which were following Sweeny's division along the road.
Corse described the attack:

> . . .without any warning, the enemy sprang from cover in line
> of battle, and charging the thin skirmish line drove it, in some
> confusion, back across the Rome Road. . . .it was here that
> Colonel [Patrick E.] Burke, commanding 2nd Brigade, was
> severely wounded in the leg, and Captain [George A.] Taylor,
> Sixty-sixth Illinois Infantry, shot through the head, being in-
> stantly killed while trying to steady his men. At the time of
> this charge by the enemy, a rebel battery opened upon some
> empty caissons and the main road pursued by the troops, now
> filled with ambulances removing wounded, creating quite a
> stampede among camp followers, etc., who had by accident
> ventured too near the front. . . .[4]

Following the Battle of Rome Crossroads, Hardee held his position
until 1:00 p.m. on the morning of May 17, by which time the wagon
trains had cleared Calhoun and were well on their way to Adairsville.[5]

According to Johnston, he hoped to make a stand near Calhoun, but
Oothkalooga Creek would have divided any position taken and, "would
have been a great impediment." He then halted a mile or two north of
Adairsville, where maps prepared by his engineers indicated the valley
of Oothkalooga Creek was narrow enough for a line of battle to be
effectively formed across it. On the night of May 17, Johnston called his
subordinate commanders into a council of war. He posed the question

[4] *OR* 38, pt. 3, p. 402.

[5] Ibid., p. 704,

whether, if forced to abandon the position, the army could safely escape by a single road to Cassville, 15 miles to the south. Hood said it couldn't be done and urged a withdrawal south of the Etowah River, while Hardee disagreed with Hood and urged making a stand where they were.[6]

Johnston failed to mention this meeting in his *Narrative of Military Operations*, but Hardee's acting assistant adjutant general, Maj. Henry Hampton, recorded his commander's position in his "Itinerary of Hardee's Army Corps" on May 17:

> . . .in this council it was understood that General Hardee advocated giving battle to the enemy in the position we then held in front of Adairsville, information having been received that McPherson's corps [sic] of the enemy were in the neighborhood of Rome and another had gone to Virginia, which would have given us greatly the advantage of the enemy, as we had our whole army massed at Adairsville.[7]

Thus surfaced for the first time a pattern which would frequently be repeated during the campaign: Hood would advocate a withdrawal, while Hardee would opt for either an attack or the defense of a specific position. Hood would subsequently fail to attack in accordance with his orders at Cassville on the morning of May 19, and again near Pickett's Mill ten days later. He would advocate a withdrawal from the second position at Cassville on the evening of May 19 and from the Chattahoochee River Line on the evening of July 7.[8]

---

[6] Joseph E. Johnston, *Narrative of Military Operations* (New York, 1876), p. 319; *OR* 38, pt. 3, p. 982.

[7] *OR* 38, pt. 3, p. 704. Hardee's intelligence was faulty, however, for it was Jefferson C. Davis' 2nd division of John Palmer's XIV Corps, Army of the Cumberland, and not James B. McPherson's corps that had been sent to Rome; no corps was detached to Virginia from Sherman's army.

[8] Francis A. Shoup, "Works on the Chattahoochee River," *Confederate Veteran* (1895), vol. 3, p. 262.

Perhaps this is what Lt. Thomas B. Mackall, aide-de-camp to Johnston's Chief of Staff, Brig. Gen. William W. Mackall, had in mind when he wrote in his journal on June 4, 1864 that "One lieutenant-general talks about attack and not giving ground, publicly, and quietly urges retreat."[9]

At this point, General Johnston developed a system of protecting his army as he retreated through relatively open country. Colonel Henry Stone of George H. Thomas' staff, wrote a vivid description of this system of tactical withdrawal used so effectively by Johnston:

> Johnston attempted no stand at Calhoun. The next day he fell back toward Adairsville, twelve miles to the south. In this movement he began that system of obstruction to Sherman's advance which he kept up whenever the open country allowed. Starting as early as light—and often at 1 or 2 o'clock he occupied all the parallel roads within reach, and, without haste or excitement, kept his columns in steady motion.

Colonel Stone continued his description:

> About 8 o'clock his [Sherman's] head of column would overtake the Confederate rear guard, which immediately showed a bold and determined resistance, behind fences, walls, or barricades of any kind, opening artillery and seeming ready for battle. Sherman's advance corps was thus compelled to deploy—an operation consuming much time—which Johnston improved by pushing along everything but the rear guard; so that when the deployed troops advanced in line of battle, they found only a beggarly array of vanishing skirmishers.
>
> About 4 o'clock in the afternoon the same operation was repeated. Thus by nightfall, Johnston had his main army far enough away to insure a peaceful rest, while Sherman's peo-

---

[9] *OR* 38, pt. 3, p. 991.

ple were tired and vexed at the resultless maneuvers. Day
after day this was done—to our great disgust.[10]

EXPEDITION TO ROME

On May 4, at the last possible moment, Confederate Adjutant and
Inspector General Samuel Cooper ordered Gen. Leonidas Polk's troops,
styled the "Army of Mississippi," to move from northern Alabama to
Johnston's support, and to concentrate on Rome, Georgia.[11]

Polk started Maj. Gen. Samuel G. French's Division from Tuscaloosa, Alabama and Maj. Gen. William W. Loring's Division from
Montevallo, Alabama in the direction of Rome, but the bishop-general
seemed oblivious to the urgency of the situation. As a result, the concentration and movement into northern Georgia was anything but expedi-
tious. General French later expressed his thoughts on the matter:

> Polk's administrative ability was not largely developed so as
> to anticipate the plainest necessity for coming events. The last
> brigade did not reach Rome until the 17th [of May] and only
> one division of the Army of Mississippi reached Johnston
> before the Battle of Resaca was fought.[12]

On May 10, Polk was ordered to concentrate his army at Resaca and
to take charge there, and on May 12, he was designated commander of
the reorganized Army of Mississippi.[13] His command consisted of his
own divisions of William W. Loring and Samuel G. French, plus Brig.
Gen. James Cantey's Division, which had been sent from Dabney H.
Maury's Department of the Gulf in Mobile, Alabama. These three infan-

---

[10] Henry Stone, "Opening the Campaign," *Military Historical Society of Massachusetts Papers,* vol. 2, p. 400.

[11] *OR* 38, pt. 4, p. 661

[12] French, *Two Wars,* pp. 193-198.

[13] *OR* 38, pt. 4, pp. 687-689.

try divisions were supported by William H. "Red" Jackson's Division of cavalry, made up of the brigades of Brig. Genls. Frank C. Armstrong, Samuel W. Ferguson and Lawrence "Sul" Ross, along with John D. Myrick's, George S. Storrs', William C. Preston's and James Waddell's battalions of artillery.[14] Polk's command would in practice constitute Johnston's third army corps, but, as was pointed out by General French, Polk's forces would not be fully concentrated with Johnston's Army of Tennessee until Mathew D. Ector's Brigade, the last element of French's Division, arrived at Cassville on May 18.[15]

On May 14, Brig. Gen. Kenner Garrard's division of Federal cavalry was sent from Villanow, down the west bank of the Oostanaula River, in the direction of Rome. On the 16th, Brig. Gen. Jefferson C. Davis' 2nd Division of Maj. Gen. John M. Palmer's XIV Corps was likewise sent down the west bank of the Oostanaula to both support Garrard and to seek a crossing of the river near the mouth of Armuchee Creek—where it was assumed a bridge crossed the Oostanaula, over which Davis could pass and cut the railroad between Kingston and Rome.[16]

Colonel Robert H. G. Minty's 1st Brigade led Garrard's cavalry column and encountered Sul Ross' Texas Brigade at Farmer's Bridge over Armuchee Creek, some eight miles north of Rome. Minty forced a crossing at the bridge and advanced to within sight of the buildings of Rome, but, according to Garrard, "ran into a force too large to engage, and withdrew."[17] When Jefferson Davis' infantry division arrived at Floyd Springs, twelve miles north of Rome, Davis learned from Garrard's cavalry that there was no bridge across the Oostanaula in the vicinity of Armuchee Creek. But Davis decided to push southward toward Rome on the 17th, hoping to capture the industrial town where the Oostanaula converged with the Etowah to form the Coosa River. [18]

[14] Ibid., p. 704.

[15] French, *Two Wars*, p. 194.

[16] *OR* 38, pt. 4, pp. 187-188.

[17] *OR* 38, pt. 2, p. 803.

[18] Ibid., pt. 4, p. 203.

On May 16, Confederate General French arrived in Rome from Tuscaloosa, Alabama and sent Brig. Gen. Claudius Sears' Mississippi Brigade on to join Johnston's army at Kingston that night. On the morning of May 17, French sent Brig. Gen. Mathew D. Ector's Brigade across the Oostanaula River north of Rome, to support Ross' Texas cavalry and Brig. Gen. John T. Morgan's Brigade of Alabama cavalry in opposing the advance of Jefferson Davis' Union infantry division. Other preparations were also undertaken to protect Rome. A section of the Brookhaven Artillery was posted north of town at Fort Jackson,[19] Fort Stovall was manned on Myrtle Hill, just south of the Coosa River, and the Rome garrison of about 150 men, under the command of Brig. Gen. Henry Brevard Davidson, prepared to defend the city.[20]

Jefferson C. Davis moved to within two miles of Rome during the afternoon of May 17 and deployed his forces. Davis centered Col. John G. Mitchell's 2nd Brigade on the wagon road (today's U. S. Highway 27), with Lt. Col. Oscar Van Tasell's 34th Illinois thrown out as skirmishers. Colonel Daniel McCook's 3rd Brigade was positioned east of the road, while Brig. Gen. James D. Morgan's 1st Brigade was advanced on the west of the wagon road, and Col. Robert F. Smith's 16th Illinois deployed as skirmishers. The four 3-inch ordnance rifles of Lt. Alonzo W. Coe's Company I, 2nd Illinois Artillery and four Napoleons of Capt. George Q. Gardner's 2nd Minnesota Battery were posted on Shorter Hill, near Maplehurst, and all was made ready for an assault against Rome on the morning of May 18.[21]

After a grueling march, Brig. Gen. Francis M. Cockrell's Missouri Brigade, the last of French's forces, arrived at Rome at dusk on May 17 and was sent immediately to Kingston by rail. Ector's Brigade was pulled out about midnight and followed Cockrell to Kingston, and at 3:00 a.m. on May 18, French was ordered to evacuate Rome and to

---

[19] The Rome Visitor's Center now stands on the former site of Fort Jackson.

[20] French, *Two Wars*, p. 193.

[21] *OR* 38, pt. 1, p. 629, 647. The Shorter College president's residence now stands on the former site of Maplehurst.

march with the remainder of his forces by the south side of the Etowah River to join Johnston's army at Cassville.[22]

On the foggy morning of May 18, the Confederate rear guard burned the wagon road bridge over the Oostanaula, followed by both the wagon and railroad bridges over the Etowah before abandoning the town to Davis' advancing Federals. With the fall of Rome, the Confederacy lost such important industrial facilities as the Noble Brothers Foundry (a valuable cannon factory), Howe & Rich (manufacturers of cartridge boxes and bayonet scabbards), H. K. Shackleford (manufacturers of haversacks and pistol belts), and John O'Neal's bucket factory.[23]

Two large river steamboats which the Federals had hoped to capture with the city, however, made a dramatic escape. *Laura Moore* and *Alfarata* had been used to haul large quantities of supplies and troops up the Coosa River to Rome from Alabama. The sides, decks, engine rooms and pilothouses of both vessels were shielded by tiers of cotton bales and after dark, both steamers slipped away from the docks and made their way down the waterway. Although they took a heavy shelling from Coe's and Gardner's Federal artillery batteries on Shorter Hill, which overlooked the river, the cottonbale shields served their purpose admirably. The boats made good their escape to Steamboat Island below Wilsonville, where they remained until after the war.[24]

CASSVILLE

Several miles to the east, meanwhile, Johnston developed another plan which he later described as follows:

> The breadth of the valley here [above Adairsville] exceeded
> so much the front of our army properly formed for battle, that

---

[22] Phil Gottschalk, *In Deadly Earnest: The History of the First Missouri Brigade, CSA* (Columbia, Mo., 1991), p. 349; *OR* 38, pt. p. 735; French, *Two Wars*, p. 194.

[23] *Past Times* (Rome, 1989).

[24] Ibid.

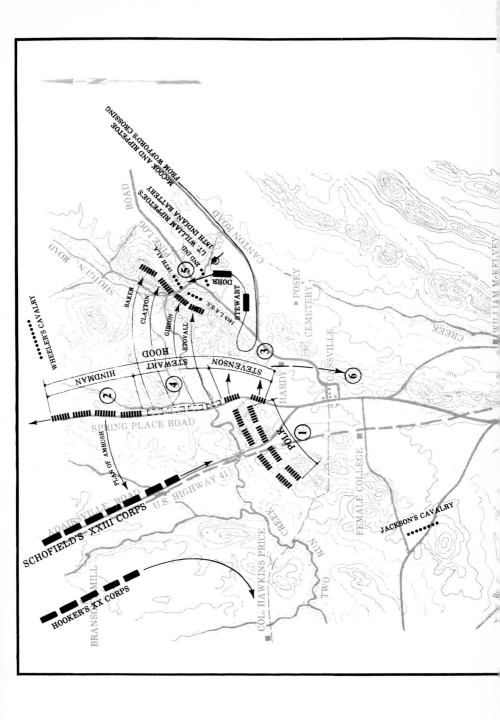

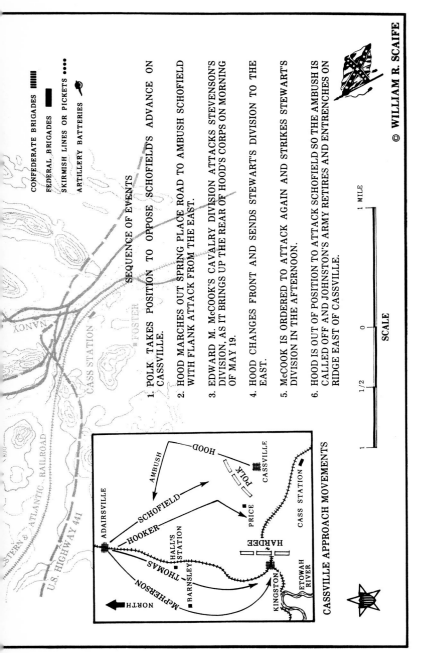

CONFEDERATE BRIGADES

FEDERAL BRIGADES

SKIRMISH LINES OR PICKETS ••••

ARTILLERY BATTERIES

SEQUENCE OF EVENTS

1. POLK TAKES POSITION TO OPPOSE SCHOFIELD'S ADVANCE ON CASSVILLE.

2. HOOD MARCHES OUT SPRING PLACE ROAD TO AMBUSH SCHOFIELD WITH FLANK ATTACK FROM THE EAST.

3. EDWARD M. McCOOK'S CAVALRY DIVISION ATTACKS STEVENSON'S DIVISION, AS IT BRINGS UP THE REAR OF HOOD'S CORPS ON MORNING OF MAY 19.

4. HOOD CHANGES FRONT AND SENDS STEWART'S DIVISION TO THE EAST.

5. McCOOK IS ORDERED TO ATTACK AGAIN AND STRIKES STEWART'S DIVISION IN THE AFTERNOON.

6. HOOD IS OUT OF POSITION TO ATTACK SCHOFIELD SO THE AMBUSH IS CALLED OFF AND JOHNSTON'S ARMY RETIRES AND ENTRENCHES ON RIDGE EAST OF CASSVILLE.

CASSVILLE APPROACH MOVEMENTS

SCALE

1/2   0   1 MILE

AFFAIR AT CASSVILLE
MORNING OF MAY 19, 1864

© WILLIAM R. SCAIFE

we could obtain no advantage of ground; so after resting about eighteen hours, the troops were ordered to move to Cassville.[25]

The Confederate commander explained his plan to defeat a portion of Sherman's army in greater detail:

Two roads lead southward from Adairsville—one following the railroad through Kingston, and, like it, turning almost at right angles to the east at that place; the other, quite direct to the Etowah Railroad-bridge, passing through Cassville, where it is met by the first. The probability that the Federal army would divide—a column following each road—gave me a hope of engaging and defeating one of them before it could receive aid from the other.[26]

On the morning of May 18, Johnston began to bait his trap. He sent Lt. Gen. William Hardee's Corps, with all the wagons and ambulances of the army, directly south from Adairsville along the main road to Kingston. He then sent the corps of Leonidas Polk and John Bell Hood, two-thirds of his army, in tight marching order over a less traveled, but shorter route across the Gravelly Plateau to Cassville.[27]

Upon reaching Adairsville, Sherman was fooled by the ground evidence he found and believed exactly what Johnston intended for him to believe—that the bulk of the Confederate army had taken the main road to Kingston. He therefore sent George H. Thomas' ponderous Army of the Cumberland along the main road after Hardee—while sending McPherson's Army of the Tennessee in another flanking movement to the west through Barnsley Gardens. Sherman then sent John Schofield's XXIII Corps directly across the Gravelly Plateau toward Cassville, with

---

[25] Johnston, *Narrative*, p. 320.

[26] Ibid.

[27] Ibid.

Hooker's XX Corps on Schofield's right flank. Late on the night of May 18, Sherman sent a dispatch to Schofield which revealed his uncertainty as to the dispersement of his army, while at the same time rationalizing his decision:

> All the signs continue of Johnston's having retreated to Kingston, and why he should lead to Kingston, if he desires to cover his trains to Cartersville, I do not see. But it is probable he has sent to Allatoona all he can by cars, and his wagons are escaping south of the Etowah by the bridge and fords near Kingston. In any hypothesis our plan is right. . . .If we can bring Johnston to battle this side of the Etowah we must do it, even at the hazard of beginning battle with only part of our forces.[28]

REAR GUARD ACTION AT ADAIRSVILLE

To gain the time necessary to get his baggage trains clear of Adairsville, Johnston left Maj. Gen. Benjamin F. Cheatham's Division of Hardee's Corps as a delaying force about three miles north of Adairsville. Cheatham deployed the brigades of Brig. Gens. George Maney, John C. Carter, and Alfred J. Vaughan in the vicinity of the Robert C. Saxon (or Octagon) House.[29]

Colonel Francis Sherman's 1st Brigade of Maj. Gen. John Newton's 2nd Division, Howard's IV Corps, led the Federal advance down the wagon road,[30] but was delayed for several hours by Cheatham's stubborn defense. Colonel Wallace W. Barrett of the 44th Illinois led the skirmishers of Sherman's brigade and ran into such heavy resistance that he called on Maj. Arthur MacArthur's 24th Wisconsin Regiment for

---

[28] *OR* 38, pt. 4, p. 242.

[29] Near where U. S. Highway 41 now crosses the Gordon-Bartow county line.

[30] Today's U. S. Highway 41.

support. Major MacArthur, who would father Gen. Douglas MacArthur, gave some indication of the intensity of the fighting in his report of the action:

> I immediately deployed two more companies on the right and the remaining four companies on the left of the road. The united efforts of the two regiments [44th Illinois and 24th Wisconsin] made no visible impression on the enemy. The fighting was very severe and lasted from about 3:00 p.m. until after dark.[31]

Private Sam Watkins of the 1st Tennessee Regiment, Cheatham's Division, described in excellent detail the action at the Octagon House from the Confederate perspective:

> Our regiment was in the rear of the whole army. I could hardly draw anyone's attention to the fact that the cavalry had passed us and that we were on the outpost of the whole army, when an order came for our regiment to go forward as rapidly as possible and occupy an octagon house in our immediate front.
>
> The house was a fine brick, octagon in shape, and as perfect a fort as could be desired. We ran to the windows, upstairs, downstairs and in the cellar. Colonel [Hume R.] Field told us we had orders to hold it until every man was killed, and never to surrender the house. It was a forlorn hope.
>
> Our cartridges were almost gone, and Lieutenant Joe Carney, Joe Sewell and Billy Carr volunteered to go and bring a box of one thousand cartridges. They got out of the back window, and through that hail of iron and lead, made their way back with the box of cartridges. Our ammunition being renewed, the fight raged on.

[31] Ibid., pt. 1, p. 327.

Watkins continued his narrative of the delaying action:

> About twelve o'clock, midnight, the 154th Tennessee,
> commanded by Colonel McGevney, [Col. Michael
> Magevney] came to our relief. The firing had ceased, and we
> abandoned the octagon house.
>
> Our dead and wounded— there were about 30 of them—
> were in strange contrast with the furniture of the house—fine
> chairs, sofas, settees, pianos and Brussels carpeting saturated
> with blood.[32]

When Johnston learned that Sherman had taken the bait and divided
his forces at Adairsville, he moved ahead to spring his trap on the morning of May 19 at Cassville. Johnston placed Polk's Corps astride the
Adairsville Road behind Two Run Creek, just north of Cassville, and
sent Hood's Corps out the Spring Place Road, which ran parallel with
and slightly to the east of the Adairsville Road. As Schofield's Union
column approached from Adairsville, Polk was to strike him in front
while Hood ambushed him in the left flank and hopefully annihilated the
smaller Federal force.[33]

The plan was well-timed. The last of Polk's troops had just joined
Johnston's army and his strength was about as great as it would ever be
during the campaign,[34] while Sherman's troops were marching confi-
dently on, expecting little opposition north of the Etowah River.
Johnston seemed confident that the time for the long-awaited counter-
stroke was at hand and issued enthusiastic orders to his men on the
morning of May 19:

---

[32] Samuel R. Watkins, *"Co. Aytch," Maury Grays, First Tennessee Regiments; or, A Side Show of the Big Show* (Dayton, 1985), p. 135.

[33] Johnston, *Narrative*, p. 320; *OR* 38, pt. 3, p. 621.

[34] Editor's Note: See Richard M. McMurry's essay "A Policy So Disastrous: General Joseph E. Johnston's Atlanta Campaign," which opens this collection, for a insightful inspection of the strength of Johnston's Army of Tennessee.

Soldiers of the Army of Tennessee, you have displayed the highest quality of the soldier—firmness in combat, patience under toil. By your courage and skill you have repulsed every assault of the enemy. . . .You will now meet his advancing columns. . .I lead you in battle![35]

After issuing his proclamation, Johnston rode out the Spring Place road with corps commanders Hood, Polk and Hardee, to show Hood precisely where he should form for the attack. Polk deployed on the high ground just south of Two Run Creek, while Hood moved his column out the Spring Place Road with Maj. Gen. Thomas Hindman's Division in the lead, followed by Maj. Gen. A. P. Stewart's Division. Two brigades from Maj. Gen. Carter Stevenson's Division brought up the rear.[36]

About mid-morning Johnston sent his chief of staff, Brig. Gen. William W. Mackall, out the Spring Place Road to caution Hood against moving too far to the right and thus overextending the wingspread of the army—since Hardee was being attacked in force by George Thomas' Army of the Cumberland on the left. To Mackall's admonition Hood replied, "And they are on me too! The cavalry gave me no warning. . .I am now falling back to form a new line farther to the rear."[37]

When Mackall inquired which road the enemy were moving on, Hood replied "On both the Canton and Spring Place Road; and did you not see them?" Mackall responded that he had seen no enemy and later reported to Johnston that he didn't believe Hood had seen any either.[38]

The force that caused Hood so much consternation was Brig. Gen. Edward M. McCook's division of cavalry.[39] This force consisted of the

---

[35] *OR* 38, pt. 4 p. 728.

[36] Ibid., pt. 3, p. 978.

[37] Ibid., pp. 621, 983.

[38] Ibid., pt. 3, p. 621.

[39] McCook's third brigade, under Col. Louis D. Watkins, was at Wauhatchie Station, Tennessee, recruiting horses and thus was not present at Cassville.

brigades of Col. Joseph Dorr and Lt. Col. James W. Stewart, which were supported by six 3-inch ordnance rifles of Lt. William B. Rippetoe's 18th Indiana Battery of horse artillery.   McCook had been sent to threaten the railroad south of Cassville and, finding no direct road to the east of town, had turned westward on the Canton Road and approached Cassville from the east, just as Hood's column was marching northward from the town. McCook, with Maj. David Brigg's 2nd Indiana cavalry in the lead, struck Stevenson's brigades, marching at the rear of Hood's column, in the right flank.   But Stevenson quickly formed a line of battle and forced McCook to withdraw back along the Canton Road. On learning of the attack, Hood ordered his entire corps to "change front" and sent Stewart's Division east and then south through a gap in the hills to face the threat from that direction. McCook had withdrawn only a short distance along the Canton Road when Maj. Gen. George Stoneman, the commander of Schofield's cavalry arm, ordered him to again attack. Heeding this order, McCook swung north, where he encountered Stewart's Division on the road south of the gap in the hills.[40]

The two forces quickly clashed. Major David Briggs of the 2nd Indiana Cavalry led a mounted sabre attack against Col. James Holtzclaw's 18th Alabama, which was on skirmish duty in front of Brig. Gen. Henry Clayton's Brigade. The spirited attack was such a surprise that 35 Alabamians were captured in the affair. On skirmish duty to Holtzclaw's right was Maj. John Austin's 14th Louisiana Sharpshooters, Brig. Gen. Randall Gibson's Brigade. Austin did not like what he saw of the charge, which he later described as "the disgraceful surrender of a number of men belonging to the 18th Alabama Regiment."[41] While this fighting involved a relatively small number of troops, it caused Hood to re-deploy his corps so that the ambush of Schofield became impracticable.[42]

---

[40]   Ibid., pt. 2, p. 752, 785. McCook's route of march and precise point of attack are corroborated by extensive ground evidence in the form of artifacts provided to the author by Robert M. White, Cartersville, Georgia.

[41]   Ibid., pt. 3, p. 862.

[42]   Johnston, *Narrative*, p. 321.

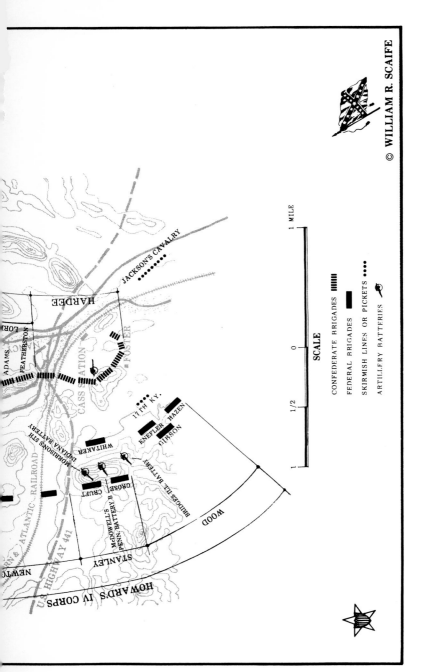

AFFAIR AT CASSVILLE
EVENING OF MAY 19, 1864

SCALE

1/2   0   1 MILE

CONFEDERATE BRIGADES ▥

FEDERAL BRIGADES ▬

SKIRMISH LINES OR PICKETS ••••

ARTILLERY BATTERIES ⚬

© WILLIAM R. SCAIFE

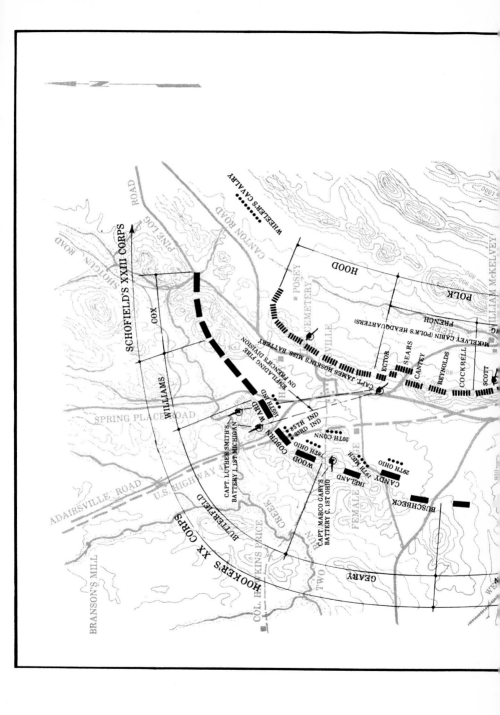

Johnston described the lost opportunity:

> When General Hood's column had moved two or three
> miles, that officer received a report from a member of his
> staff to the effect that the enemy was approaching on the
> Canton Road in the rear of the right of the position from
> which he had marched. Instead of transmitting this report to
> me, and moving on in obedience to his orders he fell back to
> that road and formed his corps across it, facing to our right
> and rear, toward Canton, without informing me of this
> strange departure from the instructions he had received. I
> heard of this erratic movement after it had caused such a loss
> of time as to make the attack intended impracticable, for its
> success depended on accuracy in timing it. The intention was
> therefore abandoned.[43]

When Hood wrote his memoirs *Advance and Retreat*, he categori-
cally denied practically everything Johnston had said. Hood even denied
that there had been any plan to ambush Schofield or that he had been
ordered out the Spring Place Road for that purpose. He went on to state
that Union general Oliver O. Howard's IV Corps was on the Ironton
(Canton) Road, and in a footnote, indicated that a "wandering contingent" of Butterfield's division of Hooker's XX Corps confronted him on
the Spring Place Road." The "wandering contingent" footnote was unfortunately accepted as reliable evidence by a number of writers and
incorporated in their work, which caused Atlanta historian Wilbur Kurtz,
Sr. to facetiously refer to it as the "wandering footnote." [44]

After-action reports and other firsthand writings indicate clearly that
Howard's Corps was proceeding toward Kingston along the railroad, at
least seven miles to the west of Hood's position. Such sources also show
that Butterfield's division was on Schofield's right flank in such position

---

[43] Ibid.

[44] Wilbur Kurtz, Comments on General Joseph E. Johnston's Review of Sherman's Memoirs,
unpublished manuscript, p. 10. Copy in author's collection.

that it would have had to pass directly through Schofield's marching column in order to reach Hood's position.[45]

In an attempt to pinpoint where Hood was attacked, Bartow County historian Robert M. White has for many years searched the Cassville area for ground evidence that might give some indication of where the action took place and the identity of the attacker. Large quantities of Spencer carbine shells were found just north of Cassville, along the old bed of Spring Place Road, which indicates the point of McCook's initial attack on Stevenson's Division as it brought up the rear of Hood's column on its northward march along the Spring Place Road.[46]

Additional quantities of Spencer's were found a short distance to the northeast, where McCook's forces struck again, this time against Stewart's Division. Both dropped and fired Confederate ammunition was also found in the areas where Spencer's were found, but no fired Confederate ammunition nor Federal ammunition of any kind was found at any other point along the Spring Place Road for a distance of some three miles north of town. McCook's two attacks are described in some detail in the *Official Records* and are consistent with this ground evidence. No other reports of any Federal units engaged in the area have been found.[47]

There is ample evidence to indicate that the force which so unnerved Hood was only McCook's cavalry supported by Rippetoe's horse artillery; there is no evidence to support Hood's contention that he was attacked by infantry from the IV and XX corps.[48]

Forced to abandon his carefully planned ambush, Johnston retired about one mile to a position on a ridge east of Cassville and prepared again to give battle. This new line ran for about 3-1/2 miles along the heavily-wooded crest of the ridge overlooking a broad, open valley to

---

[45] *OR* 38, pt. 4, pp. 232, 237, 238.

[46] Ibid., pt. 3, p. 621; pt. 2, pp. 785, 800.

[47] Brigadier General Edward McCook's brief but descriptive report of this action is located in *OR* 38, pt. 2, pp. 751-752.

[48] See the discussion regarding the ground evidence recovered from the action in the Conclusion at the end of this essay.

the west, in which sat the town of Cassville. Hood's Corps was deployed on the right of this new line, Polk's Corps in the center, and Hardee's Corps took up position on the left, south of the Western & Atlantic Railroad.[49]

Johnston, for the first time during the Atlanta Campaign, felt his flanks and communications were secure. He later described this position as "the best I saw occupied during the war—with a broad, elevated valley in front of it completely commanded by the fire of the troops occupying its crest."[50]

As Schofield's corps approached Cassville along the Adairsville Road, he deployed to his left across the valley from Hood's position on the Confederate extreme left. General Hooker's XX Corps followed and formed opposite Polk's Corps in the Confederate center, facing the village of Cassville. Oliver Howard's IV Corps formed on the right, astride the railroad and opposite Hardee. By mid-afternoon, the two armies faced each other across the valley, barely a mile separating them.[51]

Hooker's artillery unlimbered with the four Napoleons of Capt. Marco Gary's Company C, 1st Ohio, on the high ground just west of the town, near the Female College, and the six 10-pounder Parrotts of Capt. Luther Smith's Company I, 1st Michigan, on two prominent knolls, just west of the Adairsville Road—in a manner that would significantly influence events later in the day. Captain Gary's Ohio Battery shelled the Confederates in its front while a skirmish line made up of the 19th Michigan, 20th Connecticut, 73rd Ohio, 33rd Indiana, and 85th Indiana from Daniel Butterfield's 3rd Division, advanced and occupied the village of Cassville late in the afternoon.[52]

Major General Samuel G. French's Division of Polk's Corps occupied a position near the Confederate center, where a road penetrated the

---

[49] Johnston, *Narrative*, p. 322.

[50] Ibid., p. 322.

[51] The relative locations of the opposing armies can be gleaned from the remaining entrenchments and from the location of those mapped by historian Wilbur Kurtz in 1947.

[52] *OR* 38, p. 2, p. 342.

line through a gap in the ridge. French had placed Capt. James Hoskins' Brookhaven Mississippi Artillery and part of Ector's Brigade on a small knoll some 50 yards in front of the gap to repel an advance of Federal cavalry.[53]

As General Johnston rode the Confederate line late in the evening, Brig. Gen. Francis Asbury Shoup, his chief of artillery, pointed out that, if the enemy cleared the foliage masking the front of their guns, a portion of French's line might be enfiladed by Federal artillery on a small knoll about a mile away and to their far right. Shoup was referring to the six 10-pounder Parrotts of Luther Smith's Company I, 1st Michigan. Johnston, believing the danger slight, replied that the Federal artillery was located "so far as to make the damage trifling." The Confederate commander added that "No attack of infantry could be combined with fire of distant artillery, and his [French's] infantry might safely occupy some ravines immediately in rear of his position during any such fire of artillery."[54]

After dark, a meeting was initiated by General Hood between Johnston, Hood and Polk at the latter's headquarters in the William McKelvey cabin. For some reason never adequately explained, Hardee was not present until summoned by Johnston at 10:00 p.m.—after the meeting had been in progress for some time. Hardee was appalled to learn that another withdrawal had been recommended by Hood and Polk. The veteran corps commander was so opposed to the retreat that he offered to change places with either of the other corps rather than forego giving battle.[55]

Quite by accident, French met Hood on the way to the meeting and was invited to join the senior commanders for supper. According to French's account and others who were present, the division commander took no part in the discussion because he was Polk's subordinate. Johnston later described the meeting:

---

[53] French, *Two Wars*, p. 380.

[54] Johnston, *Narrative*, p. 323.

[55] French, *Two Wars*, Appendix, p. 371.

> On reaching my tent after dark, I found an invitation to meet the Lieutenant-Generals at Polk's quarters. . .the two officers, General Hood taking the lead, expressed the opinion very positively that neither of their corps would be able to hold its position next day; because they said, a part of each was enfiladed by Federal artillery. A discussion of more than an hour followed, in which I became apprehensive that as the commanders of two-thirds of the army thought the position untenable, the opinion would make it so.[56]

Johnston went on to conclude that "Although the position was the best we had occupied, I therefore yielded and the army crossed the Etowah on the 20th—a step I have regretted ever since."[57]

General Hood, in *Advance and Retreat*, took an impassioned oath that he had never recommended retreat, but instead urged Johnston to attack! He then produced testimonial letters from Francis Asbury Shoup, Johnston's chief of artillery and later Hood's chief of staff, Capt. Walter J. Morris, Polk's chief engineer, and from Polk's son, Dr. A. M. Polk—none of whom had attended the controversial meeting in question. On careful examination, these testimonials, moreover, contributed no more to Hood's credibility in the matter than they did to Johnston's.

Since Polk was killed at Pine Mountain less than a month following the evening meeting on May 19, only two key witnesses remained to shed light on the controversy: General French, who left the meeting early, and Hardee, who arrived late—both of whom later corroborated Johnston's account of the fateful meeting.[58] For the second time in only three days, the Confederate high command was divided: Hardee advocated holding their ground, while Hood urged withdrawal. And again the results were the same: a continuation of the retreat toward the Chattahoochee River.

---

[56] Johnston, Narrative, p. 324.

[57] Ibid.

[58] French, *Two Wars*, p. 374

Conclusion

The affair at Cassville has long mystified historians and students of the Atlanta campaign, and not without good reason. In Johnston's *Narrative,* the events at Cassville were covered with the minimal amount of detail and elaboration so typical of his writing. In Hood's post war *Advance and Retreat,* published in 1880—six years after Johnston's reminiscence appeared—he thoroughly confused matters by vehemently denying practically everything Johnston had written. Hood's work was characterized by historian Wilbur Kurtz, Sr., as "a tissue of denials and accusations which ignored his singular opportunity for contributing to the annals of the Atlanta Campaign." [59]

Captain Walter J. Morris, Leonidas Polk's chief engineer during the Atlanta Campaign, added to the confusion by drawing a map which depicted the positions of both armies on the afternoon of May 19. This map was reproduced in the *Official Records' Atlas,* Hood's *Advance and Retreat,* and in Samuel French's *Two Wars.* Morris' map, on casual examination appears to be well-done, complete with contour lines and graphic scale which would lead one to believe that it had been drawn to scale. In actuality, however, it is a rough sketch drawn from memory and is not drawn to scale at all. Significant errors concerning both scale and physical land features are exposed when Morris' map is compared with a modern U. S. Geological Survey study—and the entire map is misaligned with the compass by some 35 degrees. The deployment of the troops and the configuration of both the Federal and Confederate lines were inconsistent with Federal and Confederate reports of the engagement, and the detailed maps prepared by historian Kurtz for Col. Thomas Spencer's *History of Bartow County.* Consequently, those researchers who turn to Morris' cartography in the hope of clarifying some

---

[59] Wilbur Kurtz, "Comments on General Joseph E. Johnston's Review of Sherman's Memoirs," stated that "When Hood wrote his report dated Richmond, February 15, 1865, he had before him a copy of Johnston's Vineville Report, October 20, 1864 [*OR* 38, pt. 2, pp. 612-624] which by inference accuses him of blatant mendacity in his statements about the Cassville Affair as of the forenoon of May 19. Hood's reply to this charge was in the usual pattern adopted throughout his book *Advance and Retreat.*

of the controversy between Johnston and Hood, are faced with greater confusion.[60]

Military ground evidence corroborated by reports in the *Official Records* indicates with some degree of precision where Col. Edward McCook's cavalry struck Hood's force during the morning action on and near the Spring Place Road. Ground evidence was also found to be consistent with the Federal reports of John Schofield, Daniel Butterfield, Edward McCook, Maj. David Briggs, and Lt. William Rippetoe, as well as with the Confederate reports of William Mackall, Alex P. Stewart, and Maj. John Austin.[61]

This ground evidence is in conflict with Hood's contentions that: (1) Oliver Howard's IV Corps was on the Canton Road; (2) he was attacked by a "wandering contingent" of Daniel Butterfield's division of the XX Corps on the Spring Place Road; and (3) he had observed Federal troops advancing on the Canton Road, from his position at the head of his column on the Spring Place Road. Howard's IV Corps had advanced down the Western & Atlantic Railroad from Adairsville and passed through Kingston at 8:00 a.m., some seven miles to the west of Hood's position on the Spring Place Road.[62] Butterfield's division of the XX Corps was at the house of Col. Hawkins Price, some one and one-half miles west of Cassville. Butterfield would have had to pass his division through Schofield's marching column in order to reach Hood's position.[63]

While there is no Spring Place Road today, the old sunken roadbed may still be traced for several miles north from Cassville. The Canton Road runs in a northeasterly direction from Cassville and between the

---

[60] These maps, when superimposed over U. S. Geological Survey maps, indicate that the Federal and Confederate entrenchments were based on field measurements made by Wilbur Kurtz while such earthworks were relatively intact.

[61] *OR* 38, pt. 2, pp. 509, 589, 751, 785, 800; pt. 3, pp. 621, 816, 862. This evidence is also consistent with accounts found in Johnston, *Narrative*, and French, *Two Wars*.

[62] *OR* 38, pt. 1, p. 191.

[63] Ibid., pt. 4, p. 252.

two roads runs the modern Shotgun Road, two branches of the east tributary of Two Run Creek, and two prominent parallel ridges, each rising to elevations of several hundred feet above both the old Spring Place Road and the Canton Road. Because of these intervening geographic features, the Canton Road cannot be seen today from any point along the old Spring Place Road, and certainly could not have been seen by Hood from his position at the head of his corps, marching northward on the road.

Finally, Samuel G. French's precise location of James Hoskins' Brookhaven Artillery (on a knoll fifty yards in front of the gap through which ran the wagon road) provided a point from which military ground evidence could be uncovered, and a reverse azimuth projection drawn from that point clearly establishes that the position held by Capt. Luther Smith's Company I, 1st Michigan Artillery, was the only possible originating point of the enfilading fire which ultimately brought about the withdrawal of the Confederate army from Cassville.[64]

[64] Ibid., pt. 2, p. 437; French, *Two Wars*, appendix, p. 380.

The valley of Cassville. This view was taken from Hood's second position on the right of the Confederate line. Sherman's troops would have had to attack across this valley. Company I, 1st Michigan Artillery, was posted on the knoll in the distance. Photo courtesy of the author.

Dalton to Cartersville: Images of the Georgia Campaign, A Photographic Essay

William E. Erquitt

In early May 1864, Maj. Gen. William T. Sherman unleashed his three armies against Gen. Joseph E. Johnston's Confederate Army of Tennessee, which was deployed on the hills and ridges surrounding Dalton, Georgia. After some initial sparring at Rocky Face Ridge and Dug Gap, a Federal flanking maneuver through Snake Creek Gap opposite the town of Resaca, resulted in the withdrawal of the Confederate army from Dalton.

Two days of sharp combat followed the arrival of the armies at the quiet railroad town of Resaca, where more than 170,000 soldiers lined the wooded hills and valleys. The beautiful countryside was scarred by miles of artillery-studded trenches and breastworks. Johnston's new line stretched for four miles, his left flank anchored on the Oostanaula River, and his right flank on the Conasauga River. Sherman probed this line and then attacked the Confederate center, where he suffered a sharp repulse. Johnston, taking advantage of Sherman's exposed left flank, threw John Bell Hood's Corps against it, and only the arrival of a division from the Army of the Cumberland stopped Hood's steady advance.

At the opposite end of the field, Federals from James B. McPherson's Army of the Tennessee managed to capture a hill from which they could bombard the crucial bridges over the Oostanaula, an event which spelled grave danger for Johnston's Confederates. During the fighting on May 15, Sherman managed to push a division across the Oostanaula beyond Johnston's left flank. This move, which threatened Johnston's railroad communications, resulted in the Confederate evacuation that night.

The following twelve photographs—all but one of which are published here for the first time—include various wartime buildings in Dalton, the scarred battlefield in the Resaca valley, and an interesting image taken from high above the Etowah River of the important industrial town of Rome, 25 miles southwest of Resaca. Although in most cases the photographer is not known, it is probable that many of these views were taken by George N. Barnard, one of the war's most famous cameramen.

* * *

The photographs that follow are courtesy of William E. Erquitt.

Opposite: The Confederates withdrew from Dalton, Georgia on the night of May 12, 1864, and Federal troops immediately occupied the town. Dalton, unlike neighboring villages and hamlets scattered along the Western & Atlantic Railroad, was a thriving community surrounded with handsome plantations and wealthy landowners. Because of its proximity to Federally-controlled Chattanooga, Dalton was turned into a massive Confederate ordnance and supply depot for the Confederate Army of Tennessee. Food from as far away as South Carolina and Alabama was brought into the town by wagons and railroad for dispersion to Confederate forces. Valuable raw products, such as turpentine, tar, iron ore, and pig iron were shipped to Dalton for subsequent distribution. By May of 1864, Dalton was perhaps the most important Confederate town in North Georgia.

This previously unpublished view, taken in the spring of 1865, is representative of the style of homes which greeted Sherman and his army in Dalton after the Confederate evacuation. It is not known who, if anyone, occupied this particular house immediately after the war moved south of Dalton. In late February 1865, it became the headquarters of the 147th Illinois Infantry, Col. Hiram F. Sickles, commanding. Note the infantryman posed in front of the house, and the soldier—perhaps an officer—on the second story balcony.

The 147th Illinois Infantry was organized at Camp Fry, Chicago for one year of service on February 18, 1865. The Illinoisans traveled through Louisville, Nashville and Chattanooga before arriving in Dalton, where they detrained on February 27, 1865. The regiment was attached to Henry M. Judah's 1st Brigade, 2nd Separate Division, District of the Etowah, Department of the Cumberland, until July, 1865. This district was under the command of James B. Steedman. Colonel Sickles and his regiment, operating out of Dalton, protected the railroad and skirmished with roving Confederate guerrillas. After losing three killed in various skirmishes in northern Georgia and 31 dead from disease, the regiment was mustered out January 20, 1866, and discharged from service on February 8, 1866.

An inscription on the photo's reverse notes that at one point, the home also served as Henry Judah's brigade headquarters. The brigade's surgeon, Evert Van Buren, took up residence in the room on the upper left second story. A postcard view of this home, taken in the 1920s, claims that it was also Confederate Gen. Joseph E. Johnston's Dalton headquarters. A small plaque outside the residence supports this claim. Sources: Frederick H. Dyer, A Compendium of the War of the Rebellion (Dayton, 1985), p. 1102; Frank Welcher, *The Union Army, 1861-1865, Organization and Operations. Volume II, The Western Theater* (Bloomington, 1993), p. 24.

* * *

Opposite: This carte-de-visite depicts a structure constructed by Federal soldiers during their occupation of Dalton in May, 1865. After Johnston's evacuation of the city, Sherman's forces took it over and it was occupied for the remainder of the war. This previously unpublished view shows the headquarters of a Federal captain, John M----, whose boldly printed name above the doorway in the left center of the photograph is partially obstructed by a thin intervening tree. The inscription on the back of this image, claiming that one of the men in this view is "Evert Van Buren, surgeon,"—probably the fellow on the far left with his foot on the rail fence—indicates that the captain was probably a company commander in Henry M. Judah's 1st Brigade, 2nd Separate Division, District of the Etowah, Department of the Cumberland. Sources: Frank Welcher, *The Union Army, 1861-1865, Organization and Operations. Volume II, The Western Theater* (Bloomington, 1993), p. 24.

Opposite, top: This is a previously unpublished view of the Dalton headquarters of Capt. E. E. Sturtevant, who is posing in front (third from right) with members of his staff, one of whom, 1st Lt. E. H. Edward, is present in the photo but unidentified. The building was located near the Western & Atlantic Railroad. The date of this photo is unknown. These officers were with the 147th Illinois Infantry.

Opposite, bottom: Another photo from Dalton, Georgia, also previously unpublished, which depicts a large community church. Cropped from this view is a handwritten ink inscription across the bottom stating "Ward Hospital." Fortunately, an ink notation on the reverse side positively identifies this image as "Hd Qtrs Brigade Hospital—1st Brigade, 2d Sep. Division AC,—Dalton GA, May 1, 1865. Presented to Hon. E. Van Buren—by his aff. son—E. Van Buren, Jr.—Asst. Surg.—in charge."

This church was used as a hospital by Surgeon Evert Van Buren, who was assigned to Henry M. Judah's 1st Brigade, Second Separate Division, District of the Etowah, Department of the Cumberland. Note the dozen or so Federals gathered on the steps of the church.

Opposite: A handsome unpublished stereo view (date and photographer unknown) of the Chester House, a hotel at Dalton, Georgia.   Other than the absence of windows on the third floor, at first glance this three-story structure appears intact.   A closer examination, however, reveals that the hotel has been considerably damaged along its left side at the second and third story levels— apparently by artillery fire. What look to be scattered pock marks and damaged masonry on the front of the building's brick facade seem to confirm this conclusion. Also of interest are the streaks of soot along the doors and windows of the lower level, evidence that perhaps the hotel had experienced a damaging fire. Note the warehouses and shops in the background.

Opposite: This remarkable and previously unpublished ambrotype depicts the blockhouse erected just west of Dalton, Georgia. The road passing through the foreground is the Chattanooga Road, and the view is generally south, with Taylor's Ridge to the right. Note the army wagon and forge parked in the upper left portion of the image. Of particular interest is the right portion of the photograph, which, upon magnification, reveals the presence of a tent, a limber chest, and a group of soldiers standing along a split-rail fence next to what appears to be a stack of newly-made coffins.

Opposite, top: This unpublished ambrotype of the Resaca battlefield is probably another Barnard image. The caption on this print reads "Looking NW Conf. Art. on hill to right, McPherson on left in woods extreme left. Taken near the railroad." If the inscription is accurate, the Oostanaula River would be beyond the left edge of this photograph. The woods in the distance would have been occupied with brigades from John Logan's XV Corps, Maj. Gen. James B. McPherson's Army of the Tennessee. Confederate trenches and breastworks are clearly visible on the hillside in the right portion of the ambrotype. Federal troops pressed hard in this area throughout the Resaca operations.

Opposite, bottom: This is an excellent unpublished view—possibly a Barnard exposure—was taken shortly after the Battle of Resaca. The ground falling away before the camera is of the Camp Creek valley, one-half mile west of the town of Resaca. The camera is looking north by northwest, with Camp Creek itself marked by the heavy overgrowth running through the center of the image. James McPherson's Army of the Tennessee was in possession of the woods in the left distance.

Opposite: Twenty-five miles southwest of Resaca was the small industrial town of Rome, situated in the elbow formed where the Oostanaula and Etowah rivers converge to form the Coosa. Despite its small size, Rome produced a significant amount of ordnance and other war materiel for the Confederacy, including brass cannons, shot, and shell from the Noble Brothers Foundry, and cartridge boxes and bayonet scabbards, made at the firm of Howe & Rich. Pig iron was mined from the area for use in Confederate arsenals and armories.

This is a virtually unknown image of the city which, as far as this author is aware, has only been published on one occasion in a history of Floyd County, Georgia very early in the century. It was captured from atop "Myrtle Hill" looking generally north over the Etowah River. Confederate Maj. Gen. Samuel Gibbs French, with advance elements of Lt. Gen. Leonidas Polk's Army of Mississippi, held Rome May 16-18, but evacuated the city in the face of an advance by Brig. Gen. Jefferson C. Davis' 2nd Division of Maj. Gen. John Palmer's XIV Corps, Army of the Cumberland. Brigadier General William Vandever's Federal command garrisoned the city later in the year. Upon their departure on November 10-11, 1864, the heart of Rome was torched by the Federal soldiers. The photographer of this ambrotype is unknown.

Opposite, top: This previously unpublished image exhibits the ruins of the Marcus A. Cooper Iron Works, also known as the Etowah Iron Works, near Cartersville, Georgia. Some of the richest iron ore in the South was mined near Cartersville. The Cooper complex produced tons of pig iron that was eventually forged into everything from nails to artillery ammunition for the Confederacy. Although the Cooper Iron Works did not cast any artillery pieces during the Civil War, it did produce a small piece fired in celebration of the opening of the tunnel near Dalton on the Western & Atlantic Railroad during the 1840s.

Mark Cooper eventually sold his furnace and shops to Quinby & Robinson, a noteworthy cannon foundry operation based in Memphis, Tennessee. The foundry, which had produced scores of excellent artillery pieces and other valuable ordnance items, was forced to vacate Memphis in the face of advancing Federal forces. Quinby & Robinson continued to operate the foundry on the grounds of the Cooper complex until it was destroyed on May 22, 1864 by the 103rd Ohio and 24th Kentucky regiments, Second Brigade, Third Division, Army of the Ohio. Today, virtually nothing remains of the foundry except a rebuilt furnace and a small park run by the state of Georgia.

Opposite, bottom: The Cooper [Etowah] Iron Works and the Etowah Mills employed so many people that a small town grew up to serve these industries. Houses were built in the surrounding hills, merchants brought in their businesses, and even a hotel was contructed to service the populace. The town had good lines of communication, served by both the Western & Atlantic Railroad and the Etowah River. Unfortunately, the mainstays of the small population center—the foundry and mills—were built directly in the path of Sherman's Federals.

This is an excellent and previously unpublished view of the main four-story building of the Cooper [Etowah] Iron Works, which was burned during Sherman's 1864 Georgia Campaign. The narrow country road in the foreground is no longer in existence, having been reclaimed by the surrounding woods decades ago.

The Western & Atlantic Railroad in the Campaign for Atlanta

James G. Bogle

The Western & Atlantic Railroad of the State of Georgia was created by an act of the General Assembly of Georgia on December 21, 1836. Since it was to cross the state line into Tennessee and connect with the Tennessee River near Ross' Landing, companion legislation was passed by the Tennessee General Assembly on January 24, 1838. These legislative acts provided for a railroad to be surveyed and constructed from a point near present day Chattanooga, Tennessee, on the Tennessee River, to an eligible point on the southeastern bank of the Chattahoochee River in Georgia. The survey was made under the direction of Lt. Col. Stephen Harriman Long, U. S. Army. Construction began around the end of November 1839 and the last rails were laid in the spring of 1850. The total cost of building the Western & Atlantic, paid by the people of Georgia, was $4,087,925.00. With the southern end of the line established southeast of the Chattahoochee River at a place called Terminus (later known as Marthasville and then Atlanta), the Macon & Western Railroad and the Georgia Railroad were extended to that point as well.

Another important link was the Atlanta & La Grange Railroad, begun in 1849, which later formed the line from Atlanta to West Point and on to Montgomery, Alabama, via the Western Railway of Alabama, better known as the West Point Route.[1]

With so much railroad building going on in Georgia, the state of Tennessee recognized the need for land transportation, and in 1845 authorized the construction of the Nashville & Chattanooga Railroad to connect those two cities. Construction of the East Tennessee & Georgia Railroad began soon after to provide a line connecting Knoxville, Tennessee, with the Western & Atlantic at Dalton, Georgia. Later, a branch line was built from Cleveland, Tennessee, to Chattanooga using a tunnel bored through the north end of Missionary Ridge. Another line, the Memphis & Charleston Railroad, ran east from Memphis and connected with the Nashville & Chattanooga Railroad at Stevenson, Alabama, sharing the latter's tracks in order to enter Chattanooga.

The Western & Atlantic Railroad was the connecting link in a well devised system of railroads that made Georgia the "Keystone State of the South," and the future city of Atlanta, "The Gateway City." The route today remains essentially as surveyed by Colonel Long and his men in the 1830s. The W&A is a very crooked railroad, with total curvatures exceeding 10,000 degrees— meaning that in a distance of 138 miles, the road effectively makes about 28 complete circles.[2]

In his annual report of September 30, 1860, Superintendent John W. Lewis referred to the Western & Atlantic as the "crookedest road under the sun."[3] Colonel Long did succeed in laying out a line that was free of heavy grades. The ruling grade is less than one percent, which is remarkable when one considers the topography between Atlanta and Chattanooga. Colonel Long found a way to leave Chattanooga without having to tunnel under Missionary Ridge as the East Tennessee & Geor-

---

[1] James Houston Johnston, *Western & Atlantic Railroad of the State of Georgia* (Atlanta, 1952), pp 1-8; Ulrich Bonnell Phillips, *A History of Transportation in the Eastern Cotton Belt to 1860* (New York, 1908), p. 365.

[2] Employee's Educational Service, *The Nashville, Chattanooga & St. Louis Railway* (Nashville, 1941), Lesson No 1, p. 28.

[3] Annual Report, Western & Atlantic Railroad, Sept. 30, 1860, p. 5.

gia Railroad did, but as he came south through the ridge and valley section of northwest Georgia it was necessary to tunnel through Chetoogeta Mountain. This tunnel was the final obstacle to completion of the Western & Atlantic, and the headings were driven through on October 31, 1849. On May 9, 1850, the rails were finished and with much ceremony, the first train ran over the entire line.[4] The tunnel through Chetoogeta Mountain is 1,477 feet in length and extends in an east-west direction, though the Western & Atlantic generally runs north-south.[5] In spite of the importance of this tunnel to opposing armies, neither side made any attempt to block it or destroy it during the Civil War other then to remove rails. Likewise, the tunnel of the Nashville & Chattanooga at Cowan, Tennessee, which ran through the Cumberland Mountains, and the tunnel through Missionary Ridge into Chattanooga on the ET&Ga Railroad were preserved by both sides.

In his memoirs, General Sherman related a story about the Chetoogeta tunnel during the Federal advance in June 1864. On a hot day, a group of Rebels lay in the shade of a tree overlooking the Federal camps about Big Shanty. One soldier remarked to his fellows: "Well, the Yanks will have to git up and git now, for I heard General Johnston himself say that General Wheeler had blown up the tunnel near Dalton, and that the Yanks would have to retreat, because they could get no more rations." "Oh Hell," said a listener, "don't you know that old Sherman carries a duplicate tunnel along?"[6]

The organization set up to operate the W&A during its early days of operations was very simple—and probably typical of the day—for a road with 138 miles of main line track. The superintendent in charge of the operations of the line reported directly to the governor of Georgia. This relationship often required the superintendent to perform functions quite foreign to the operations of a railroad, such as the issuance of

---

[4] Johnston, *Western & Atlantic Railroad,* p. 39.

[5] Annual Report, Western & Atlantic Railroad, Sept. 30, 1849, p. 1.

[6] William T. Sherman, *Memoirs of General William T. Sherman, by Himself,* 2 vols. (New York, 1875), vol. 2, p, 151.

fractional currency during the Civil War.[7] The superintendent's principal assistants were the Treasurer, Master of Transportation, and Master Machinist. The Treasurer was in charge of all fiscal matters and handled receipts and disbursements. The Master of Transportation was responsible for the daily operation of trains and stations and the maintenance of the track and right-of-way. The Master Machinist was in charge of the shops and responsible for maintenance and repair of locomotives and rolling stock. The headquarters were located in Atlanta as were the shops and other facilities of the road.

The road bed of the W&A, as initially constructed, bears little resemblance to the line today. The ties were logs cut to length, untreated, and laid on the ground with no ballast. The rails were of the strap iron bar type, with spikes driven through holes in the bar and laid on longitudinal stringers of wood. The strap iron rails proved very unsafe and would sometimes turn up at the end, forming a so-called "snakehead," which could pierce the floor of a railcar and, on occasion, would go all the way through the top. These rails were replaced with bars which had a flange to one side through which the spikes were driven. This rail was also laid on wooden stringers, but was heavier and somewhat safer. The next type used was the "U" rail, weighing 45 pounds to the yard. These rails of rolled wrought iron did not stand up well under traffic. It was not until 1857 that the new Pear rail, forerunner of the modern "T" rail, was laid on the W&A and by 1861, a total of 50 miles of track had been laid with this new rail. The gauge of the road (the distance between the rails) was five feet.[8] While better than the flange bar rail and the "U" rail, the Pear rail of the period was also made of wrought iron, and consequently exhibited all of that metal's disadvantages. It was called Pear rail because the ball of the rail in cross-section resembled an inverted pear. The remaining 88 miles were laid for the most part with "U" rail, with some

[7] Allen D. Candler, *Confederate Records of the State of Georgia*, 5 vols. (Atlanta, 1909), vol. 2, p. 254.

[8] Interview with James Bell, Engineer,W&A Railroad, by Wilbur G. Kurtz, Kurtz Collection, Atlanta Historical Society, notebook no. 3, p. 40; Annual Report, Western & Atlantic Railroad, September 30, 1862, p. 6.

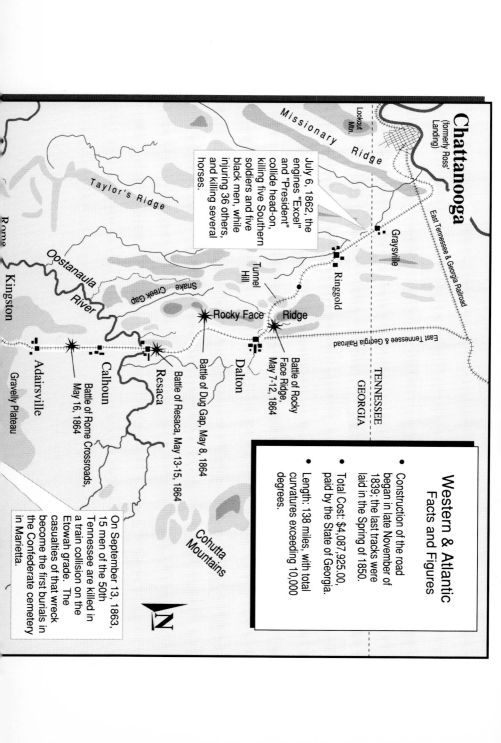

Chattanooga
(formerly Ross' Landing)

Lookout Mtn.

Missionary Ridge

Taylor's Ridge

East Tennessee & Georgia Railroad

July 6, 1862, the engines "Excel" and "President" collide head-on, killing five Southern soldiers and five black men, while injuring 36 others, and killing several horses.

Graysville

Ringgold

Tunnel Hill

Snake Creek Gap

Rome

Oostanaula River

Kingston

Rocky Face Ridge

Battle of Rocky Face Ridge, May 7-12, 1864

Battle of Dug Gap, May 8, 1864

Dalton

East Tennessee & Georgia Railroad

TENNESSEE
GEORGIA

Adairsville

Gravelly Plateau

Calhoun

Battle of Rome Crossroads, May 16, 1864

Resaca

Battle of Resaca, May 13-15, 1864

Cohutta Mountains

Western & Atlantic Facts and Figures

- Construction of the road began in late November of 1839; the last tracks were laid in the Spring of 1850.

- Total Cost: $4,087,925.00, paid by the State of Georgia.

- Length: 138 miles, with total curvatures exceeding 10,000 degrees.

On September 13, 1863, 15 men of the 50th Tennessee are killed in a train collision on the Etowah grade. The casualties of that wreck become the first burials in the Confederate cemetery in Marietta.

N

The Western & Atlantic Railroad

The "crookedest road under the sun."

```
0        10        20
M I L E S
```

Etowah River

Coosa River

Skirmishes at Cassville, May 19, 1864

Following the fall of Atlanta, Allatoona Pass, a critical supply depot for Sherman's armies, withstands a fierce assault by French's Division on October 5, 1864, as General Hood moves his Confederate army north.

Battle of New Hope Church, May 25, 1864

Battle of Dallas, May 28, 1864

Pumpkin Vine Creek

Battle of Pickett's Mill, May 27, 1864

Lost Mtn.

Battle of Kennesaw Mtn., June 27, 1864

Battle of Kolb's Farm, June 22, 1864

Allatoona

Big Shanty

Marietta

"The Great Locomotive Chase," or Andrews' Raid. On the evening of April 12, 1862, twenty-two Union volunteers commandeered the engine "General" at Big Shanty, and traversed 90 miles before being captured near Graysville.

On the evening of September 1, 1864, five locomotives and 81 cars of ammunition are set afire as Hood's forces evacuate Atlanta.

Chattahoochee River

Battle of Jonesboro, August 31–September 1, 1864

Atlanta & West Point Railroad

East Point

Western & Macon RR

Jonesboro

Atlanta
(originally named "Terminus," then "Marthasville.")

Battle of Ezra Church, July 28, 1864

Decatur

Vinings Station

Peachtree Creek

Battle of Peachtree Creek, July 20, 1864

Battle of Atlanta, July 22, 1864

flange bar rail on the northern end. Such was the condition of the track and road bed of the W&A at the outset of the Civil War.[9]

The locomotives in use were very light, and all but one locomotive owned by the W&A was of the American type, 4-4-0, i.e., with four driving wheels, four leading truck wheels and no trailing truck wheels. The one exception was the oldest locomotive on the road, an 0-6-0 type, used primarily in switching service, with six driving wheels and no leading or trailing truck wheels. Two classic examples of the locomotives used by the W&A of the Civil War period survive today in the *General* and the *Texas,* both of Andrews' Raid fame, with the *Texas* retaining more of its 1860s authenticity. At the start of the Civil War, the newest locomotives on the road were five purchased in 1857, while the oldest had been in service since 1847.[10]

A typical train at the war's outset consisted of six to 10 loaded cars—none weighing more than 16,000 pounds—travelling at an average speed of roughly ten miles per hour. The engine crew included an engineer, fireman, and a wood-passer. All locomotives burned wood as fuel, and for the year ending September 30, 1862, the 46 locomotives in service on the W&A consumed 14,403 cords of wood to travel 542,253 miles. The average locomotive ran 37.65 miles on a single cord of wood. Thus it took about three and a half cords of wood to move a train from Atlanta to Chattanooga.[11]

When the Civil War began in 1861, the W&A Railroad was a critical link in the western rail system, connecting the Nashville & Chattanooga, the Memphis & Charleston, and the East Tennessee and Georgia lines with Atlanta, together with the roads fanning out south, east, and west from that city. Operation of these railroads was in the hands of individual owners and the officers of each line, and in many cases the various lines did not connect at terminals. The Confederacy was never able to create a central authority over the several railroads of the south as the

[9] Annual Report, Western & Atlantic Railroad, Sept. 30, 1862, p. 6.

[10] Richard E. Prince, *The Nashville, Chattanooga & St. Louis Railway* (Green River, 1967), pp. 48-49.

[11] Annual Report, Western & Atlantic Railroad, Sept. 30, 1862, p. 17.

Federal government was able to do with its rail lines. This failure to establish a coordinating authority resulted in many problems between the state of Georgia, the Confederate government in Richmond, and the Confederate Army over the use of railroad equipment. The W&A was operated by the state of Georgia with general supervision in the hands of the superintendent, whose duty and responsibility it was to conduct operations of the road and to appoint subordinate officers, subject to the approval of the governor. He was also vested with power to make contracts, settle claims, and to ensure repair and maintenance of equipment for the road.[12] Effective January 1, 1858, Governor Joseph Brown of Georgia appointed longtime friend and associate Dr. John W. Lewis as superintendent of the W&A.[13] Lewis proved to be a very competent superintendent, and during his nearly three years in office made considerable improvements to the physcial condition of the road, primarily by laying new Pear rail, improving bridges, and widening cuts and embankments. The road was profitable, enriching the state treasury by several hundred thousand dollars each year. Dr. Lewis was replaced in 1861 by John S. Rowland, another long time associate of Governor Brown's. Rowland died in 1863, however, and was replaced by Dr. George D. Phillips, who remained as superintendent until operations were taken over by the United States Military Railroads (U.S.M.R.R.) on September 2, 1864.[14]

The year 1861 was a good one for the W&A, with net earnings reported at $547,041.73. Several new bridges were constructed and improvements made to the road bed. Camp McDonald, a camp of military instruction and training was established at Big Shanty on June 11, 1861, and the year saw several troop movements to the Virginia theater by way of the W&A. There were 47 locomotives on hand in 1861, and as of September 30, 1861, ten were in need of repair.[15]

---

[12] Johnston, *Western & Atlantic Railroad,* p. 43.

[13] Ibid., p. 51.

[14] Ibid., p. 57.

[15] Annual Report, Western & Atlantic Railroad, Sept. 30, 1861, Locomotive Table.

In October 1861, Governor Brown had his first major conflict with the Confederate government over operation of the W&A, when Secretary of War Judah P. Benjamin ordered the W&A to provide six locomotives and 70 box cars for use in military operations in East Tennessee. The result was an angry exchange of telegrams between Richmond and Milledgeville, and in the end, the Secretary of War gave way. At one point Governor Brown wired Richmond "If you seize our cars or engines I shall by military force if necessary, make counter seizures."[16]

The increased traffic on the W&A in 1862 is reflected in the net earnings increase to $998,270.41, although damage to the railroad by the enemy was beginning to become a factor. In the early part of the year, two important bridges across Chickamauga Creek on the northern end of the line were burned. Another attempt at destruction of the road was foiled when the Andrews Raid of April 12, 1862 failed in its mission to disable the road. As the first serious attempt by the Federals to damage the railroad, the raid did alert the Southern authorities to the need to guard the bridges, and a system was created for that purpose. Andrews' Raid was soon established as one of the most colorful and daring events of the war; some of the participants in the raid were the first recipients of the Medal of Honor, the United States' highest award for valor.[17]

The summer of 1862 saw the first large Confederate troop movement by rail. On June 27, Gen. Braxton Bragg ordered the movement of Maj. Gen. John P. McCown's division of about 3,000 men from Mississippi to Chattanooga. The troops were routed via Mobile, Montgomery and Atlanta, with the last leg on the W&A to Chattanooga. The movement of 776 miles took only six days, ending on July 3, 1862.[18]

A few days later, on July 6, 1862, there occurred a tragic accident on the W&A near Johnson's Station south of Graysville, Georgia. A head-on collision killed five soldiers, seven blacks, six horses and injured 36 other soldiers.[19] The engineer of the north-bound train, Sylvester M.

---

[16] Robert C. Black, *The Railroads of the Confederacy* (Chapel Hill, 1952), pp. 68-69.

[17] The Andrews' Raid is best described in Charles O'Neill, *Wild Train* (New York, 1956).

[18] Black, *Railroads of the Confederacy,* p. 181.

[19] *The Daily Intelligencer,* Atlanta, GA, July 8, 1862.

Cannon, and his fireman, George Prince, were also killed. The two
W&A locomotives involved were the *Excel* and the *President,* and the
Annual Report for 1862 reports both locomotives in the shop for repairs.
Superintendent John S. Rowland investigated the accident and reported
it was due to military interference by officers and men on the north-
bound train. It was not uncommon in accidents of this nature for the
soldiers aboard the train to make a quick judgment as to fault, and the
train crew involved would immediately take to the woods. Tom Haney,
engineer on the south-bound train, jumped from the train and fled from
the accident.[20] An interesting sequel to this story occurred some years
after the war when the widow of Engineer Cannon brought suit against
the State of Georgia to recover damages due to the death of her husband.
During the appeal process, the case came before the Georgia Supreme
Court, with ex-Governor Joseph E. Brown presiding as Chief Justice.
The suit was denied, with Chief Justice Brown declaring that the state
could pay no damages because Sylvester M. Cannon, an engineer of a
train hauling armed soldiers in time of war, was aiding and abetting
rebellion against the peace and dignity of the government of the United
States of America.[21]

Superintendent Rowland, in his report to the governor of October 1,
1862, indicated that the W&A had suffered a good bit that year. Rolling
stock of every description had been terribly cut up and abused, and in
many cases completely ruined, in the transportation of Confederate
troops. According to the superintendent, the troops themselves were responsible for the damage:

> . . .closed box cars were used principally, and the weather
> being very warm, in order to get fresh air, and prevent suffer-
> ing, they cut the cars to pieces. Many also rode on top of the
> cars, thereby tearing loose, and wearing out the tin covering
> which cannot now be replaced. Our cars have been pressed
> by the military authorities and taken on other roads. We have

[20] Ibid., July 9, 1862.

[21] Georgia Supreme Court Reports, Atlanta, 1867, vol. 34, p. 422.

lost 180 cars, many of which are on the Mobile & Ohio
Railroad in Mississippi, and other roads.[22]

The W&A had 46 locomotives still on hand at the end of September
1862. Two were in the shop undergoing repairs and five others were
reported as needing repairs, leaving a balance of 39 locomotives reported
as in "Good Order."[23]

Although the annual report of the superintendent of the W&A for the
year ending September 30, 1863 is not available, Governor Brown related some information in his annual message to the General Assembly
of November 5, 1863. The railroad had paid into the state treasury for
that fiscal year $1,650,000.00, and there was due from the Confederate
government the sum of $427,586.75. Governor Brown also reported on
the deterioration of the road bed and equipment because of the heavy
military traffic the Road was called upon to handle.[24]

Military activity increased in the state in 1863, and demands upon
the W&A became even greater. April of that year saw a second attempt
at destruction of the road as Col. Abel D. Streight with some 1,700
Federal mounted infantry, most of whom were riding mules, moved
across northern Alabama with Rome, Ga. as their objective. Streight
planned to cut the W&A east of Rome, but he failed in his mission when
he was forced to surrender to a much smaller force commanded by
Nathan Bedford Forrest near Cedar Bluff, Alabama, on May 3, 1863.

During September of 1863, the greater part of Lt. Gen. Longstreet's
corps was moved west from Virginia to augment Braxton Bragg's forces
in northern Georgia. The troops moved by way of the W&A for the final
leg from Atlanta to Catoosa Platform Station, three miles east of Ringgold.[25] Colonel G. Moxley Sorrell, Longstreet's chief of staff, wrote
with respect to this movement: "Never before were so many troops
moved over such worn-out railways, none first class from the beginning.

---

[22] Annual Report, Western & Atlantic Railroad, Sept. 30, 1862, p. 7.

[23] Ibid., pp. 16-17.

[24] Johnston, *Western & Atlantic Railroad*, p. 55.

[25] Black, *Railroads of the Confederacy*, p. 190.

Never were such crazy cars—passenger, baggage, mail, box, platform, all and any sort wabbling on the Jumping strap-iron—used for hauling good soldiers."[26]

John Coxe, a member of Joseph Kershaw's Brigade, LaFayette McLaws' Division, made this move via Petersburg, Weldon, Wilmington, Florence, Charleston, Savannah, Millen, Macon to Atlanta and thence the W&A to Catoosa Platform Station. He wrote:

> we arrived at Atlanta about noon. We found a railroad con-
> gestion there in consequence of a block of troops and freight
> on the W&A, then the only direct line open to Chattanooga
> and Bragg's Army. A train was made up for us and we got
> aboard, but didn't start until 9 PM. But here occurred more
> engine trouble. Our little engine, named *Kentucky,* was too
> light for the weight of our train and had much difficulty
> climbing grades. I went to sleep, but was waked up a little
> before daylight by the noise of the *Kentucky* trying to 'puff
> up' the grade of Allatoona Mountain. She made three efforts
> before she made it to the station at the top by daylight. We
> ran to Cartersville, and stopped two hours to allow our engi-
> neer to work on the cylinders of the engine. Apparently he
> made a good job of it, because we ran on without further
> hitch till we got to Dalton about the middle of that cold and
> dreary afternoon. And here we found a complete tie-up.
> There were many trains there, and every piece of siding was
> jammed with them. On account of burned bridges, trains
> could run only 12 miles further, and though there was a large
> railroad water tank at Dalton, yet there was no water for the
> engines, and the tender of our engine was nearly empty. It
> was said that the pump of the tank was broken. There was
> great confusion, engineers, conductors, firemen, and many
> army officers and soldiers making all sorts of suggestions for
> relieving the situation, but no relief came. The weather was
> windy and cold. At last toward night, General Kershaw took
> the matter in hand as far as our train was concerned. Procur-

---

[26] G. Moxley Sorrell, *Recollections of a Confederate Staff Officer* (Jackson, 1958), p. 180.

ing about 20 water buckets from somewhere, he ordered our train to a creek about two miles distant. Here a bucket squad from water to tender was formed. This was in the nature of an endless chain, and after an hour's such work, the tank of our tender was supplied sufficiently for all present needs. And our train then proceeded to the burned bridge over the west branch of the Chickamauga River, where it stopped about 11:00 PM in a cornfield. Most of us were asleep when the order to disembark was shouted through the freight coaches and waked us up. We got off on the right and saw across the field a large clump of trees, about a quarter of a mile away, and we were at once ordered to march over there and build up fires, for the night air was frosty.[27]

The movement of Longstreet's Corps over the W&A was not without serious mishap, however. On Sunday, September 13, 1863, a northbound train pulled by the locomotive *Senator*

and loaded with troops of the 50th Tennessee Infantry Regiment of Gen. John Gregg's Brigade, Johnson's Division, ran off the track some two miles north of Marietta. Once the derailed cars were pushed off the track, the train continued northward, now behind schedule. That evening this same train collided with a southbound train, pulled by the locomotive Chieftain, on the Etowah grade at Stegall's Station. Fifteen soldiers of the 50th Tennessee Regiment were killed and 40 wounded. The southbound train was carrying wounded men from the fighting around Ringgold."[28]

The casualties from this wreck were taken to Marietta and were the first to be buried in the Confederate Cemetery in that city.[29] The remainder of the 50th Tennessee finally reached Bragg's Army on September

---

[27] John Coxe, "Chickamauga," in *Confederate Veteran,* 40 vols. (Nashville, August 1922), 30, p. 292.

[28] *The Daily Intelligencer,* Sept. 15 and Sept. 16, 1863.

[29] *Georgia Historical Markers* (Helen, 1983), p. 151.

18 and was heavily engaged in the opening phases of the Battle of Chickamauga, a battle in which the regiment would nearly be annihilated.

After the abandonment of Chattanooga by the Confederates following the Battle of Missionary Ridge on November 25, 1863, the W&A was used primarily by the military in support of the Confederate Army of Tennessee in northwest Georgia. General Bragg (and subsequently Joseph E. Johnston) headquartered the army at Dalton through the winter of 1863-1864. There was some skirmishing along the northern end of the W&A during November and December 1863 primarily in the vicinity of Ringgold.

In late 1863, the employees of the W&A were organized into two military companies forming a State Road Battalion under the command of Maj. George Hillyer, who also served as auditor of the railroad. The State Railroad Battalion was encamped at Griswoldville. Conductor William A. Fuller was placed in command of one of these companies and commissioned a captain in the "Independent State Road Guards" by Governor Brown.[30] Fuller's unit never performed any military service, and after removal of the headquarters of the W&A from Atlanta to Griswoldville in 1864, he had problems controlling his troops. He complained of the fact that the superintendent detailed engine crews all over the state without coordination and that many employees of the road and members of the unit were given passes, or else left of their own accord, to care for families and personal property. Major Hillyer kept a tighter rein over the track men and shop hands whose duties, at that time, did not require them to be on the road.[31]

The annual report of the superintendent as of September 30, 1864 reported net earnings of $1,114,752.70. Governor Brown had ordered a 100% increase in freight rates charged to the Confederate government and the W&A had the sum of $977,774.60 due from the Confederate

---

[30] It was Fuller's train which was stolen at Big Shanty on the morning of April 12, 1862, by the Federal raiding party under James J. Andrews. Fuller's military rank, so often cited in accounts of the Andrews Raid, is in reference to this 1863 commission.

[31] Major George Hillyer Letters, August 1864, Griswoldville, GA., Department of Archives & History, State of Georgia, Atlanta, GA.

government—which constituted most of the profit for the year. Depreciated currency had its effect on the real earnings of the road. Depreciation notwithstanding, the W&A paid into the state treasury $278,000 and also invested $180,000 in the "Blockade Company."[32] Heavy losses were suffered in rolling stock and locomotives. A review of the earnings by month for the year ending September 30, 1864, indicates that February was the peak month with a high of $411,932.66 in income, dropping to $16,678.93 in July (reflecting the withdrawal of Confederate forces to the south in the Atlanta Campaign, as well as the "refugeeing" of citizens of northwest Georgia. No earnings were reported for August and September because the W&A of the State of Georgia was no longer in operation.[33]

In spite of the Federal forces in Chattanooga and the need for rail transportation to support them, it was not until January 1864 that the Nashville & Chattanooga Railroad bridge over the Tennessee River at Bridgeport, Alabama, was repaired and put back in service. The first supply train ran over this bridge and into Chattanooga on January 14, 1864.[34] This bridge had been out of service since July 1863 and reflected the poor effort of the Federal forces at that time to keep the railroads running. Finally, on December 19, 1863, the War Department ordered Col. Daniel C. McCallum, Chief of the U. S. Military Railroads,

---

[32] The Blockade Company was apparently a company set up at the instigation of Governor Brown of Georgia to enable the state to run the Federal naval blockade of Southern ports. Louise B. Hill, in *Joseph E. Brown and the Confederacy* (Westport, 1972), p. 157, indicated that Brown had previously purchased shares in shipping companies for the State of Georgia, and that on March 1, 1864, Brown chartered four vessels to engage more extensively in the shipping business, though no mention is made of the Blockade Company. Historian E. Merton Coulter, in *A Short History of Georgia* (Chapel Hill, 1933), p. 305, fails to mention the Blockade Company but discusses two other enterprises: the Belgian American Company, incorporated by the Georgia legislature in 1860 and pledged $100,000 annually as a guarantee to it of profits of not less than 5% on the investment, and the Direct Trade & Navigation Co., chartered to engage in domestic and foreign commerce. James H. Johnston, in his *Western & Atlantic RR*, p. 110, adds the following: "During the War between the States an allotment of $180,000 was made in 1864 to the 'Blockade Company.' The cash books of the road's treasurer carries no explanation of this item, but it was issued upon warrant of the Governor, and the use to which it was put is self-evident." It appears that this expenditure from W&A profits was a low-key affair handled by Governor Brown, and reflects his tight control over the railroad.

[33] Annual Report, Western & Atlantic Railroad, Oct. 1, 1864, p. 5.

[34] Jesse C., Burt, Jr., *The Nashville, Chattanooga & St. Louis Railway, 1854-1872: The Era of Transition,* The East Tennessee Historical Society, Knoxville, TN., Publication No. 23, 1951, p. 63.

to Tennessee to examine the Nashville & Chattanooga Railroad and help in its reconstruction in order to support the forces at Chattanooga.[35] The War Department in Washington, soon after the beginning of the Civil War, recognized a need for military units trained to operate the railroads. In order to maintain and operate the railroad facilities required in the war effort, the Secretary of War set up a para-military command and dispensed army rank to experts selected for their achievements in civilian life. In this way, the War Department was able to attract the services of able railroad administrators like Herman Haupt, Daniel C. McCallum and others to serve with the U. S. Military Railroads.

Colonel McCallum was a Scottish immigrant who, as a young boy, settled with his parents in Rochester, New York, in the 1820s. After an elementary schooling, he went to work for the New York & Erie Railroad and by 1854 was made general superintendent of that road. On February 11, 1862, he was appointed Military Director and Superintendent of Railroads in the United States pursuant to an act of January 31, 1862, which gave the government the authority to control and operate captured Southern railroads. He was commissioned with the rank of colonel. While he often acted in an independent capacity, Colonel McCallum and the U . S. Military Railroads were under the Quartermaster General of the U. S. Army.[36]

By the end of 1863, operation of U.S. Military Railroads in the Eastern Theater was pretty routine, and with the movement of Maj. Gen. U.S. Grant to Chattanooga and the subsequent buildup of forces there, the railroads of that area required special attention. As a consequence, Colonel McCallum was assigned to Chattanooga along with his chief of construction, Col. W. W. Wright and a portion of one division of the Construction Corps consisting of 285 men. In 13 days, Colonel Wright had the Nashville & Chattanooga bridge over the Tennessee River at Bridgeport restored and then went to work to put the 151 miles of the

---

[35] U.S. War Department, *The War of the Rebellion: The Official Records of the Union and Confederate Armies,* 128 vols. (Washington, D.C., 1890-1901), series III, vol. 5, p. 934. Hereinafter cited as *OR.*

[36] Thomas Weber, *The Northern Railroads in the Civil War* (Westport, 1970), p. 135.

Nashville & Chattanooga into condition to support the Union forces in and around Chattanooga.[37]

After the war, General Johnston inquired of General Sherman who the chief railroad engineer was for his command. When told it was Col. W. W. Wright, a civilian, Johnston was apparently surprised, and told Sherman that the Federal feats of bridge building and repairs of roads had "excited" his imagination. Johnston went on to relate an incident during the Battle of Kennesaw Mountain. An officer from Maj. Gen. Joseph Wheeler's cavalry reported they had made a break in the W&A near Tilton Station which he said would take at least a fortnight to repair. During their discussion, a train was seen coming down the road which had passed that break. General Sherman went on to write "I doubt whether the history of war can furnish more examples of skill and bravery than attended the defense of the railroad from Nashville to Atlanta during the year 1864."[38]

The U.S.M.R.R. had a very simple organizational structure. There were two major departments, one for transportation and one for construction. The Transportation Department was assigned three functions: first, conducting transportation or managing the movements of trains; second, maintenance of roads and structures; and third, maintenance of rolling stock and locomotives. The Construction Department had but one function: the repair and construction of railroads. This department was organized into divisions, the number of which was increased or diminished as needs required. At its peak, there were six Construction Divisions on the U.S.M.R.R. in the Military Division of the Mississippi, which generally included the western theater of operations. On February 10, 1864, Col. Adna Anderson was appointed General Superintendent of Transportation, and Col. W. W. Wright was appointed as Chief Engineer of Construction. Most of the personnel of the U.S.M.R.R. were civilians.[39] Earlier, Anderson had been engineer of the Virginia railroads terminating at Alexandra, and since January 1, 1863, chief engineer of

[37] Burt, *Nashville, Chattanooga & St. Louis Railway,* p. 63.

[38] Sherman, *Memoirs,* 2, pp. 151-152.

[39] *OR* 5, series III, p. 982.

the military railroads in Virginia. Wright had also gained valuable experience on the Virginia railroads, as well as during the Gettysburg campaign under Brig. Gen. Herman Haupt, then Chief of the U.S.M.R.R.[40]

General Sherman assumed command of the Military Division of the Mississippi on March 18, 1864, and on April 6, 1864, issued General Order No. 6 from his headquarters in Nashville. This order restricted the railroads of the U.S.M.R.R. to carrying food, ammunition, and army supplies. Troops and cattle were to be moved on foot and private shipments were allowed only on return trips. Private citizens were allowed to travel on the railroads only when issued a permit by one of the commanders of military departments or the commander of the Military Division of the Mississippi. This order enabled the U.S.M.R.R. to fulfill its mission of supplying the armies in the field.[41]

A division of the Construction Corps of the U.S.M.R.R. consisted of a total of 777 men. In overall charge was a division engineer, directing five subdivisions in specific missions, incuding the repair and construction of bridges and trestles; track construction; the creation and maintenance of water stations; masonry work as might be required; and internal transportation support with oxen and 18 authorized ox drivers. In addition, the division was assigned a railroad train complete with crew so that the entire unit could be moved on short notice with its equipment and supplies.[42]

The Transportation Department included the operating crews of trains, dispatchers, clerks, maintenance of way personnel, machinists, and shop personnel for the maintenance of locomotives and rolling stock. Generally, each railroad was operated by a Superintendent of Transportation who was responsible for the complete operation of the railroad and who reported to Col. Adna Anderson, General Superintendent of Transportation, U.S.M.R.R. For operating purposes of the U.S.M.R.R., the W&A was merged with the East Tennessee and Georgia

---

[40] Weber, *Northern Railroads in the Civil War,* p. 192.

[41] Duncan K Major and Roger S. Fitch, *Supply of Sherman's Army During the Atlanta Campaign* (Ft. Leavenworth, 1911), pp. 15-16.

[42] *OR* 5, series III, pp. 968-969.

Railroad—Col. L. P. Wright was general superintendent of both roads until July 1, 1864, with his headquarters in Chattanooga. He was relieved by W. C. Taylor on July 1, 1864, who was in turn replaced by A. A. Talmage on January 1, 1865.[43]

As Colonel McCallum and the U.S.M.R.R. took over the Nashville & Chattanooga and later the W&A and other connecting lines, there was an urgent need for locomotives and rolling stock, as little or none were to be found on the captured roads. Colonel McCallum was authorized to procure new locomotives without delay, and to expropriate them from other railroads when practicable. Demonstrating the industrial capability of the North during the Civil War, beginning in April of 1864, 140 new locomotives were delivered to Nashville for the U.S.M.R.R., and 18 locomotives were borrowed from five-foot guage railroads in Kentucky, 14 of which came from the Louisville & Nashville Railroad. Other cars were procured from elsewhere in the North.[44]

As the Confederate forces fell back deeper into Georgia, the U.S.M.R.R. took over operations of the W&A. It quickly became apparent to the Federals that considerable construction was required to put the line back in shape, and the task of maintaining it once repaired would be no less difficult. Colonel Wright, in his final report to Colonel McCallum on April 24, 1866, stated that "the reconstruction and maintenance of this line was in many respects the most difficult and interesting of any military operation during the War."[45] As General Johnston gave up portions of the W&A, he damaged the road so as to delay the Federal advance. Regardless of the damage done, however, the railroad was quickly repaired by the Construction Corps of the U.S.M.R.R. Small, skilled detachments placed along the line with tools and supplies took care of small breaks in the tracks. When a big break occurred, a complete division of the Construction Corps, and more if necessary, was moved in to do the work. Repair work began on the W&A on March 1, 1864, and

---

[43] Talmage remained in charge until September 1, 1865, when he was succeed by A. J. Cheeny. Cheeny remained in that position until September 25, 1865, when the road was returned to Georgia and Campbell Wallace was appointed to the position. Ibid., p. 993.

[44] Weber, *Northern Railroads in the Civil War,* pp. 194-195.

[45] *OR 5*, series III, p. 950.

by March 20, the road was in service a short distance south of Ringgold in support of the Federal army.

From May 7 to May 8, 1864, heavy fighting took place along the W&A at Tunnel Hill and Rocky Face Ridge near Dalton. This action is often referred to as the beginning of The Atlanta Campaign, which for the most part, followed the tracks of the W&A from Dalton south to Atlanta. On May 9, when Maj. Gen. James B. McPherson's Army of the Tennessee came through Snake Creek Gap and threatened Johnston's rear, the Confederates began falling back along the W&A to Resaca. After the fighting at Resaca on May 13-15, the Southerners fell back across the Oostanaula River, burning the railroad bridge behind them.

The Federal construction train ran into Resaca with the advanced elements of the army on the night of May 15, and began work on the Oostanaula Bridge while the iron parts were still hot. By May 20 the bridge was completed, and Federal supply trains were running to Kingston.[46]

The next project for the Construction Corps was the Etowah River bridge, destroyed by General Johnston's forces on May 20 as they fell back to the Allatoona Mountain range. Two thousand construction troops rebuilt the 600-foot long, 67-foot high bridge in five and one half days, completing their work at noon on June 11.[47]

On May 22, General Sherman began his flanking movement to the Dallas-New Hope Church-Pickett's Mill area, and for the first time during the campaign moved away from the W&A. After the fighting there, and the capture of Allatoona Pass by Maj. Gen. George Stoneman's cavalry on June 1, Sherman began moving his forces eastward back to the W&A. There was fighting along the W&A at Acworth and Big Shanty on June 4 as the troops on both sides arrayed themselves before Kennesaw Mountain. Diners at the Lacy Hotel in Big Shanty were quite startled that evening when a solid shot fired by a gun of the Chicago Board of Trade Battery hit one of the upper rooms of the hotel, rolled

[46] Sherman, *Memoirs,* 2, p. 44.

[47] Ibid., p. 51.

down the stairs, out the back door and into the yard, striking the iron pot in which the family wash was boiling.[48]

Mr. C. J. Hevey of Rome, Ga., who was an engineer for the U.S.M.R.R. in 1864, reminisced in the *Locomotive Engineer,* December 1891, of train operations on the W&A in 1864. He wrote:

> All engines were double-crewed and they never got cold. We ran by orders something after this style: 'Engines Nos. 133, 134 and 135 will meet engines Nos. 126, 127 and 128 at Graysville.' There was no superiority, the orders were emphatic, and no trouble ever experienced. Rear collisions [were] few. All trains were supplied with a train guard of soldiers, who soon became expert brakemen, so that trains at the low speed we ran could be stopped very quickly. For fear of becoming tiresome, I will shut off here by telling you that myself and Charlie Biggs, with Conductors Ostin and James Sanderson with engine No. 26 hauled the timber for the bridge built by McDonald over the Etowah River under penalty of being placed in the front ranks with a musket if he did not finish said bridge in a very short specified time. McDonald saved his 'bacon' and had about 13 hours to spare. I ran that engine over the bridge that number of hours ahead of Sherman's schedule.[49]

The Battle of Kennesaw Mountain took place on June 27, and again the scene of action was close to the tracks of the W&A. The Federal forces were using the W&A as far south as Allatoona Pass, where they had established a large depot to handle rations and ammunition. The Confederate forces were using the south end of the line to bring up supplies to Marietta and to evacuate the wounded south to Atlanta and beyond. One of the locomotives supporting the Confederates at Kennesaw Mountain was the *General* of Andrews' Raid fame, and according to

---

[48] Wilbur G. Kurtz, "Historic Big Shanty Now Known as Kennesaw," *The Atlanta Constitution Sunday Magazine,* Oct. 23, 1938.

[49] William McDonald was assistant engineer of the 3rd Division of the Construction Corps, U.S.M.R.R., and was in charge of building the Etowah River Bridge.

an account in a local newspaper, she almost came under fire of the Federal batteries during this battle:

> When the battle began during the early morning General Johnston sent up a train load of ammunition, etc., to the Confederate lines at the eastern base of Kennesaw Mountain. The ammunition, etc., was unloaded and carried to the front as quickly as possible, but the engine and train were detained at that point, by order of General Johnston, to carry back the wounded at the close of the battle. During the entire morning the 'General' and her train stood at the point where now is Elizabeth station, and some of the Federal bombshells, flying over the Confederate entrenchments exploded almost in her neighborhood. In the afternoon, wounded soldiers from [Brig. Gen. Winfield S.] Featherstone's [Featherston's] Division, and others in that portion of the field, were placed aboard the train and the 'General' brought them down to Marietta and thence on to Atlanta.[50]

After the Battle of Kennesaw, Johnston fell back towards the Chattahoochee River line. When Maj. Gen. John A. Schofield's Army of the Ohio crossed the Chattahoochee above Johnston's right on July 8, the Confederate commander determined to fall back still further.[51] On July 9, the Confederates crossed the Chatthoochee River and destroyed the W&A bridge over that river.[52] The Federal forces soon had the W&A open to Marietta, and Vinings Station by July 6.

On July 17, Johnston was replaced as commander of the Confederate Army of Tennessee by Gen. John Bell Hood. This change in command was followed by the battles of Peachtree Creek (July 20), and Atlanta (July 22). The latter battle was General Sherman's effort to cut the Georgia Railroad, thereby eliminating Confederate support from the

---

[50] *The Kennesaw Gazette,* Atlanta, GA., March 1886, p. 6.

[51] E. B. Long, *The Civil War Day by Day, An Almanac, 1861-1865* (Garden City, NY., 1971) p. 535.

[52] Sherman, *Memoirs,* 2, p. 70.

east and northeast. The July 27 battle at Ezra Church occurred as Sherman's forces attempted to encircle Atlanta from the west.[53]

The Construction Corps rebuilt the bridge over the Chattahoochee River, and the first train ran over the bridge at noon on August 5. Working only during daylight hours, the bridge, 780 feet long and 92 feet high, was built in four and one half days.[54] Herman Haupt, who created the organization of the U.S.M.R.R., and who had gathered such men as McCallum, Anderson, and Wright to assist him, later wrote that the construction of the "Chattahoochee bridge is the greatest feat of the kind that the world has ever seen."[55] On August 16, the Confederate cavalry under Joseph Wheeler attacked the Federal supply depot at Allatoona Pass with little damage. Atlanta was under bombardment during August as General Sherman moved his forces west around the city, cutting the railroad connections to the southwest and the south.[56]

On August 28 and 29, the Federal troops under Maj. Gens. George Thomas and Oliver O. Howard fought the Confederates at the Battle of East Point and destroyed the Atlanta & West Point Railroad from there down to Fairburn. According to Sherman,

> The track was heaved up in sections the length of a regiment, then separated by rail, bonfires were made of the ties and fence rails on which the rails were heated, carried to trees or telegraph poles, wrapped around and left to cool. Such rails could not be used again; and, to be still more certain, we filled up many deep cuts with trees, brush and earth, and commingled them with loaded shells, so arranged that they would explode on an attempt to haul out the bushes. The explosion of one such shell would have demoralized a gang

[53] Long, *Civil War Day by Day,* pp. 540, 542, 543, 547.

[54] *OR* 5, series III, p. 951. The work was commenced on July 23 and halted the next day. Orders were received to start again on on the 2nd of August, and the bridge was finished on the 5th, taking 4-1/2 days altogether.

[55] Herman Haupt, *Reminiscences of General Herman Haupt* (Milwaukee, 1901), p. 318.

[56] Long, *Civil War Day by Day,* p. 549.

of negroes, and thus would have prevented even the attempt
to clear the road.[57]

Several times during August 1864, as Federal patrols were guarding
the railroad south of Acworth, Confederate raiders threw trains off the
track, often through the use of an iron shoe and a wooden wedge. Many
Federal guards were taken prisoner, as the Confederates then ransacked
the wrecked cars.

Private W. B. Smith of Company K, 14th Illinois Volunteer Infantry
Regiment, was part of a detail guarding the W&A between Big Shanty
and Acworth during August 1864. After chasing a Confederate detachment
bent on wrecking a train near Moon's Station, he described the
device used by the train wreckers.

> Soon after taking our position one of our boys found the iron
> shoe and the wooden wedge. . .secreted under some leaves.
> The iron shoe was made out of an old plowshare, having a
> groove in it so as to catch the flange of a car wheel and run it
> upon and over the rail. The wooden wedge was about eight-
> een inches long and four inches thick at the large end, and
> both had clamps with which to fasten them to the rails. The
> two were designed to be used on rails opposite each other,
> and could not have failed to accomplish the work.[58]

By the end of August, it was apparent to General Hood that Atlanta
would have to be abandoned to the advancing Federal forces. Every
effort had been made by Superintendent George D. Phillips and his staff
of the W&A to move locomotives and rolling stock south over the
Macon & Western Railroad and thus save this equipment from the Federals. The act of "refugeeing" equipment was also carried out by other
railroads that served Atlanta.[59]

---

[57] Sherman, *Memoirs,* 2, p. 105.

[58] W. B. Smith, *On Wheels and How I Came There* (New York, 1893), p. 179.

[59] Annual Report, W&A RR, Oct. 1, 1864, Macon GA; Intelligencer Steam Power Press.
Supt. Phillips wrote his section from Griswoldville, GA., and dated it Oct. 20, 1864; Jesse C. Burt,

Around noon on September 1, 1864, the *General* and the *Missouri* left Atlanta on the Macon & Western Railroad, each pulling a train of military supplies picked up in the East Point yards, namely ammunition, guns, and quartermaster supplies. Atlanta was beset from the direction of Jonesboro but no one in Atlanta knew exactly where the Federal forces were. The trains came to a halt near Rough & Ready when artillery of the XXIII Corps opened up, and both trains were backed to the car shed in Atlanta. They were then moved to the Georgia Railroad yards between Oakland Cemetery and the Schofield & Markham Rolling Mill. The supplies could not be removed so the authorities decided to destroy them, for the city was to be abandoned that night. Dave Young, the engineer, assigned to the *General* at this time, was ordered to damage the engine sufficiently to render it useless to the Federals. This was hardly necessary in view of the damage incurred by the later burning of the car loads of ammunition and other supplies. The *Missouri* was run backward into a line of cars and the *General* was run backward into the *Missouri,* and then the cars were set ablaze. The *Missouri* was the last locomotive purchased by the W&A prior to the war. Built by the Rogers Locomotive works in 1857, she was placed in service on the W&A in March of that year. A total of five locomotives and 81 cars of ammunition and other supplies went up in flames the evening of September 1, 1864 as General Hood's Confederate forces left Atlanta.[60] This scene was vividly portrayed many years later by David O. Selznick in his production of *Gone With the Wind* with the burning of Atlanta. The seven locomotives were badly damaged and all the cars were destroyed along with the supplies.

Jr., "The Savor of Old Time Railroading," Bulletin No. 84, The Railway & Locomotive Historical Society, Boston, MA., 1951, pp. 36-45; Letter, William A. Fuller, W&A RR, Apr. 20, 1903 (copy in author's possession).

[60] Letter from Wilbur G. Kurtz to Albert Hirsch, dated September 26, 1950 (copy in author's collection); In a message to Henry W. Halleck, Maj. Gen. H. W. Slocum mentions the destruction of seven locomotives, but other sources confirm the destruction of only five. *OR* I, 38, pt. 5, p. 778, Slocum to Halleck; pt. 3, p. 992, Court of Inquiry findings; Robert U. Johnson and Clarence C. Buel, eds., *Battles and Leaders of the Civil War,* 4 vols. (New York, 1884-89), vol. 4, p. 344, Hood's account of the defense of Atlanta. The information is also corroborated by the late Wilbur G. Kurtz in interviews with James Bell and Anthony Murphy of the W&A.

After the fall of Atlanta on September 1-2, 1864, the U.S.M.R.R. completed the railroad into the city on September 3, 1864.[61] The W&A, as far as the State of Georgia was concerned, had ceased to exist. By the end of September 1864, the number of locomotives had been reduced to 28 and the total number of cars was 391. All of this equipment had been moved south over the M&W Railroad to Macon and beyond on the Central Railroad of Georgia. The headquarters of the W&A had been established at Griswoldville on the Central Railroad of Georgia a few miles east of Macon.[62]

During September and October 1864, the W&A was used to build up supplies in Atlanta to support Sherman's army and prepare it for the next movement. There were frequent interruptions by Confederate forces in spite of Federal guards at cities and bridges along the route. The cavalry raids did little damage to the W&A but in early October, General Hood began to move his infantry around to the west of Atlanta with the intention of destroying the W&A north of Marietta. Hood later succeeded in destroying the line from Big Shanty to Allatoona, some 15 miles in length, but the subsequent Battle of Allatoona on October 5 and 6 failed to dislodge the Federals from the road. Soon after this battle some 10,000 Federal soldiers were distributed along the break to replace the ties and to prepare the roadbed. Colonel Wright came down from Chattanooga with his regular crews and the necessary iron and spikes, and within seven days the W&A was back in operation.[63]

By October 12, 1864, General Hood had moved further north and demanded the surrender of the Federal garrison at Resaca. Colonel Claude R. Weaver, the commanding officer, replied: "If you want it, come and take it." General Hood declined to make the assault on Resaca and continued moving north, tearing up the railroad all the way to Tunnel Hill.[64] No effort was made to destroy the tunnel.

---

[61] *OR* 5, series III, p. 952.

[62] Annual Report, W&A Railroad, Oct. 1, 1864, pp. 3-4.

[63] Sherman, *Memoirs,* p. 151.

[64] Ibid., p. 155.

After this action, General Hood marched west towards Alabama and Tennessee. About this time General Sherman received word from Washington that his proposal to march to the sea would be approved. Sherman then directed the rebuilding of the W&A from Atlanta to Chattanooga so that he could remove from Atlanta the sick and wounded and all surplus supplies. By November 1, the road was back in operation and on November 2, General Sherman received word from General Grant that he was free to leave Atlanta and make the "March to the Sea."[65]

As soon as men and material not required for the march to the sea were removed from Atlanta, General Sherman ordered the destruction of the W&A. Federal wrecking parties went to work and destroyed 84 miles of track between Atlanta and Resaca, heating the rails upon flaming piles of ties and then twisting them into uselessness. Such treated rails were commonly referred to as "Sherman Neckties." North of Resaca, the iron was pried loose for 20 miles and deposited at Dalton, where it would remain in Federal hands. Stations were destroyed by burning and only the stone walls of a few would survive. The Etowah River bridge was dismantled and carried to the rear for storage. Rolling stock and locomotives were destroyed. Everything in the city of Atlanta that could prove useful to the Confederates in the waging of war was set afire, including the Union Station and the shops and facilities of the W&A and other railroads in the city.[66] On the morning of November 15, 1864, General Sherman's forces marched out of Atlanta in two wings and began their famous march.[67]

Atlanta was a devastated city cut off from the rest of the Confederacy by the destruction of all the railroads leading into it. The W&A had been destroyed and rebuilt twice during the Campaign of 1864. All of the railroad's locomotives and rolling stock that were not destroyed had been removed and were being used on other railroads to the southeast.

General Sherman's memoirs summarize the role played by the railroads in the Atlanta Campaign:

---

[65] Ibid., p. 166.

[66] Black, *Railroads of the Confederacy,* p. 258.

[67] Sherman, *Memoirs,* p. 171.

Our trains from Nashville forward were operated under military rules, and ran about ten miles an hour in gangs of four trains of ten cars each. Four groups of trains daily made one hundred and sixty cars, of ten tons each, carrying sixteen hundred tons, which exceeded the absolute necessity of the army, and allowed for accidents that were common and inevitable. But, as I have recorded, that single stem of railroad, four hundred and seventy-three miles long (the length from Louisville to Nashville to Chattanooga and on to Atlanta) supplied an army of one hundred thousand and thirty-five thousand animals for the period of one hundred ninety-six days, viz., from May 1 to November 12, 1864. To have delivered regularly that amount of food and forage by ordinary wagon would have required thirty-six thousand eight hundred wagons of six mules each, allowing each wagon to have hauled two tons twenty miles each day, a simple impossibility on roads such as then existed in that region of the country. . . I reiterate that the Atlanta Campaign was an impossibility without these railroads; and only then, because we had the men and the means to maintain them and defend them, in addition to what were necessary to overcome the enemy.[68]

After the war Sherman wrote on January 18, 1886, to Joseph M. Brown, son of the war-time governor of Georgia and then traffic manager of the W&A Railroad Company, lessee of the W&A, an endorsement for his booklet, *The Mountain Campaigns in Georgia.* In these words he placed in proper perspective the role of the W&A in 1864:

. . .the Atlanta Campaign of 1864 would have been impossible without this road, that all our battles were fought for its possession, and that the W&A Railroad of Georgia should be the pride of every true American, because, by reason of its existence the Union was saved. . . .every foot of it should be sacred ground, because it was once moistened by patriotic blood; and that over a hundred miles of it was fought a con-

[68] Ibid., p. 399.

tinuous battle of one hundred and twenty days, during which, day and night, were heard the continuous boom of cannon and the sharp crack of the rifle.[69]

*   *   *

It was not until the Spring of 1865, after the war had ended, that the W&A was put back in service. General Thomas ordered the rebuilding of the line and work began on May 10, 1865. It was operational to Atlanta on July 4, 1865. On September 25, 1865, the W&A was returned to the State of Georgia and operations resumed under state control. It was described as "A rough patchwork of damaged and crooked rails, laid on rotten cross-ties and or rough poles and other makeshifts; eight miles of track at the upper end was entirely missing and the rolling stock was more nearly fit for the scrap heap than for traffic."[70]

Campbell Wallace was appointed superintendent and began the job of getting the road back to normal operations. There was a great deal of traffic to supply Atlanta and Georgia, resulting from the delay in reopening the seaboard lines. Wallace was replaced by Col. Edward Hulburt, a very capable administrator who later made a name for himself as an organizer of narrow guage railroads. Hulbert was replaced by Foster Blodgett, a close accomplice of Reconstruction Governor Rufus B. Bullock. Blodgett is said to have stated "that he took charge of the road to manage its public and political policy."[71] Hundreds of employees were discharged to make room for Republican favorites. William A. Fuller, the conductor of the stolen train pulled by the *General* on April 12, 1862, was "discharged for being a Democrat."[72]

Conditions on the W&A soon became intolerable, and the people of the state demanded that control of the road be removed from the political arena. Legislation was enacted that permitted the lease of the W&A on

---

[69] Joseph M. Brown, *The Mountain Campaigns in Georgia* (Buffalo, 1890) p. 73.

[70] Phillips, *Transportation in the Eastern Cotton Belt,* pp.331-332.

[71] Ibid., p. 332.

[72] Johnston, *Western & Atlantic Railroad,* p. 62.

December 27, 1870 for a period of 20 years to the W&A Railroad
Company, headed by war-time governor Joseph E. Brown.[73]

The road was promoted as the "Kennesaw Route" and the "Battlefield Route," and prospered under this lease. In 1890, the line was leased
to the Nashville, Chattanooga & St. Louis Railway, then the Louisville &
Nashville Railroad, and is today operated by CSX Transportation. During the days of fine passenger trains, the W&A carried the famous *Dixie
Flyer* and other Chicago to Florida trains. It remains today a vital link in
the CSX rail network and is still owned by the State of Georgia.

---

[73] Ibid., p. 69.

THE FORGOTTEN "HELL HOLE"

The Battle of Pickett's Mill

Jeffrey S. Dean

Twenty years after the war, Federal Maj. Gen. William B. Hazen, in his *A Narrative of Military Service,* recalled: "The Battle of Pickett's Mill was fought toward the evening of the 27th of May, 1864, and has generally been confounded with the action at New Hope Church fought two days before. . . .It is scarcely noticed in any reports of the Union commanders, and is ignored by Maj. Gen. William T. Sherman in his memoirs; but it was the most fierce, bloody, and persistent assault by our troops in the Atlanta Campaign, and the Confederates, who were victorious, have described it at length."[1]

Pickett's Mill and New Hope Church were often confused even by those who fought there, such as Hazen's fellow brigade commanders John H. King and Benjamin F. Scribner, both of whom referred to the area as "New Hope Church." Still another Union soldier, reminiscing on

---

[1] William B. Hazen, *A Narrative of Military Service* (Boston, 1885), p. 276.

his regiment's role at Pickett's Mill, recorded the fight as "The Battle of New Hope." A Hoosier in Hazen's brigade called it the "Hell Hole."[2]

Disregarded or overlooked by General Sherman in his memoirs, the Pickett's Mill assault was nevertheless judged notable by many in both armies. Brigadier General Thomas J. Wood, whose division led the assault, unequivocally characterized the Pickett's Mill offensive as "the best sustained and altogether the fiercest and most vigorous assault that was made on the enemy's intrenched positions during the entire campaign."[3] Joseph E. Johnston's chief of staff, Brig. Gen. William W. Mackall, echoed Wood's sentiments from the Confederate perspective, writing on the day after the battle: "In every encounter thus far we have beaten them, but have had no general engagement; last evening's was the most important and severe."[4]

The battle may have been "confounded" with New Hope Church, as General Hazen pointed out, but judging from reports and reminiscences, Pickett's Mill was anything but "scarcely noticed" by those who saw combat in this *forgotten* "Hell Hole."

* * *

At this phase of the Campaign for Atlanta, along what came to be known as the "Dallas Line," the two armies opposed each other from Dallas northeast to New Hope Church, a line of some four miles. It was at New Hope Church on May 25 that Sherman came up short in his efforts to capture a vital road intersection, losing 1,600 men in the attempt. Along the Dallas Line the relative strengths of the opposing armies was as comparable as at any time in the campaign. With the XVII Corps not yet up, and 11,000 men of Baird's and Hovey's divisions detached to guard the wagon trains at Burnt Hickory, the Federal front-

---

[2] U.S. War Department, *The War of the Rebellion: The Official Records of the Union and Confederate Armies,* 128 vols. (Washington, D.C., 1890-1901), Series I, vol. 38, part 1, pp. 561, 594. Hereinafter cited as *OR.* All references are to series I unless otherwise noted; R. M. Collins, *Chapters from the Unwritten History of the War Between the States* (Dayton, 1988), p. 209; C.C. Briant, *History of the Sixth Regiment, Indiana Volunteer Infantry* (Indianapolis, 1891), p. 316.

[3] *OR* 38, pt. 1, p. 379.

[4] W. W. Mackall, *A Son's Recollections of His Father* (New York, 1930), p. 211.

line strength in late May numbered 92,000 men. Johnston, having received significant reinforcements since the commencement of the campaign, now counted 70,000 soldiers with which to oppose Sherman.[5] On the defensive and occupying earthen entrenchments, Johnston would never again enjoy a more favorable match-up.

On May 26 Sherman renewed his flanking strategy, stretching his lines to the east in an attempt to turn the Confederate right. Major General Oliver O. Howard, holding the line opposite John B. Hood's Confederate corps, was ordered to move his IV Corps to the left and dig in. Howard deployed John Newton's Second Division to the right of Joseph Hooker, with the bulk of David Stanley's First Division positioned behind it in reserve. Instructed to take position on Newton's left, Wood's Third Division passed the day, according to Wood, "In very brilliant and successful maneuvering to determine the exact position of the enemy's intrenched line."[6] This involved heavy skirmishing to drive away Confederate screening troops, crossing of Brown's Mill Creek, and the occupation, according to Howard, of "an important hill, then apparently opposite the enemy's right flank." This position, at some points within 100 yards of the Confederate main line, was the scene of constant firing and significant losses.[7]

Major General John Schofield's XXIII Corps also moved up and took position astride the Dallas-Acworth road on Wood's left. Satisfied with the disposition of his troops on the enemy's right, Sherman ordered an assault. The men selected for this duty—Wood's division and Brig. Gen. Richard W. Johnson's First Division of the XIV Corps—were under the overall command of Oliver Howard. Brigadier General Nathaniel C. McLean's First Brigade of the XXIII Corps completed the force, which totalled some 14,000 soldiers.[8] General Howard, however, along with Army of the Cumberland commander George Thomas, determined that Confederate artillery enfilading fire would render too vulner-

---

[5] *OR* 38, pt. 1, p. 733; Sydney C. Kerksis, ed., *The Atlanta Papers* (Dayton, 1980), p. 81.

[6] *OR* 38, pt. 1, p. 377.

[7] Ibid., p. 193.

[8] Ibid., pt. 4, p. 359.

able the point of assault chosen by Sherman. The flanking assault would require another approach.[9] This last-minute change in tactics, made in the absence of reliable information about the enemy's movements, would have enormous ramifications for the impending battle at Pickett's Mill.

Major General David S. Stanley's First Division relieved Wood at 10:00 a.m., allowing Wood's men to pull back and form for the assault in a tree-shrouded field behind the extreme left of the XXIII Corps line. Assembled in column six lines deep, with Johnson bringing up the rear, Wood's three brigades began moving east at 11:00 a.m.[10]

Federal efforts to extend their line were duly noted by the Southerners. Confederate General Johnston anticipated Sherman's movements and countered on May 26 by extending his own line to the east. Johnston ordered Maj. Gen. Thomas Hindman's Division of Hood's Corps to move from New Hope Church to the right of the line, and Maj. Gen. Patrick Cleburne, summoned from Hardee's Corps at Dallas, marched his division to a position on Hindman's right.[11] Cleburne reached Pickett's Mill between 2:00-3:00 p.m. on May 26. The Irish-born general positioned Brig. Gen. Lucius Polk's Brigade on Hindman's immediate right. The twelve guns of Maj. T. R. Hotchkiss' Battalion, followed by one of Brig. Gen. Daniel C. Govan's regiments, were sent to bolster Polk's right.

The balance of Cleburne's command—the brigades of Brig. Gens. Hiram Granbury and Mark P. Lowrey, and the rest of Govan's Brigade—formed in echelon in Polk's rear. After this deployment was completed, Johnston's extreme right flank extended one mile to the northeast of New Hope Church. Throughout the night of the 26th and into the following morning, Cleburne's Confederates erected entrenchments along the line. The new line, Cleburne reported, "was, in the main, covered with trees and undergrowth, which served as a screen along our lines

---

[9]   Ibid., pt. 1, p. 194, 377.

[10]   Ibid., p. 193-194.

[11]   John B. Hood, *Advance and Retreat* (Secaucus, 1985), p. 119.

[and] concealed us, and were left standing as far as practicable for that purpose."[12]

Sherman's flanking column, meanwhile, continued eastward through rough country, described by General Wood as "dense forests of the thickest jungle, a country whose surface was scarred by deep ravines and intersected by difficult ridges."[13] Colonel Robert Kimberly and his 41st Ohio of Hazen's brigade led the way, struggling to carry out Wood's verbal instructions to "march in line of battle, skirmishers out, a mile and a half due southeast by the compass; then wheel to the right and march due southwest until the enemy [is] found." The rest of the brigade, Kimberly recalled, was to ". . .follow in column by battalion front, and behind were to come four other brigades. The order was explicit and emphatic to attack the instant the enemy was found, waiting for no further orders under any circumstances, whether the enemy were found in position or not, behind fortifications or otherwise."

Colonel Kimberly moved the prescribed distance to the southeast, wheeled to the southwest as ordered, and moved the column a mile before spying soldiers along a tree-lined crest directly to his front: "There, in full view, 500 yards away, was a large force in position, the men busily intrenching their line. The column of attack had come upon the rear of that line, which faced the wrong way for the enemy. . ." The attacking force was in rear of the left flank of the Union Army, instead of behind the right flank of the Confederates.[14]

General Howard quickly ordered the assault force to march another mile farther east. Arriving in the area of Pickett's Mill between 2:00-3:00 in the afternoon, Wood and Howard cautiously reconnoitered the front, the latter observing "a line of works to our right, but they did not seem to cover General Wood's front, and they were new, the enemy still working hard upon them." Finally in position on the Southerners' flank, the Federal assault force was realigned, with Johnson's division formed

[12] OR 38, pt. 3, p. 724.

[13] Ibid., pt. 1, p. 377.

[14] Robert L. Kimberly and Ephraim S. Holloway, *The Forty-First Ohio Veteran Volunteer Infantry in the War of the Rebellion. 1861-1865* (Cleveland, 1897), pp. 83-84.

on Wood's left.[15] At 4:35 p.m., Howard dispatched a message to Thomas to report on his progress, stating that he was ". . .on the ridge beyond the hill that we were looking at this morning. No person can appreciate the difficulty in moving over this ground unless he can see it. I am. . .now turning the enemy's right flank, I think.[16]

While the Federals moved into position, General Wood considered the portentous state of affairs: "When all these movements, so well calculated to try the physical strength of the men, were concluded, and the point gained, from which it was believed that the column could move directly on the enemy's flank, the day was well spent. It was nearly 4:00 p.m. The men had been on their feet since early daylight, and of course were much worn."[17]

In order to intensify the fire upon a small section of the Confederate line, which would facilitate a breach and further weakening of the enemy's flanks, Wood's three brigades would go forward in column of battalions. William Hazen's Second Brigade was slated to lead the assault, closely followed by the First and Third brigades under Brig. Gen. William Gibson and Col. Frederick Knefler, respectively. Only two days earlier, however, a similar formation was repulsed with heavy losses at New Hope Church. Whether or not he was recalling that earlier debacle, General Howard, just prior to the assault, determined to alter the plan of attack. As Hazen stood by, Wood suggested to Howard, "We will put in Hazen and see what success he has." Hazen later recalled: "This was a revelation to me, as it was evident there was to be no attack by column at all."[18]

Lieutenant Ambrose Bierce of Hazen's staff witnessed Hazen's response: ". . .my commander and friend, my master in the art of war. . . uttered never a word, rode to the head of his feeble brigade and patiently

[15] *OR* 38, pt. 1, p. 194, 377.

[16] Ibid., pt. 4, p. 324.

[17] Ibid., pt. 1, p. 377.

[18] Hazen, *Narrative*, p. 257.

awaited the command to go. Only by a look which I knew how to read did he betray his sense of the criminal blunder."[19]

Hazen's brigade was formed in two lines of two battalions each, just as it had been on the march. Four Ohio regiments—from left to right, the 124th, 93rd, 41st and 1st—made up the first line. The second line, left to right, included the 23rd Kentucky, 6th Indiana, 5th Kentucky, and 6th Kentucky. Protecting Hazen's right flank was Brigadier General McLean's brigade, positioned along the edge of a wheatfield. McLean, Howard reported, was "sent to a place in full view of the enemy's works, a little to the right of the point of attack, with a view to attract the enemy's attention and draw his fire."[20] It appears that a breakdown in Federal communications took place on the Federal left. It seems clear that Hazen, Howard, and Wood *expected* Col. Benjamin F. Scribner's brigade (Johnson's division) to support Hazen's left. Scribner, however, thought he was to support Gibson's brigade, the second in line *behind* Hazen[21] Thus at the very start of the advance potential problems loomed: Hazen would have questionable support on his left flank, and, if the column attack was not properly supported, he would lack support from behind as well. Bierce summed up the unfolding drama: "That, then, was the situation: a weak brigade of fifteen hundred men, with masses of idle troops behind in the character of audience, waiting for the word to march a quarter-mile uphill. . . ." At 4:30 p.m., on May 27, General Wood ordered the advance to begin, and Hazen's troops moved forward without support and without knowledge of what lay ahead.[22]

While the Federals were marching to Pickett's Mill, Cleburne was industriously strengthening his defense for the anticipated assault. Early on May 27, Govan's Brigade was advanced closer to the Federal line in order to observe any enemy movement. About the time the Federal flanking column began its march, around 11:00 a.m., Govan informed

---

[19] Ambrose Bierce, "The Crime at Pickett's Mill," *The Collected Works of Ambrose Bierce,* 2 vols. (New York, 1966), vol. 1, pp. 284-285.

[20] *OR* 38, pt. 1, p. 194.

[21] Compare *OR* 38, pt. 1, pp. 423, 866 with ibid., pt. 1, p. 594.

[22] Bierce, "Pickett's Mill," pp. 284-285; *OR* 38, pt. 1, p. 377.

Cleburne that Federals were beginning to move to the right in force. Cleburne ordered Govan to position his men on Polk's right, where, according to the division commander, ". . .he covered himself in rifle pits." Cleburne further strengthened his line by placing Capt. Thomas J. Key and two 12-pounder howitzers from Hotchkiss' Battalion on the right of Govan's Arkansans. Key's howitzers were sighted into a deep ravine near Cleburne's front, situated to provide an enfilading fire into the area over which Cleburne anticipated the main Federal assault would be directed.[23]

While the Federal assaulting column was forming, Cleburne sent Hiram Granbury's Texas brigade hurrying to Govan's right at 4:00 p.m.[24] One of Granbury's men, Lt. R. M. Collins of the 15th Texas, recalled the urgency of the moment:

> a courier dashed up to Granbury's headquarters under a great oak, and handed him a dispatch. The General did not wait to send orders to the commanders of regiments to get their regiments ready to move but rose up at once and gave the command: 'Attention Brigade!' We were in line, every man in his place, in less time than it requires to pencil four of these lines, at the command 'Right face, forward, double quick march!' we were off on a run.[25]

Moving toward the right flank the length of their brigade, Granbury's men formed a line of battle and advanced downhill a short distance to receive the oncoming Federals. Granbury's line bisected a spur ridge running northeast from a point near where the left of his brigade met Govan's right. Beginning opposite Granbury's left, Cleburne later reported, was ". . .a deep ravine, the side of which next to Granbury was very steep, with occasional benches of rock, up to a line within 30 or 40 yards of Granbury's men, where it flattened into a natural glacis. This

---

[23] Ibid., pt. 3, pp. 724-725.

[24] *OR* 38, pt. 3, p. 724.

[25] Collins, *Chapters*, p. 211.

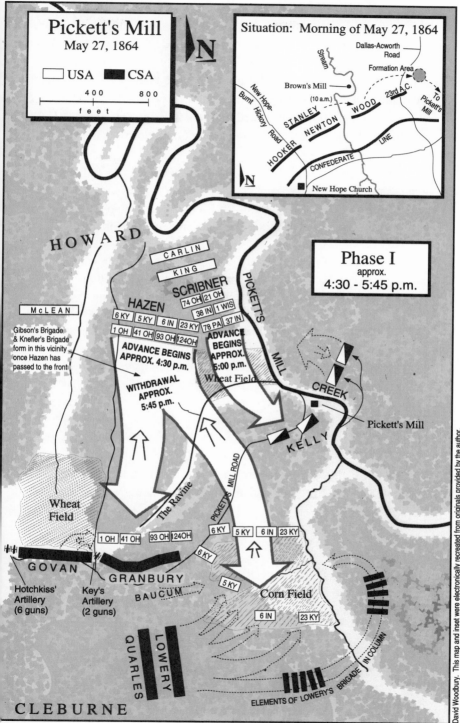

Pickett's Mill
May 27, 1864

□ USA   ■ CSA

400   800
feet

Situation: Morning of May 27, 1864

Dallas-Acworth Road

Stream

Formation Area

Brown's Mill

(10 a.m.)

STANLEY

NEWTON

WOOD

23rd A.C.

To Pickett's Mill

HOOKER

CONFEDERATE LINE

New Hope Church

New Hope-Burnt Hickory Road

N

HOWARD

CARLIN

KING

SCRIBNER

HAZEN

74 OH | 21 OH

38 IN | 1 WIS

6 KY | 5 KY | 6 IN | 23 KY

78 PA | 37 IN

1 OH | 41 OH | 93 OH | 124 OH

McLEAN

Gibson's Brigade & Knefler's Brigade form in this vicinity once Hazen has passed to the front

ADVANCE BEGINS APPROX. 4:30 p.m.

ADVANCE BEGINS APPROX. 5:00 p.m.

WITHDRAWAL APPROX. 5:45 p.m.

Wheat Field

PICKETT'S MILL

CREEK

Pickett's Mill

KELLY

Phase I
approx.
4:30 - 5:45 p.m.

Wheat Field

The Ravine

PICKETT'S MILL ROAD

6 KY | 5 KY | 6 IN | 23 KY

6 KY

1 OH | 41 OH | 93 OH | 124 OH

GOVAN

Hotchkiss' Artillery (6 guns)

Key's Artillery (2 guns)

GRANBURY

BAUCUM

5 KY

Corn Field

6 IN | 23 KY

LOWERY

QUARLES

ELEMENTS OF LOWERY'S BRIGADE IN COLUMN

CLEBURNE

David Woodbury. This map and inset were electronically recreated from originals provided by the author.

glacis was well covered with well grown trees, and in most places with thick undergrowth."[26] Such terrain, with the addition of fieldworks—not entrenchments—made Granbury's line doubly formidable and easy to defend, as would soon be demonstrated.[27] The balance of the Confederate line, from Granbury's right east-northeast to Pickett's Mill Creek, was manned by 1,000 dismounted troopers of Brig. Gen. John H. Kelly's cavalry division, of Maj. Gen. Joseph Wheeler's Corps.[28]

Hazen's men began moving up to challenge the Confederate defenses and were quickly bogged down amidst the choking undergrowth in the ravine. Staff officer Ambrose Bierce, who would later gain fame as a writer, described the start of this unpromising movement:

> We moved forward. In less than one minute the trim battalions had become simply a swarm of men struggling through the undergrowth of the forest, pushing and crowding. The front was irregularly serrated, the strongest and bravest in advance, the others following in fan-like formations, variable and inconstant, ever defining themselves anew. . . .The color bearers kept well to the front with their flags, closely furled, aslant backward over their shoulders. Displayed, they would have been torn to rags by the boughs of the trees. Horses were all sent to the rear; the general [Hazen] and staff and all the field officers toiled along on foot as best they could.[29]

As the Federals approached the Confederate line, the woods were suddenly filled with flying lead and the hoarse, fierce yells of a thousand throats:

---

[26] *OR* 38, pt. 3, pp. 724-725.

[27] Fieldworks, also referred to as "barricades," consisted of rocks, logs, dirt, and limbs piled on top of the ground, while entrenchments were dug into the ground. Fieldworks were used when there was no time to dig entrenchments.

[28] Hood, *Advance and Retreat,* p. 117.

[29] Bierce, "Pickett's Mill," pp. 287-288.

Suddenly there were [sic] a ringing rattle of musketry, the
familiar hissing of bullets, and before us the interspaces of
the forest were all blue with smoke. . . .The forward fringe of
brave and hardy assailants was arrested in its mutable exten-
sions; the edge of our swarm grew dense and clearly defined
as the foremost halted, and the rest pressed forward to align
themselves beside them, all firing. The uproar was deafening;
the air was sibilant with streams and sheets of missiles. In the
steady, unvarying roar of small-arms the frequent shock of
the cannon was rather felt than heard, but the gusts of . . .
[canister] which they blew into that populous wood were
audible enough, screaming among the trees and cracking
against their stems and branches. We had, of course, no artillery to reply.[30]

Hazen's right elements began to suffer heavily from the furious fire
delivered by Granbury's Texans. Cleburne recorded that the charging
Federals shouted

'Ah, damn you, we have caught you without your logs now.'
[a reference to New Hope Church]. Granbury's men, needing
no logs, were awaiting them, and throughout awaited them
with calm determination, and as they appeared on the slope
slaughtered them with deliberate aim. The piles of his dead
on this front, pronounced by the officers of this army who
have seen most service to be greater than they had ever seen
before, were a silent but sufficient eulogy upon Granbury and
his noble Texans.[31]

The plight of the Federals on the Union right had grown desperate.
Hazen's men, crowded into a ravine less than 100 yards from a barri-
caded enemy, were receiving deadly waves of canister fire from Key's
howitzers and musketry from Granbury's Texans. On the Federal left,

[30] Ibid.

[31] *OR* 38, pt. 3, p. 725.

however, it was a different story. In the jumbled confusion of the forward movement, the two battalion line assigned to support Hazen lost contact ("on account of the thick wood," according to Hazen) and began veering to the left. Whether accidentally or by design, this move had the effect of bringing the second line up to a cornfield on the left flank of the first line. Here, the flanks were joined, even as the first line continued to engage Granbury.[32]

As Hazen's brigade stretched toward the east, the original column formation, in effect, was transformed into an ordinary line of battle. Had Hazen's men maintained their initial formation, Granbury's line would have overlapped them. As it was, Hazen's second line extended the Federal left well beyond the Confederate right flank, reaching all the way to the cornfield, as much as 40 to 50 yards in Cleburne's rear. With an open door to the enemy rear in front of them, and what Hazen reported as "no works and but slight resistance in [their] front," the second Federal line moved out across the cornfield with the 23rd Kentucky on the left, anchored along a stream, the 5th and 6th Kentucky on the right, and the 6th Indiana holding the center.[33]

Cognizant of the potential for disaster, General Granbury forwarded a message to Govan summoning help to extend the line. As it was, Govan did not have significant numbers of the enemy on his front, contrary to Howard's plans. Rather than serving to ". . .attract the enemy's attention and draw his fire," as ordered, McLean's brigade remained concealed in the woods along the border of the wheatfield.[34]

With McLean's brigade out of the picture, Govan reacted promptly to Granbury's call for support. The 8th and 19th Arkansas Regiment (consolidated) under Col. G. F. Baucum was hastily pulled from the line and moved to the extreme right flank. Here Baucum's Arkansans confronted Hazen's brigade, which had just overrun the works held by Kelly's dismounted cavalry. In the opinion of his division commander, Baucum made a "sweeping charge," but ultimately being flanked him-

[32] Hazen, *Narrative,* p. 257.

[33] *OR* 38, pt. 1, p. 423.

[34] Ibid., pp. 194-195.

self, was unable to check the Federal advance. Cleburne, aware of the unfolding crisis on his right, sent his only remaining brigade under Mark Lowrey to the threatened sector. "His arrival was most opportune," Cleburne wrote, "as the enemy was beginning to pour around Baucum's right." Lowrey made an immediate impact, "throwing his regiments in successively as they unmasked themselves by their flank march." The Federals soon learned that what Hazen described as "slight resistance" was turning out to be something much more.[35]

In an outstanding account of the fighting in the cornfield, C. C. Briant of the 6th Indiana described the situation at that time from the Federal perspective. As the 23rd Kentucky and 6th Indiana moved up to the south end of the cornfield, the 5th Kentucky, which had started out on the right flank of the 6th Indiana, pulled up short in the woods at the southwest corner of the field. Briant was dispatched to bring the 5th Kentucky forward to shield the Federal right. Briant delivered his message to Col. William W. Berry of the 5th, then returned to his unit and discovered Capt. Samuel McKeehan, the ranking officer in that sector, lying on the ground with a bullet wound in the mouth. Briant provided a gripping account of the action:

> I laid his [McKeehan's] head back on the ground and straightened up with my face full to the front. The first look discovered a rebel column in good order [Lowrey] moving at quick time toward Pumpkin Vine Creek. I thought this meant mischief, and broke at the top of my speed to the left, down the line toward the creek, passing to the bluff beyond the extreme left of the Twenty-third Kentucky. From here I could see no help anywhere; but this rebel column had passed by our left, down the creek, and were just coming into the field at the mouth of the ravine [in the cornfield], and in five minutes more time would have been completely in our rear. I instantly gave the command to retreat, and at the same time, with all possible speed, went back up to my own regiment, yelling at the top of my voice all the way up, 'Retreat! Re-

---

[35] Ibid., pt. 3, p. 725; Ibid., pt. 1, p. 423.

treat!' and as soon as I arrived at my own regiment and
company I gave the order, 'Retreat square to the rear or we
will be captured.'

It is needless to say that both regiments broke in wild disorder for a place of safety. But the amusing part of this performance was to see the rebel commander ride in the midst of
the Twenty-third Kentucky boys, and with a very gentle,
sweet voice, tell them to halt and form their lines, while his
own men, with fixed bayonets, were coming as fast as their
legs would carry them. The boys did not halt, all the same.
But the curious part was that they were so much excited that
they did not notice the rebel Colonel, but made their way into
our own line and were saved, except a few on the extreme
left, near the creek.[36]

Although the Federals fell back in wild disorder across the cornfield,
they managed to reform along the fence at the far end. Hazen recalled
that during this retreat, "The left flank fell back along the fence near my
position [the fence] running at right angles to the line of battle. . .and
here fired with great execution upon the enemy advancing across the
cornfield from our left. The enemy came on in fine style, coming up
from the ravine beyond; but after one volley from our men along the
fence they were out of sight, to a man, in twenty seconds."[37]

The onrushing Confederates, Cleburne reported, "finding themselves suffering from the enemy's direct and oblique fire, withdrew,
passing over the open space of the field behind them." Some of Cleburne's staff, however, mistook the withdrawal for a repulse and consequently believed the Confederate line had ruptured. William A. Quarles'
Brigade of Maj. Gen. Alexander P. Stewart's Division was ordered up to
restore the line. When Quarles was unable to locate a break in the line,
he took up a position in reserve behind Lowrey's regiments. The Con-

[36] Briant, *History,* pp. 319-320.

[37] Hazen, *Narrative,* p. 258.

federate line now extended along the south edge of the cornfield, traversing a creek, and continuing east to a hill.[38]

This action on the Federal left was the closest Howard's men would come to victory at Pickett's Mill. Ironically, it was the result of an unplanned change in formation. Only by an alert Confederate response was the Federal assault on Granbury's flank repulsed and disaster averted. In the words of Lowrey, ". . .the position [of Granbury] could not have been held had not the right flank been secured. . . .Indeed it was one of those times in which the victory trembled in the scale, and the lives of many men, and probably the destiny of an army, hung upon a moment of time."[39] The scale may indeed have been tipped in favor of the Federals had their efforts in pushing forward Scribner's brigade on Hazen's left proved successful. This was prevented by the action of Brig. Gen. John H. Kelly's cavalry in the vicinity of Pickett's Mill.[40]

Expecting a Federal advance along the creek, Kelly wisely dismounted his men and deployed them along a hill southwest of the mill. Soon after Hazen's assault began, Scribner's Federal brigade moved forward with its left on the creek. As Scribner's regiments advanced, some of Kelly's dismounted troopers crossed to the east side of the stream at the mill, occupied a hill, and directed a deadly enfilading fire into the exposed Federals. Unaware of Hazen's predicament and in dire need of support, Scribner halted his advance in order to eliminate the threat to his left flank. He sent three regiments over the creek just north of the mill and assaulted the Confederate position there. Scribner drove the Confederates off the hill but lost critical time in the process while Hazen was heavily engaged in the cornfield and in sore need of Scribner's support.[41]

Pressed on the left by the brigades of Lowrey and Quarles and taking heavy casualties on his unprotected right flank in the ravine,

---

[38] *OR* 38, pt. 3, p. 725.

[39] Mark P. Lowrey, "General M. P. Lowrey, An Autobiography," *Southern Historical Society Papers,* 52 vols. (Richmond, 1876), vol. 16, p. 372.

[40] Jacob D. Cox, *Atlanta* (New York, 1882), p.79; *OR* 38, pt. 1, p. 865.

[41] *OR* 38, pt. 1, p. 595.

Hazen's regiments were quickly reaching the limits of their endurance. Hazen sent numerous messages to the rear asking for support, but many of the couriers were either shot on the way or else failed to locate Federal reinforcements.[42] With no relief forthcoming and intensified pressure on both of his flanks, Hazen ordered a withdrawal. A number of units remained in the line, unable to disengage in the face of the steady Confederate fire, while others along the line began to retreat from ravine to cornfield. Bierce described the fitful withdrawal:

> The battle, as a battle, was at an end, but there was still some slaughter that it was possible to incur before nightfall; and as the wreck of our brigade drifted back through the forest we met the brigade (Gibson's) which, had the attack been made in column, as it should have been, would have been but five minutes behind our heels, with another [brigade] five minutes behind its own. As it was, just forty-five minutes had elapsed, during which the enemy had destroyed us and was now ready to perform the same kindly office to our successors.[43]

Several fragments of regiments, which had assembled in the rear after the Federal withdrawal, passed by both Howard and Hazen. As recorded by Pvt. Silas Crowell of the 93rd Ohio Infantry, a lieutenant leading this group stepped up to Hazen and asked, "General, where is our brigade?. . . .We wish to report our regiments. General Hazen looked at him a moment. The tears began to roll down his cheeks and he said, 'Brigade, hell, I have none. But what is left is over there in the woods.'"[44]

General Hazen later praised his brigade for its valiant efforts in that bloody battle: "It is due the brave brigade. . .to say that this battle of the 27th of May is its first and only unsuccessful effort during the war, and at this time, as its dead list will show, went at its work with an honest

---

[42] Ibid., p. 442.

[43] Bierce, "Pickett's Mill," p. 294.

[44] Silas Crowell, "The General Wept," in *The National Tribune,* December 31, 1896.

good will which deserved a better result. I shall ever believe its part bravely and well done."[45]

The Federal failure to execute the original plan of action had a telling effect on the outcome of the battle. As Bierce indicated, Gibson's brigade was not in close support of Hazen. That General Wood was compelled to order Gibson to "renew the assault" suggests that the plan for an attack by column of brigades was not vigorously pursued after it began, or was not properly communicated to the commanders involved.[46] Many of Hazen's regimental commanders maintained in their after action reports that, with a second line in support, they could have penetrated the Confederate line. Although it's difficult to know with any certainty, poor visibility and rough terrain probably explain why the supporting brigades of Wood's division were not in position behind Hazen as planned. Neither Wood nor Howard could view enough of the field to recognize Hazen's predicament. Whatever the case, as Bierce recorded, Gibson's supporting troops arrived too late.

For a number of reasons, General Wood expected that a renewed attack by Gibson would succeed: Gibson's advance would not need to cover as much ground as Hazen's had; he was now familiar with the ground as a result of Hazen's experience; and if all went well, Scribner would be in position to cover the left flank of the assaulting column.[47] In the interval between Hazen's withdrawal and Gibson's advance, however, Cleburne had further fortified the Confederate line with fieldworks, bolstered his front with reinforcements, and resupplied the men with ammunition. In spite of Wood's optimism, the reception awaiting Gibson would prove significantly worse than the bloody repulse suffered by Hazen.

About 6:00 p.m., Gibson advanced into the all-but-impenetrable woods that had caused Hazen so much trouble. According to one of Gibson's soldiers, "The woods and undergrowth were so dense that nothing could be seen for a distance of one-hundred fifty yards." Conse-

---

[45] *OR* 38, pt. 1, p. 424.

[46] Ibid., p. 378.

[47] Ibid., p. 378.

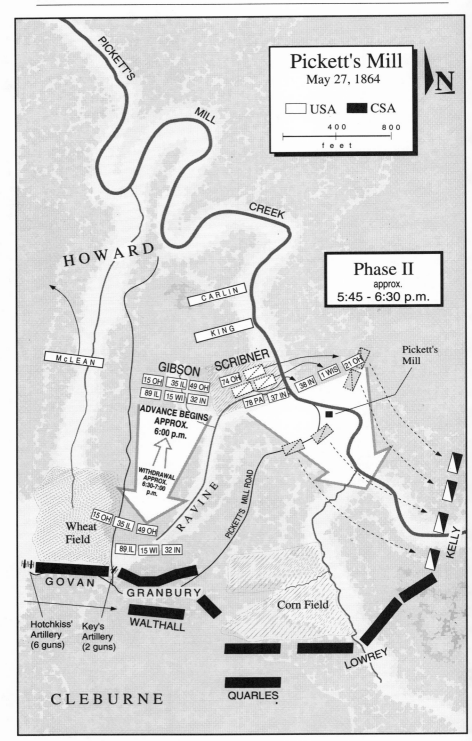

Pickett's Mill
May 27, 1864

☐ USA   ■ CSA

400   800

feet

N

PICKETT'S

MILL

CREEK

HOWARD

Phase II
approx.
5:45 - 6:30 p.m.

CARLIN

KING

McLEAN

GIBSON   SCRIBNER   Pickett's
                                                                      Mill

15 OH 35 IL 49 OH   74 OH   38 IN 1 WIS 21 OH

89 IL 15 WI 32 IN

ADVANCE BEGINS   78 PA 37 IN
APPROX.
6:00 p.m.

WITHDRAWAL.
APPROX.
6:30-7:00
p.m.

RAVINE

PICKETT'S MILL ROAD

KELLY

15 OH 35 IL 49 OH

Wheat
Field

89 IL 15 WI 32 IN

GOVAN   Corn Field

GRANBURY

Hotchkiss' Key's   WALTHALL
Artillery   Artillery
(6 guns)   (2 guns)   LOWREY

CLEBURNE   QUARLES

quently, Gibson's two advancing lines diverged, with the first line drifting to the left. An officer in the 49th Ohio, Lt. Col. Samuel F. Gray, now finding his unit in the front line, described the advance: "I could see no organized force in my front, but the woods full of men seeking shelter from the terrible storm of shot and shell." About this time the Adjutant General of Hazen's brigade informed Gray that the Southern battle line was on the other side of a ravine, "a few yards in advance." Arriving at the ravine, Gray's Ohioans observed a tattered remnant of Hazen's brigade on the other side, taking cover from the Confederate line by hugging the hill just under the crest. Gibson's troops charged up the hill directly into a heavy fire, all the while enfiladed from the right by artillery and musketry. Even through this storm of fire they moved forward to within 10 paces of the Confederate line "occupying one side of his [Confederate] barricade and he the other." At "one or two points," Gray reported, "[we] got within bayonet reach of the rebels. . ." but found it "impossible for us to take a position before which line after line had melted away. . . ."[48]

Like Hazen's men before them, Gibson's soldiers sought cover on the hillside, waiting in vain for support. Pressured on both flanks and with heavy fire on his front, Gibson was forced to withdraw. Those that could fell back to the protection of the ravine and ultimately escaped to the rear. As in the first assault, however, a number of units close to the enemy line preferred to cling to the cover amidst the trees and rocks on the hillside, rather than retreat under a murderous enemy fire. From these precarious hillside positions, mixed remnants of Gibson's and Hazen's brigades kept up a steady fire on the enemy. Later tallies revealed that heavier casualties were suffered in the second assault, for Gibson's loss numbered 681, compared with the 467 casualties in Hazen's brigade. Andrew Gleason, a sergeant in the 15th Ohio, succinctly summarized the day's carnage: "This is surely not war, it is butchery."[49]

[48] Ibid., pp. 392, 413-414.

[49] Ibid., p. 387; Andrew J. Gleason, "Confusion as to Names," in *The National Tribune*, February 11, 1897.

As darkness approached, generals Wood and Howard determined that additional assaults would be fruitless. This decision was probably a result of a message received about this time from General Thomas. As recorded in the IV Corps journal, this dispatch ordered Howard to "connect his right with General Schofield's left, and to take up a strong position which he could hold until he can be re-enforced, and if necessary to do this our left must be refused; that he must not place his troops in such a position as to risk being turned, and to say to General Johnson that he must place his troops so as to secure our left flank."[50]

A good many Federal dead and wounded, however, were still in the ravine or clinging to the hillside before the Confederate works. In order to retrieve these soldiers, Wood turned to Colonel Knefler, his last fresh brigade, and ordered it to advance and cover the removal of the wounded—but not to assault. Thus, two hours after the first assault, a third Federal brigade followed the steps of its comrades, moving through the ravine and losing formation in the choking woods. Just as Hazen's and Gibson's before him, Knefler found that upon reaching the Confederate line he was "completely enfiladed by the enemy's artillery, suffering severely." Amidst this intense fire, Knefler's men fought desperately to maintain their position in the ravine and along the north edge of the cornfield, constructing barricades where possible.[51]

Back in the vicinity of Pickett's Mill, meanwhile, Scribner's men were again advancing south astride the creek after clearing Confederate cavalry from the hill opposite the mill. Scribner's soldiers probably did not have any knowledge of the consecutive repulses of Hazen and Gibson until they connected with the 17th Kentucky—Knefler's left flank regiment in the cornfield. With Scribner in position, the Federal line was finally established on Wood's left, albeit far too late to carry out the original plan. Hoping to fall upon an exposed enemy flank—as might have been the case earlier—Scribner's troops instead discovered fieldworks at the southern boundary of the cornfield, fully manned by the Confederate brigades of Lowrey and Quarles. As reported by Scribner,

[50] *OR* 38, pt. 1, pp. 865-866.

[51] Ibid., p. 447, 467.

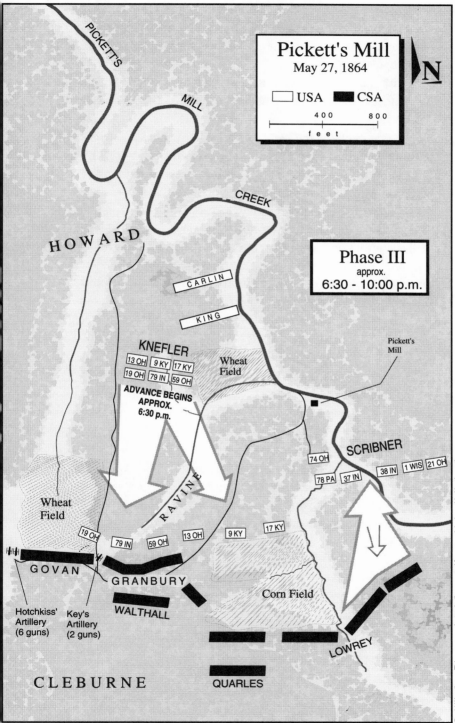

Pickett's Mill
May 27, 1864

☐ USA ■ CSA

400   800
feet

N

Phase III
approx.
6:30 - 10:00 p.m.

PICKETT'S

MILL

CREEK

HOWARD

CARLIN

KING

KNEFLER

| 13 OH | 9 KY | 17 KY |
| 19 OH | 79 IN | 59 OH |

Wheat
Field

Pickett's
Mill

ADVANCE BEGINS
APPROX.
6:30 p.m.

SCRIBNER

74 OH

78 PA | 37 IN

38 IN | 1 WIS | 21 OH

RAVINE

Wheat
Field

19 OH | 79 IN | 59 OH | 13 OH

9 KY | 17 KY

GOVAN

Corn Field

GRANBURY

WALTHALL

Hotchkiss'
Artillery
(6 guns)

Key's
Artillery
(2 guns)

LOWREY

CLEBURNE

QUARLES

"The enemy, emboldened by his success in checking our progress, furiously assaulted the whole line; this was repeated several times and as often repulsed.[52]

With the onset of darkness, the fighting subsided, though both sides maintained a sporadic fire. Knefler's objective of retrieving the wounded had to be abandoned. In his official report that fall, Knefler acknowledged that many of the wounded were left behind due to "the impossibility of bringing ambulances to the scene of action, it being an almost impenetrable jungle, cut up by ravines, creeks, and swamps, without roads, or even paths, for vehicles of any description."[53]

Soldiers in both armies took what rest they could under the circumstances, separated as they were by less than 100 yards along some parts of the line. "For some hours afterwards" wrote Cleburne, "a desultory dropping fire, with short, vehement bursts of musketry, continued, the enemy lying in great numbers immediately in front of portions of my line, and so near it that their footsteps could be distinctly heard."[54]

Since resting his men seemed out of the question in such extreme circumstances, Granbury sought and received sanction from Cleburne to launch an assault on the Federals to his front (primarily Knefler's brigade, with remnants of Hazen's and Gibson's brigades mixed in). Around 10:00 p.m., Granbury's men moved forward, their places in line being immediately occupied by Brig. Gen. Edward C. Walthall's Brigade of Hindman's Division. Lieutenant Collins of the 15th Texas recalled the night movement: ". . .at the sound of the bugle we dashed down, with a yell, into that dark gorge, like a whirlwind."[55] Cleburne added: "The Texans, their bayonets fixed, plunged into the darkness. . .and with one bound were upon the enemy; but they met with no resistance. Surprised and panic-stricken, many fled, escaping in the darkness; others surrendered and were brought into our lines."[56]

[52] Ibid., p. 595.

[53] Ibid., p. 448.

[54] Ibid., pt. 3, p. 725.

[55] Collins, *Chapters*, p. 214.

[56] *OR* 38, pt. 3, p. 726.

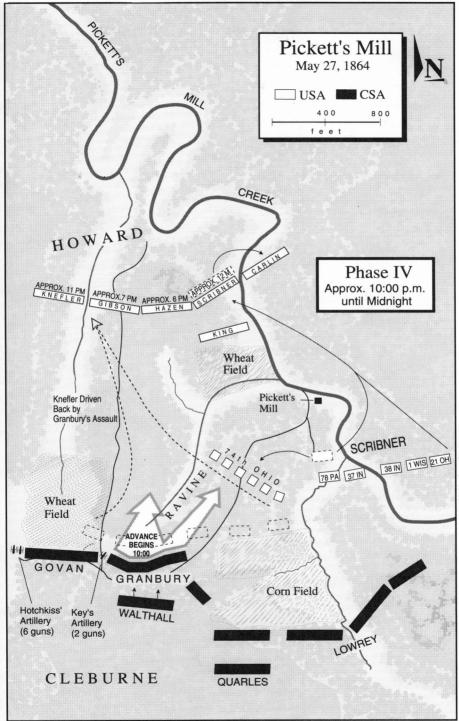

Pickett's Mill
May 27, 1864

☐ USA   ■ CSA

400   800
feet

N

Phase IV
Approx. 10:00 p.m.
until Midnight

PICKETT'S

MILL

CREEK

HOWARD

CARLIN

APPROX. 11 PM
KNEFLER

APPROX. 7 PM
GIBSON

APPROX. 6 PM
HAZEN

APPROX. 12 M.
SCRIBNER

KING

Wheat
Field

Pickett's
Mill

SCRIBNER

Knefler Driven
Back by
Granbury's Assault

78 PA   37 IN   38 IN   1 WIS   21 OH

74th OHIO

RAVINE

Wheat
Field

ADVANCE
BEGINS
10:00

GOVAN

GRANBURY

Corn Field

Hotchkiss'
Artillery
(6 guns)

Key's
Artillery
(2 guns)

WALTHALL

LOWREY

CLEBURNE

QUARLES

Not surprisingly, the Federal perspective of the night attack differs in the telling. According to Wood's version of events, Knefler's men unleashed a volley into the onrushing Southerners, which brought the Texans to a "dead halt." Knefler was then "handsomely and skillfully withdrawn," and "not the slightest pursuit was attempted."[57]

A careful reading of the various accounts clearly paints the picture of some Federals fleeing before the charging Southerners. Most of the Federals, however, maintained their line long enough to deliver a volley before withdrawing in either great haste or outright panic. Another Confederate reminiscence, this from Capt. Samuel T. Foster, seems to substantiate this view:

> In about an hour from the time we rec'd Granbury's order to charge. . .we raised a regular Texas yell. . .and started forward through the brush, and so dark we could not see *anything at all*. We commenced to fire as soon as we started, and the Yanks turned loose, and the flash of their guns would light up the woods like a flash of lightning, and by it we could see a line of blue coats just there in front of us. . . .[58]

With Knefler's retreat, Scribner's right flank became dangerously exposed as Granbury's Confederates pushed forward. Scribner wisely shifted his reserve regiment, the 74th Ohio, into the area vacated by Knefler's left, to maintain a protective skirmish line. As Granbury's right flank skirmishers pushed forward and felt Scribner's left, meeting the line of the 74th Ohio in the process, "they were not aware of any material change in our lines," wrote Scribner.[59] Scribner was later withdrawn around midnight and the field of conflict was left in Confederate hands.

Pulling back about a half-mile to the rear, the Federal brigades began manning a line of new breastworks which had been constructed even as

---

[57] Ibid., pt. 1, p. 379.

[58] Norman D. Brown, ed. *One of Cleburne's Command, The Civil War Reminiscences and Diary of Capt. Samuel T. Foster, Granbury's Texas Brigade, CSA* (Austin, 1980), p. 85.

[59] *OR* 38, pt. 1, p. 595.

the battle was raging. Probably built as a result of the message from Thomas to Howard, the breastworks were begun by the brigades of Carlin and King. Brigadier General William P. Carlin's brigade, placed on the east side of Pickett's Mill Creek, now held the left of the newly formed Federal line. The troops of King's brigade, with Scribner in reserve behind them, occupied the works just west of the creek. Continuing the line roughly to the right were the remnants of Hazen's, Gibson's, and Knefler's brigades. Being the only fresh troops and holding the far left flank, Carlin and King prepared to receive a possible Confederate counterattack the following day. Looking back toward the battlefield as they dug in, one soldier described "a weird and gloomy light. . ." which permeated the dark woods—the result of dead pine trees set ablaze during the fighting.[60]

Neither side was able to renew the fight on May 28, spending the day instead regrouping, fortifying, and surveying the carnage before them. One Federal soldier observed: "I was over the battleground. . .and never even at Shiloh, have I seen trees on the ground, marked as these. In one tree we counted two hundred bullet marks."[61] Close by the Confederate line, large numbers of Federal dead lay where they had fallen. Lieutenant Collins, of Granbury's Texas Brigade, noticed that dawn on the day after the battle at Pickett's Mill:

> . . .revealed a sight on that hill side that was sickening to look upon. All along in front of the center and left of our brigade the ground was literally covered with dead men. To look upon this and then the beautiful wild woods, the pretty flowers as they drank in the morning dew, and listen to the sweet notes of the songsters in God's first temples, we were constrained to say, 'What is man and his destiny, to do such a strange thing?'[62]

[60] G.W. Lewis, *The Campaigns of the 124th Regiment Ohio Volunteer Infantry* (Akron, 1894), p. 152.

[61] Frederick C. Cross, ed. *Nobly They Served the Union* (Frederick C. Cross, 1976), p. 88.

[62] Collins, *Chapters,* p 215.

Captain Foster recorded in his diary one of the most grisly accounts of the Pickett's Mill battlefield:

> May 28th
> About sun up this morning we were relieved and ordered back to the Brigade--and we have to pass over the dead Yanks of the battle field of yesterday; and here I beheld that which I cannot describe; and which I hope never to see again, dead men meet the eye in every direction, and in one place I stopped and counted 50 dead men in a circle of 30 ft. of me. Men lying in all sorts of shapes and [illegible] just as they had fallen, and it seems like they have nearly all been shot in the head, and a great number of them have their skulls bursted open and their brains running out, quite a number that way. I have seen many dead men, and seen them wounded and crippled in various ways, have seen their limbs cut off, but I never saw anything before that made me sick, like looking at the brains of these men did. I do believe that if a soldier could be made to faint, that I would have fainted if I had not passed on and got out of that place as soon as I did—We learn thru [sic] Col. [Franklin C.] Wilkes that we killed 703 dead on the ground, and captured near 350 prisoners.[63]

Various accounts indicate that anywhere from 500-700 Federal soldiers were buried along the line of Confederate works.[64] Irrespective of the burials, however, the smell of death was pervasive. One Federal soldier recalled, "The stench from dead horses and dead men between the lines was almost intolerable. No wonder the boys named it 'Hell Hole.'"[65]

---

[63] Brown, *One of Cleburne's Command*, p. 88.

[64] Collins, *Chapters*, p. 215. There are indications that these dead were buried in a mass grave, which, although researched by the author, has never been located.

[65] Henry Fales Perry, *History of the Thirty-Eighth Regiment, Indiana Volunteer Infantry, One of the Three Hundred Fighting Regiments of the Union Army in the War of the Rebellion, 1861-1865* (Palo Alto, 1906), p. 138.

Cleburne's losses numbered 85 killed and 363 wounded at Pickett's Mill. Relying on the commonly used one-to-four ratio of dead-to-wounded, Cleburne estimated that the Federal casualties totaled at least 3,000 killed and wounded.[66] Pickett's Mill, however, was exceptional for a number of reasons, and typical casualty ratios did not apply. Ambrose Bierce gave one explanation for such an anomaly: "I remember that we were all astonished at the uncommonly large proportion of dead to wounded—a consequence of the uncommonly close range at which most of the fighting was done."[67] Wood's division suffered an astounding 1-to-2.5 dead-to-wounded ratio (not counting Scribner's brigade, whose precise losses were not found) exceeding similar ratios in most other Civil War battles, and certainly in all other battles in the Atlanta Campaign. Federal losses were in the neighborhood of 1,600 soldiers.[68]

The close range at which the two sides fought certainly accounts for the unusually high Federal killed-to-wounded casualty ratio at Pickett's Mill, but those losses also illustrate the resoluteness displayed by the attacking Federals. The Confederates were equally determined in their successful defense, but the efforts demonstrated by Howard's soldiers under such unfavorable circumstances are praiseworthy. Hazen, who believed his men deserved a better result, was openly critical of Howard's handling of the Pickett's Mill battle. His criticisms, as well as others, are summarized as follows.

Both Hazen and Ambrose Bierce were vehement in their complaints that the initial plan of attack—a massed assault in column of brigades—was abandoned just prior to the start of the battle. Instead of a concentrated assault on a narrow front, Howard sent in his brigades individually, at intervals, allowing the Confederates breathing room between attacks. Several other Federal officers in the attack later reported that if support had been available, they could have broken the enemy line.

---

[66] *OR* 38, pt. 3, p. 726.

[67] Bierce, "Pickett's Mill," pp. 295-296.

[68] Study by author based on casualty reports in *OR*.

A second criticism of Howard's generalship concerned his handling of the Federal left flank along Pickett's Mill Creek. Brigadier General Jacob D. Cox, who commanded a division of the XXIII Corps at the time of the battle, commented after the war that "had Johnson [Scribner's division commander] noticed that he was first attacked in flank by cavalry only, and pushed Scribner's brigade straight on in support of Hazen, whilst he took care of the horsemen with another brigade of his division, the determined attack of the Fourth Corps men would probably have been successful."[69]

Howard himself chastises General McLean for failure to make a demonstration against the Confederate left. It was this failure, so Howard alleges, that allowed the Confederates to reinforce their right by withdrawing Baucum's Arkansas troops from their left.

The foregoing criticisms, based on hindsight, must be tempered by the consideration of how Howard perceived the tactical situation as it unfolded. It is instructive to examine a few issues in this regard. First and most important, the Federal march to Pickett's Mill stretched the Union line beyond the point of continuity. When Thomas and Howard changed the initial point of attack on the morning of the 27th, they did not realize that the Confederates had extended their right flank by shifting Hindman's and Cleburne's divisions to the right. This move forced Howard's flanking force to make a longer march to their left than was originally anticipated. McLean's brigade, which was to make a demonstration on the right, was also expected to maintain communication with the left flank of the army at New Hope Church. McLean, at that start of the battle, had lost contact with the XXIII Corps on his right, essentially isolating the 14,000 Federals at Pickett's Mill, with no readily accessible road for supply or reinforcement. The Confederates, by contrast, could, with relative ease send reinforcements along the roads from the area around New Hope Church to Cleburne's position at Pickett's Mill. And this is exactly what took place, for during the battle, the brigades of Quarles and Walthall traveled this route. These brigades increased Cleburne's strength from 5,700 men at the start of the fight, to roughly

---

[69] Cox, *Atlanta*, pp. 79-80.

10,000 troops (cavalry included) before it was over.[70] The quickness with which Cleburne was able to support his line, coupled with Howard's isolation from the main Federal army, quite likely led the Union commander to surmise that, if his troops failed at Pickett's Mill, a Confederate counterattack was inevitable. If one is to second-guess Howard, these facts are essential for a fair appraisal.

Howard's decision not to pursue the column attack, as well as his apparent reluctance to support his left flank, can be justified by the fact of his isolation from the rest of the Federal Army. Undoubtedly he was aware of this situation when he arrived at Pickett's Mill; at the same time he was unaware of the strength of his enemy. If indeed this was the case, sending Hazen in on a forced reconnaissance was a reasonable decision, as was his decision not to support Scribner on the left (if such a decision was ever made). At that point his last fresh troops (the brigades of King and Carlin) were in position. There was no hope of reinforcement or resupply that day. Without artillery and in the face of an aggressive enemy able to readily reinforce himself, holding King and Carlin in reserve was a prudent choice. Even had he failed to realize this predicament, Thomas' message around 6:30 p.m. would have had the same effect. Indeed, the entrenching begun by King's brigade while in reserve was probably a result of Thomas' dispatch.

In fairness to Howard, one must also consider the formidable disadvantages in terrain with which he was forced to grapple. According to Cox, the ground

> was a dense wood broken into ravines, where nothing could be seen, and where the embarrassments were scarcely less than in a night attack. Under the circumstances the wonder is, not that the attack failed, it is rather that Howard was able to withdraw in order, carrying off his wounded; and that he did so proves the magnificent steadiness and courage of his officers and men.[71]

---

[70] *OR* 38, pt. 3, pp. 677, 726, 987.

[71] Cox, *Atlanta,* p. 80.

Given the broken terrain and uncertainty about enemy strength, a detailed reconnaissance would be an essential prelude to launching an assault. Unfortunately for Howard, he lost a great deal of time searching for the Confederate flank, and once found, the urgency to attack it before the enemy could establish defensive works left time for only limited reconnaissance. Howard found himself trying to effectively coordinate and maneuver bodies of soldiers through thick woods, while lacking information critical to the successful prosecution of the battle. Ordinarily, a commander garnered information from messengers or direct line of sight; Pickett's Mill, however, was an exception, for the range of visibility was extraordinarily limited and numerous message-bearing couriers were lost or killed during the battle. Consequently, as a battlefield commander, Howard was effectively blind. This by no means exonerates Howard, since rough-terrain attacks were, by this time, normal fare for the Federals.

*   *   *

The Federal and Confederate troops remained in position for several days after the battle. Each side entrenched, the Confederates along the Pickett's Mill road, the Federals one-half mile north. During the night of May 27, a road was constructed from the Federal rear to the nearest existing road, which allowed ammunition and artillery to be brought up in support of the weary infantry. Also that night, Carlin's brigade of Johnson's division was placed across Pickett's Mill Creek on the left of King's brigade.[72] This action was in compliance with General Thomas' earlier message to Howard ordering him to protect his left flank. By the 28th, the Federals had been resupplied and communication with the rest of the Federal Army had been reestablished.[73]

While the Federals remained relatively motionless, the Confederates planned to take the initiative on May 29 with an attack by Hood's Corps on the Federal left. On the 28th, Hood had received information from

---

[72] *OR* 38, pt. 1, pp. 523, 527.

[73] Ibid., p. 867. The artillery was entrenched as well and engaged in counter-battery fire with Confederate cannon.

Wheeler's cavalry that "the enemy had its left flank beyond this stream [Pickett's Mill Creek], in a position which was exposed. . . ."[74] This presented the Confederates with a perfect opportunity to cross the stream and attack the "exposed" enemy (Carlin's brigade).

Hood proposed to Johnston that his corps be withdrawn from the vicinity of New Hope Church and deployed to attack Carlin on the next day. According to Hood, "the whole of the proposed movement was to depend upon the enemy's left flank remaining as represented [by Wheeler]."[75] Johnston approved the plan and Hood set out to fall upon the Federal left. Arriving at the point of attack on the morning of the 29th, Hood professed that the enemy's exposed position had been abandoned and that he had moved to the west side of the stream, where he had been reinforced. Hood informed Johnston of these developments and requested instructions. Johnston, assuming from the reported actions of the enemy that the element of surprise had been lost, ordered Hood to cancel the attack. There is no mention in the Federal accounts of any withdrawal to the west side of Pickett's Mill Creek. Conversely, Carlin's brigade was reinforced on the *east* side of the creek. It is highly probable that Hood was in error in his recollection of this event.[76]

Succeeding days brought renewed and incessant skirmishing, with some units reporting heavy losses. Finally, as the Confederate line was stretched to the limit, a June 2 attack by the Federal XXIII Corps on the Confederate right flank at Foster's Farm forced Johnston to make a critical decision. The Federals had gained a foothold from which a massed attack might roll up the Confederate line. Rather than risk that possibility, Johnston evacuated the Dallas-New Hope Church-Pickett's Mill line on the night of June 4, and retreated to the Lost Mountain line a couple of miles north of Kennesaw Mountain. The next day Sherman's men finally occupied the empty Confederate line at Pickett's Mill, where one week earlier so many lives had been lost.

---

[74] Hood, *Advance and Retreat,* p. 120.

[75] Ibid., p. 121.

[76] Ibid., pp. 121-122; *OR* 38, pt. 1, pp. 523, 527. This decision would add another chapter to the bitter dispute between Hood and Johnston.

FROM ATLANTA to SAVANNAH

A Sociological Perspective of William T. Sherman's March Through Georgia

Charles E. Vetter

O n the evening of September 1, 1864, Confederate Gen. John Bell Hood, after experiencing six weeks of Union bombardment, evacuated Atlanta, Georgia, making it possible for Maj. Gen. William T. Sherman to issue his long-awaited announcement to the North: ". . .Atlanta is ours and fairly won."[1] The long advance from Chattanooga, Tennessee, by the Army of the West was at last completed, and as a mid-nineteenth-century city, "Atlanta was dead."[2]

The fall of Atlanta, wrote correspondent David P. Conyngham, was "the crowning point in Sherman's great campaign."[3] The red-haired

---

[1] William Sherman to Henry W. Halleck, September 3, 1864, U.S. War Department, *The War of the Rebellion: The Official Records of the Union and Confederate Armies,* 128 vols. (Washington, D.C., 1890-1901), series I, vol. 38, pt. 5, pp. 777. Hereinafter cited as *OR.* All references are to series I unless otherwise noted.

[2] William Key, *The Battle of Atlanta and the Georgia Campaign* (New York, 1958), p. 76.

[3] David P. Conyngham, *Sherman's March Through the South with Sketches and Incidents of*

soldier from Lancaster, Ohio, who had viewed much of his life's efforts as of no great consequence, had succeeded in outgeneraling, outmaneuvering, and outflanking his Confederate opponents. The success of Sherman's army fixed the eyes of the world on this West Point graduate. Sherman became an instant hero and received letters of praise from people all over the world. The North saw him as a great leader, Europe looked to him as a strategic genius, and the South condemned him. Students of warfare would study his campaign and "haughty professionals of the Old World would talk less, after this, of the American war as merely the scramble of two armed mobs."[4] General Ulysses S. Grant would say that Sherman "had accomplished the most gigantic undertaking given any general in the war."[5] In honor of his victory, Grant ordered "a salute to be fired, with *shotted* guns, from every battery bearing upon the enemy [in Virginia]."[6]

Sherman had displayed imagination, resourcefulness, versatility, boldness, determination, patience, and a genuine power of leadership—all fundamental characteristics of a great military commander. He had adhered to many of the orthodox teachings of warfare, yet he had also shattered some of those theories by broadening a military objective to include a geographical destination. He had captured Atlanta while inflicting his unorthodox concept of warfare upon the people of the South. Although he had not broken up Hood's army, he had dealt it a heavy blow and disoriented it. Tactically he had made errors, but they did not detract from his victory.

President Abraham Lincoln decreed a day of thanksgiving for Sherman's capture of Atlanta:

> . . .Major-General William T. Sherman and the gallant officers and soldiers of his command before Atlanta, for the dis-

---

the Campaign (New York, 1865), p 213.

[4] Lloyd Lewis, *Sherman, Fighting Prophet* (New York, 1932), p. 420.

[5] William T. Sherman, *Memoirs of W.T. Sherman, by Himself,* 2 vols. (New York, 1931), vol. 2, p. 113.

[6] Ibid., p. 110.

tinguished ability and perseverance displayed in the campaign in Georgia, which, under Divine favor, has resulted in the capture of the City of Atlanta. The marches, battles, sieges, and other military operations, that have signalized the campaign must render it famous in the annals of war, and have entitled those who have participated therein to the applause and thanks of the nation.[7]

For almost three months Sherman occupied Atlanta. He reorganized his army, directed operations against the forces of Hood still within fighting distance, and prepared for his next move: the march across Georgia to the sea. "I will make the interior of Georgia feel the weight of war," he wrote Maj. Gen. John M. Schofield in October.[8] This was not a sudden careless expression of revenge, but simply the utterance of a long-held belief that until the full weight of war should be felt by the South, the conflict would continue. Mercy lay in hastening the war's end.

Shortly after noon on September 2, 1864, troops under the command of Maj. Gen. Henry W. Slocum, XX Corps, Army of the Cumberland, entered into the city of Atlanta. It was essentially a victory parade, as regiment after regiment marched to the tunes of "Yankee Doodle" and "The Battle Hymn of the Republic." The city they entered was thrown into a state of anarchy. There was no government, nor was there any evidence of military or police protection. Looters of all ages were ransacking and plundering stores, vacant buildings, and abandoned homes, intent on taking whatever they could before the Federals arrived. Destruction was everywhere. Correspondent Conyngham examined the city after its bombardment and told his readers of how "the suburbs were in ruins, and few houses escaped without being perforated." Citizens were killed "and many more had hair-breath escapes."[9] The psychological effect of the sociological devastation was perhaps best described by

---

[7] Ibid.

[8] William Sherman to John M. Schofield, October 17, 1864, *OR* 39, pt. 3, p. 335.

[9] Conyngham, *Sherman's March Through the South*, p. 218.

historian Wallace Reed who observed, "In the dread silence of that memorable morning [before Sherman's troops entered at noon] ten thousand helpless people looked at each other's faces for some faint sign of hope and encouragement. . . ."[10] Atlanta had become a desolate place, its foundations had been destroyed and now it was at the mercy of its destroyer.

Five days later, Sherman entered the city. Prior to his entrance into Atlanta, Sherman had made the decision that the city would not be a military post, occupied and controlled by the army. Past experience had taught him that using a captured city for a permanent garrison was simply another way of giving aid and comfort to the enemy.

He had seen how the captured cities of Memphis, Vicksburg, Natchez, and New Orleans had required a full division of troops and he wanted none of that. He felt that "success was actually crippling our armies in the field by detachments to guard and protect the interests of the hostile population."[11] It was his goal to abandon Atlanta after thoroughly destroying its means of supply and lines of communication. He had no intention of leaving Union troops to garrison it. Temporarily and only out of necessity, while he planned and prepared for his next move, it would become a military garrison; all military personnel would have precedence over the civilian population. To accomplish this end, Sherman in early September ordered:

> The city of Atlanta, belonging exclusively for war-like purposes, it will at once be vacated by all except the armies of the United States. . . .At a proper time full arrangements will be made for a supply to the troops of all articles they may need. . . .The same military principles will apply to all military posts south of Atlanta.[12]

[10] Wallace Reed, *History of Atlanta* (Syracuse, 1889), p. 188.

[11] Sherman, *Memoirs*, 2, p. 111.

[12] Willis Fletcher Johnson, *Life of William Tecumseh Sherman, Late Retired General, U.S.A.* (Philadelphia, 1891), p. 349.

On the same day, Sherman gave notice to Washington of his drastic proclamation and wrote Maj. Gen. Henry Halleck:

> I propose to remove all the inhabitants of Atlanta, sending those committed to our cause to the rear, and the rebel families to the front. I will allow no trade, manufactories, nor any citizens there at all, so that we will have the entire use of [the] railroad back, as also such corn and forage as may be reached by our troops. If the people raise a howl against my barbarity and cruelty I will answer that war is war, and not popularity-seeking. If they want peace they and their relatives must stop war.[13]

They could go north or south but as far as Sherman was concerned, they had to go. He had seen and suffered too long the drain of strength because of the permanent garrisoning of towns.

Sherman's order fell on the citizens of Atlanta "like a thunder-bolt."[14] They had never imagined that the war would reach their city. Sherman knew the measure would be severely criticized, but he "made up his mind to do it with the absolute certainty of its justness and that time would sanction its wisdom." He believed "the people of the South would read in this measure two important conclusions: one, that we were in earnest; and the other, if they were sincere in their common and popular clamor 'to die in the last ditch,' that the opportunity would soon come."[15]

Sherman also believed that his operations in the Deep South, if harsh enough, would have a negative impact on the morale of Robert E. Lee's Army of Northern Virginia, which was involved in protracted siege operations with Ulysses S. Grant and the Armies of the Potomac and James before Richmond and Petersburg. Georgia was home to many of Lee's soldiers. A threat to their homes and families would have a devastating

---

[13] William Sherman to Henry W. Halleck, September 4, 1864, *OR* 38, pt. 5, p. 794.

[14] Samuel Millard Bowman and Richard Bache Irwin, *Sherman and His Campaigns: A Military Biography* (New York, 1865), p. 221.

[15] Sherman, *Memoirs*, 2, pp. 111-112.

psychological effect on the soldiers fighting in Virginia. The result would be to increase an already rising desertion rate within that army. It would also act as a mortal blow against those who had families in the upper states; if it could happen in Georgia, it could happen in Virginia as well.

Once Atlanta was secure, Sherman began planning his next move. His philosophy of war and entire personality would not permit him to remain idle and rest on his hard-won laurels. The objective of the war was the conquest and defeat of the South. Simply because Atlanta, one of the citadels of the South, had fallen, did not mean the war was over. He would not subscribe to the mistaken belief that the Confederate armies would cease their resistance and the Rebel government would sue for peace. He had fallen into that trap following the victory at Vicksburg, but did not make the same mistake after the capture of Atlanta. He realized that the war must be fought to the bitter end, that the will of the South had to be conquered.

Sherman left Slocum's corps to defend Atlanta and on October 3, began his pursuit of Hood and the Army of Tennessee. For almost a month he chased Hood 150 miles northwest over much of the same territory he had traveled on his approach to Atlanta. But he could not bring Hood to battle and soon decided it would be futile to continue the pursuit. Hood "is eccentric and I cannot guess his movements as I could those of [Joseph E.] Johnston, who was a sensible man and only did sensible things," wrote Sherman to a fellow officer.[16]

Colonel Horace Porter, an aide to Grant, recalled Sherman's thinking at this time. After lunching together, Sherman and Porter retired to a house the general was using as headquarters, and there Sherman elaborated on his next move. He felt it vital that a definite "objective point or points" should be established. To march in a general manner "through Georgia for the purpose of inflicting damage would not be good generalship." Instead, he had settled on a definite point. "I want to strike out for the sea. . . ."[17] The idea was not new to Sherman. At least as far

---

[16] William Sherman to John Corse, October 7, 1864, *OR* 39, pt. 3, p. 135

[17] Horace Porter, *Campaigning With Grant* (Secaucus, 1887), p. 292.

back as May 1864, he had contemplated such a raid. Colonel Willard Warner, recently assigned as inspector general, recalled an interesting conversation with the general. After Sherman explained his intentions to march from Chattanooga to Atlanta, Warner inquired as to what Sherman would do if and when he was in Atlanta. Warner pointed out to the general that his army would be 450 miles from its main supply base and that he would be dependent on a single line of railroad to provide material for his army. According to Warner, Sherman, "Stopping short in his walk and snapping the ashes off his cigar in a quick, nervous way he replied in two words—'Salt water.'" At first Warner did not fully understand, until he gave a map a more thorough examination. Then he asked Sherman if he meant Savannah or Charleston, to which Sherman replied, "yes."[18]

There was serious danger in such a plan. As long as Sherman could keep his armies moving through the interior of the state, he could subsist off the land, ". . .but if I should have to stop and fight battles the difficulty would be greatly increased," he noted. There was also the matter of Hood and the lingering Army of Tennessee. What would Hood do? Would he follow and attempt to interfere, or would he move north or northwest into Tennessee? Sherman disposed of Hood in one statement when he told Porter that "I don't care much what he does." He felt sure he would never succeed in bringing Hood to battle, and he had no intention of following him all over Georgia and/or Tennessee, or wherever he might choose to go. Sherman hoped Hood would move his army north. ". . .I would be willing to give him a free ticket and pay his expenses," he told Porter, "if he would decide to take that horn of the dilemma." That way Sherman ". . .could send enough of his army to delay his progress. . ." and eventually ". . .destroy him. . . ." This would then free ". . .the bulk of my army. . ." to ". . .cut a swath through to the sea. . . ." Once there, Sherman believed he could move north to the rear of Lee, ". . .or do almost anything else Grant might require of me."[19] Sherman had concluded that a slow pursuit of Hood would only add to

[18] Basil Henry Liddell Hart, *Sherman: Soldier, Realist, American* (New York, 1958), p. 10.

[19] Porter, *Campaigning With Grant*, p. 293.

the strength of the enemy. The most effective use of his army would be a destructive march to the sea. Sherman, however, would have to convince Grant.

Throughout the month of September and into October the two generals debated the issue. On October 1, Sherman telegraphed Grant, raising the question:

> . . .why will it not do to leave Tennessee to the forces [Maj. Gen. George] Thomas has, and the reserves soon to come to Nashville, and for me to destroy Atlanta and march across Georgia to Savannah or Charleston, breaking roads and doing irreparable damage?[20]

Grant was skeptical of the move because it would take Sherman farther away from his base of supply into a hostile country with an enemy army at his rear. He wanted Hood's army destroyed before Sherman started on a raid through Georgia. But Sherman disagreed and was determined to have his way. He argued:

> The possession of the Savannah River is more fatal to the possibility of a Southern Independence; they may stand the fall of Richmond, but not all of Georgia. . . . [I] admire your dogged perseverance and pluck more than ever. If you can whip Lee and I can march to the Atlantic, I think Uncle Abe will give us a twenty day's leave of absence to see the young folks.[21]

Sherman pressed his point even further, declaring that no longer could his army remain on the defensive; no longer did he want to guess at what his enemy might do. Cutting loose from Atlanta and heading east would place him on the offensive and would force his enemy into

---

[20] Sherman, *Memoirs*, 2, p. 145.

[21] William Sherman to U.S. Grant, September 20, 1864, *OR* 39, pt. 2, pp. 412-413.

guessing at his plan.[22] If Grant would approve his proposal, then he felt
sure he could "make this march, and make Georgia howl."[23]

After serious deliberation and raising such issues as the inability to
prepare a coastal base, fear of being attacked by hostile citizens, and the
strength of George Thomas' army, Grant wired Sherman from City
Point, Virginia and approved the plan. Since Sherman had left a strong
force under the command of Thomas to keep watch over Hood, Grant
felt it would indeed be better for Sherman to move south rather than
north. He told Sherman

> . . .Hood's army, now that it had worked so far north, be
> looked upon more as the objective. With the force, however,
> that you have left with Thomas, he must be able to take care
> of Hood and destroy him. I do not really see that you can
> withdraw from where you are to follow Hood, without giving
> up all we have gained in territory. I say, then, go as you
> propose.[24]

Sherman answered Grant immediately, assuring his commander that
his proposed march ". . .would produce fruits more compensating for the
expense, trouble, and risk."[25]

Writing to Chief of Staff Halleck, Sherman said," I now consider
myself authorized to execute my plan. . . ." Sherman told Halleck that
he would strike out into the heart of Georgia, and make for Charleston,
Savannah, or the mouth of the Appalachicola. "I must have alternates,"
Sherman explained, "else, being confined to one route, the enemy might
so oppose that delay and want would trouble me, but, having alternates, I
can take so eccentric a course that no general can guess at my objective."
Sherman also urged Halleck to "have lookouts at Morris Island, S.C.,
Ossabaw Sound, Ga., Pensacola and Mobile Bays. I will turn up some-
where, and believe I can take Macon and Milledgeville, Augusta and

---

[22] October 11, 1864, Ibid., pt. 3, p. 202.

[23] October 9, 1864, Ibid. p. 162.

[24] U.S. Grant to William Sherman, November 2, 1864, Ibid. p. 594.

[25] William Sherman to U.S. Grant, November 6, 1864, Ibid. p. 660.

Savannah, Ga., and wind up with closing the neck back of Charleston so that they will starve out."[26] Describing his view of warfare, Sherman explained to Halleck that his movement through Georgia "is not pure military or strategic, but it will illustrate the vulnerability of the South." He was prepared to make people of all ages and all social classes understand the real meaning of war.[27] To Thomas, Sherman wrote, ". . .I propose to demonstrate the vulnerability of the South and make its inhabitants feel that war and individual ruin are synonymous terms."[28] Sherman was intent on conquering not only the South but the Southerner as well.

With the agreement reached between Grant and Sherman, a profound change took place in the American Civil War. Total war, though not officially adopted, had been sanctioned by the two generals. Grant and Sherman had ascended to the two most powerful positions in the United States Army, and, as military historian Russell Weigley observed, the war had descended into a "remorseless revolutionary struggle," and Lincoln "had had to abandon nearly all hopes for reconciliation. . . ."[29] Therefore, Weigley added, the possible "dangerous effects of military means upon the ultimate ends of postwar sectional understanding had to be sacrificed to the immediate quest for victory. . . ." Nothing short of total war seemed to offer complete victory and thus reunion. Two strategies of war were being combined to form a grand strategy. According to Weigley, Sherman's was to wage war against "the enemy's mind," while Grant's was to bring complete destruction to the enemy's armies."[30] The Northern generals were pulled toward both methods because their aim was the complete conquest of the South. As of November 1864, the Civil War ceased being a war of reconciliation and became officially a

---

[26] William Sherman to Henry W. Halleck, October 19, 1864, Ibid., pp. 357-358.

[27] Ibid.

[28] William Sherman to George Thomas, October 20, 1864, Ibid. pp. 377-378.

[29] Russell F. Weigley, *The American Way of War: A History of United States Military Strategy and Policy* (Bloomington, 1973), pp. 150-151.

[30] Ibid., pp. 150-151.

war of conquest. The move was made to take the historical development of war into a new era.

Even before Sherman received official approval for his march to Savannah he had begun preparations for the endeavor. As early as October 19, almost one month before the beginning of the march, he ordered his chief commissary of subsistence, Col. Amos Beckwith, to begin preparing for the move:

> I want to prepare for my big raid. On the 1st of November I want nothing but what is necessary for war. Send all trash to the rear at once and have on hand thirty days' food and but little forage. I propose to abandon Atlanta and the railroad back to Chattanooga, and sally forth to ruin Georgia and bring up on the seashore. Make all dispositions accordingly.[31]

Fenwick Y. Hedley, adjutant of the 32nd Illinois Infantry Regiment, recalled the heady days preceding the drive for the sea:

> Events during the last week in October and the first ten days in November, 1864, were stirring enough. The railroad. . .was repaired from Chattanooga to Atlanta, where the bulk of Sherman's army was assembling. Every train going north was loaded to its utmost capacity with the wounded and infirm; [and with] almost everything that the men could not carry on their backs. Returning trains brought only the most needed articles—hard bread, pork, coffee, sugar, and ammunition. It was evident even to those in the ranks that some important, if not desperate, undertaking was at hand.[32]

Now that Grant had approved the campaign, Sherman stepped up his preparations. He issued orders making it clear that men during marches

---

[31] Sherman, *Memoirs*, 2, p. 159; William Sherman to A. Beckwith, October 19, 1864, *OR* 39, pt. 3, pp. 358-359.

[32] Fenwick Y. Hedley, *Marching Through Georgia: Pen-Pictures of Every-Day Life*, (Chicago, 1884), p. 245.

and in camps must keep their places and not scatter about to be picked up by the hostile people. It was of the utmost importance that "our wagons should not be loaded with anything but provisions and ammunition," ordered Sherman.[33] There was to be no general train of supplies because the army was to forage liberally off the country during the march. To the corps commanders alone was "entrusted the power to destroy mills, houses, cotton-gins, &c. . . ."[34]

Determined to make as great a psychological and sociological impression on the people of Georgia as possible, Sherman decided not to start his march until the presidential election of 1864 had been decided. He believed the news of Lincoln's victory would add to Southern consternation and to the damage he proposed as a military move. Sherman, unlike many of his soldiers, did not bother to vote. Instead, he spent time studying the latest United States Census statistics regarding those counties in Georgia through which he proposed to pass, in order to determine where he would march and what he should destroy.[35] He was determined "not to stand on the defensive," and was confident that his wife would soon "hear of me on a bigger road than that of Meridian."[36]

From Kingston, Georgia on November 9, Sherman issued orders dividing his army into two wings. The right wing was placed under the command of Maj. Gen. Oliver O. Howard and consisted of the XV and XVII infantry corps.[37] Sherman's left wing was led by Maj. Gen. Henry W. Slocum and consisted of the XIV and XX infantry corps.[38] A cavalry

---

[33] Special Field Orders No. 119, November 8, 1864, *OR* 39, pt. 3, p. 701.

[34] Special Field Orders No. 120, November 9, 1864, Ibid. pp. 713-714.

[35] Lewis, *Sherman, Fighting Prophet,* p. 432.

[36] William Sherman to Ellen Sherman, October 19, 1864, Mark Antony DeWolfe Howe, ed, *Home Letters of General Sherman* (New York, 1909), p. 312.

[37] Special Field Orders N. 120, November 9, 1864, *OR* 39, pt. 3, p. 713. Howard had replaced James B. McPherson as commander of the Army of the Tennessee after the latter's death at the Battle of Atlanta on July 22, 1864. Major General Peter J. Osterhaus's XV corps was composed of the divisions of Brig. Gens. Charles R. Woods (1st Div.), William B. Hazen (2nd Div.), John E. Smith (3rd Div.), and John M. Corse (4th Div.). The XV Corps artillery was commanded by Maj. Charles J. Stolbrand. Major General Frank P. Blair's XVII Corps was composed of the divisions of Maj. Gen. Joseph A. Mower (1st Div.), and Brig. Gens. Mortimer D. Leggett (3rd Div.), and Giles A. Smith (4th Div.). The XVII Corps artillery was commanded by Maj. Allen C. Waterhouse.

[38] Brigadier General Jefferson C. Davis' XIV corps was composed of the divisions of Brig.

division commanded by Brig. Gen. Judson Kilpatrick composed Sherman's mounted arm. On November 12, Sherman ordered the Western & Atlanta Railroad—his only reliable line of communication and supply— torn up from Atlanta to Dalton. Historian William Key equated Sherman's decision to destroy the railroad as tantamount to Ceasar's crossing of the Rubicon: there would be no turning back.[39]

One of the last orders to be carried out before the march began was the destruction of the city of Atlanta. Sherman assigned Chief Engineer Orlando M. Poe "to take special charge of the destruction in Atlanta." Poe was ordered to destroy ". . .all depots, car-houses, shops, factories, foundries, &c., being careful to knock down all furnace chimneys, and break down their arches. . ."[40] The destruction of Atlanta was extensive. One historian described it as a "cataclysm which increased in fury over four volcanic days of flame, smoke, and exploding dynamite. . ."[41] The depot, roundhouse, and machine shops of the Georgia Railroad, plus a large number of houses and shops, were leveled.[42]

A few days before the beginning of the burning of Atlanta, Sherman sat down and wrote his farewell letter to Grant. It proved to be a restatement of why the march to the sea had to be made. He wrote:

> . . .I propose to act in such a manner against the material resources of the South as utterly to negative Davis' boasted threat and promises of protection. If we can march a well-appointed army right through his territory, it is a demonstration to the world, foreign and domestic, that we have a power which Davis cannot resist. This may not be war, but rather

---

Gens. William P. Carlin (1st Div.), James D. Morgan (2nd Div.), and Absalom Baird (3rd Div.). The XIV corps artillery was led by Maj. Charles Houtaling. Brigadier General Alpheus S. Williams' XX corps was composed of the divisions of Brig. Gens. Nathaniel J. Jackson (1st Div.), John W. Geary (2nd Div.), and William T. Ward (3rd Div.). The XX Corps artillery was led by Maj. John A. Reynolds.

[39] Special Field Orders No. 165, November 12, 1864, Ibid. pp. 750-751; Key, *The Battle of Atlanta and the Georgia Campaign*, p. 82.

[40] William Sherman to Capt. O. M. Poe, November 7, 1864, *OR* 39, pt. 3, p. 680.

[41] Samuel Carter, III, *The Siege of Atlanta, 1864* (New York, 1973), p. 358.

[42] Sherman, *Memoirs*, vol. 2, p. 177.

statesmanship, nevertheless it is overwhelming to my mind
that there are thousands of people abroad and in the South
who will reason thus: If the North can march an army right
through the South, it is proof positive that the North can
prevail in this contest.[43]

Not only would such an act give proof to the world of the power of
the Union, but more important—and perhaps more practical—was the
fact that it "was a direct attack upon the rebel army and the rebel capital
at Richmond," wrote Sherman after the war, and "it would end the
war."[44]

On November 16, 1864, at about 7:00 a.m., Sherman—unquestionably the most unwelcome visitor Atlanta ever experienced—rode out of
the devastated city, leaving behind his line of supply and communication
and a hostile army. "Behind us lay Atlanta," he later wrote, "smoldering
and in ruins, the black smoke rising high in the air, and hanging like a
pall over the ruined city." A band struck up a marching tune, noted
Sherman, and ". . .we turned our horses' heads to the east. Atlanta was
soon lost behind the screen of trees, and became a thing of the past."[45]

Sherman was taking an enormous risk. Not only was he turning his
back on a hostile army, he was breaking his lifeline and moving into the
heart of enemy territory. With this action he was taking a step into the
future. But he did so with confidence. Not only was he sure of what he
was doing, he wanted to do it and believed it would succeed. He had
learned his trade from Grant, one of the best in the military world. He
had seen Grant make a similar move at Vicksburg. Now he was confident enough to do the same thing but on a much larger scale. Moving
three-fourths of his army to another objective while the enemy's power
was so close at hand was a move that entailed not only a risk, but nerve
and boldness. It was a decision that proved successful and demonstrated
on Sherman's behalf, according to one historian, "a refreshing combina-

---

[43] William Sherman to U.S. Grant, November 6, 1864, *OR* 39, pt. 3, p. 660.

[44] Sherman, *Memoirs*, vol. 2, p. 177.

[45] Ibid., pp. 178-179.

tion of shrewdness and willingness to take risks that are the hall mark of a great commander."[46]

The point of least resistance became Sherman's goal. While Grant held the main forces of the Confederacy under Lee in Virginia and Thomas kept Hood's army occupied in Tennessee, Sherman marched south and southeast into the enemy's rear. Grant's force became the massive body of the Union while Sherman and his forces became the swinging, long-reaching arms which destroyed the Confederacy's stores, railways, and food, reducing it to impotency by the use of the incendiary torch as much as by the weapons of war. Grant ". . .practiced naked attrition," according to one historian describing the relationship between Grant and Sherman during this stage of the war, "while his lieutenant practiced wholesale slaughter of cattle and pigs and, in South Carolina, marched day after day under clouds of black smoke." This was the grand strategy arrived at by Grant and Sherman to bring the Civil War to a rapid close.[47]

If Sherman had been thorough in his preparations for the Atlanta campaign, then his designs for the Georgia march were meticulous. Whenever possible, his troops marched by four roads and each corps carried its own ammunition and provision trains. They were ordered to "forage liberally on the country during the march."[48] Each brigade was ordered to organize its own foraging party. The cavalry would be permitted to appropriate horses, mules, and wagons. Blacks were to be put to work whenever and wherever possible. Sherman also ordered that artillery and wagon trains be reduced to the minimum. Wagon loads were to be kept light and each soldier would carry forty rounds of ammunition. Beef would be driven on the hoof and oats were to be supplied through wide-spread foraging across the Georgia landscape.[49]

---

[46] Alfred Higgins Burne, *Lee, Grant, and Sherman: A Study in Leadership in the 1864-65 Campaign* (New York, 1939), pp. 80-81.

[47] Cyril Falls, *The Art of War, From The Age of Napoleon to the Present Day* (London, 1961), p. 76.

[48] Special Field Orders No. 120, November 9, 1864, *OR* 39, pt. 3, p. 713.

[49] Ibid., pp. 713-714.

The point of Sherman's in-depth preparations, according to English historian Liddell Hart, was to "develop the mobility of his army to such a pitch that it should be a huge 'flying machine' of light infantry."[50] Sherman realized the great risk he was taking and had to be sure he was fully prepared, for as he put it, "Success would be accepted as a matter of course, whereas, should we fail, 'this march' would be adjudged the wild adventure of a crazy fool."[51]

From the beginning the tactic of deception was utilized as a means of confusing the Confederates and keeping them off balance. Initially, the right wing of Sherman's army under Howard headed south toward Jonesboro, while the left wing under Slocum marched east through Madison. These divergent lines of march were designed to simultaneously threaten both Macon and Augusta. This maneuver kept the Confederate high command in a state of disarray and confusion as to Sherman's ultimate objective—thereby preventing a concentration in front of Milledgeville, the capital of Georgia and Sherman's initial destination. Sherman asked the War Department to assist him in deceiving the enemy as to his true objective by releasing false information to the press.[52]

Sherman's 62,000 veterans marched out of Atlanta "into the fat fields of Georgia. . .like locusts devouring a land," wrote one Sherman biographer.[53] It was one of the finest veteran armies the world had seen up to that time. "A remarkable body of men," is how Adjutant Hedley described it, an army of young men, all veterans "who had served an apprenticeship of more than three years at their profession. . . ." Many were too young to vote, Hedley noted, yet they could be counted on to "carry their load." Each was "practically a picked man," bragged the adjutant, resourceful and self-sufficient.[54]

---

[50] Liddell Hart, *Sherman*, p. 331.

[51] Sherman, *Memoirs*, 2, p. 179.

[52] Ibid. p. 177; William Sherman to C. A. Dana, November 9, 1864, *OR* 39, pt. 3, p. 727.

[53] Lewis, *Sherman, Fighting Prophet*, p. 442.

[54] Hedley, *Marching Through Georgia*, pp. 258-259.

Spreading his columns across some sixty miles, Sherman tore up large sections of railroad track and destroyed almost every station along his line of march. Miles of railroad track were ripped from the ground and the ties were arranged in piles and burned. Sections of rails were heated over the ties, then twisted around trees to form what the men called "Sherman's neckties" and "Sherman's hairpins." Railroad cars were burned, wheels broken, axles made unusable, boilers punctured, and cylinder heads cracked. Major James A. Connolly, inspector general of the Army of the Cumberland, reported on the widespread destruction:

> . . .every 'Gin House' we pass is burned; every stack of
> fodder we can't carry along is burned; every barn filled with
> grain is destroyed. . .everything that can be of use to the
> Rebels is either carried off by our foragers or set on fire. . .[55]

According to Connolly, the army's separated columns were able to determine each other's progress, route, and location by watching "smoke by day and pillars of fire by night. . . ."[56]

The army marched as if embarking on a holiday, and at certain points the men got out of hand as they looted town dwellings and farms of provisions of a private nature.[57] Though under orders to limit their seizures to necessary items, Sherman's "bummers,"—as the more enthusiastic foragers were commonly denoted—stole silver, jewelry, and personal property, bayoneted and ripped apart furniture, battered magnificent pianos and spinets into kindling, slaughtered cattle, and carried off pigs, sheep and poultry for their suppers.[58]

Correspondent Conyngham recorded a graphic portrait of Sherman's bummers and the criminal work they performed in Georgia. "He pried

---

[55] James Austin Connolly, "Major James Austin Connolly's Letters to his Wife, 1862-1865," *Transactions of the Illinois State Historical Society*, no. 35 (Springfield, 1928), p. 406.

[56] Ibid.

[57] James M. Merrill, *William Tecumseh Sherman* (Chicago, 1971), p. 270.

[58] Richard Harwell and Philip N. Racine, eds., *The Fiery Trail: A Union Officer's Account of Sherman's Last Campaigns* (Knoxville, 1986), p. 54; Oliver Otis Howard, *Autobiography*, 2 vols. (New York, 1907), vol. 2, pp. 77-78.

open chests to take the personal valuables of families; knocked to pieces tables, pianos, and chairs; tore bed clothing in strips and scattered then about the yard," noted the newspaperman. "Color is no protection from these roughriders. They go through a negro cabin, in search of diamonds and gold watches, with just as much freedom and vivacity as they 'loot' the dwelling of a wealthy planter. . . ." The bummer would return to camp, wrote Conyngham, "loaded down with silver ware, gold coin, and other valuables. I hazard nothing in saying that three-fifths (in value) of the personal property of the counties we passed through was taken."[59]

In Covington, some 20 miles east and south of Atlanta, Federal troops invaded the plantation of Dolly Sumner Lunt, who recorded the event with a colorful flair:

> . . .like demons they rushed in! To my smokehouse, my
> Dairy, Kitchen and Cellar, like famished wolves they come,
> breaking locks and whatever is in the way. The thousand
> pounds of meat in my smoke-house is gone in a twinkling,
> my flour, my meat, my lard, butter, eggs, pickles of various
> kinds, both vinegar and brine, wine, jars, and jugs are all
> gone. My eighteen fat turkeys, my hens, chickens, fowls, my
> young pigs, are shot down in my yard and hunted as if they
> were rebels themselves.[60]

Ten days later after assessing her losses, she recorded that she was "poorer by thirty thousand dollars."[61]

It did not take long before Sherman's troops realized why they had been ordered to travel so lightly. It was not only to ensure a quick march. Instead of the scheduled fifteen miles a day, they were averaging only ten. The reduction had been made in order to enable them to thoroughly lay waste the resources of the region through which they

---

[59] Conyngham, *Sherman's March Through the South*, p. 314.

[60] Dolly Sumner Lunt, *A Woman's Wartime Journal, An Account of the Passage over a Georgia Plantation of Sherman's Army on the March to the Sea, as Recorded in the Diary of Dolly Sumner Lunt* (Macon, 1927), pp. 34-36.

[61] Ibid.

were marching. In his official report filed after the end of the march, Sherman wrote that "This may seem a hard species of warfare, but it brings the sad realities of war home to those who have been directly or indirectly instrumental in involving us in its attendant calamities."[62]

The impact of Sherman's march on the civilians in its path was devastating. At first, word was out in the form of rumor that only a large raiding party was approaching. As refugees from Atlanta came into contact with other Georgians, however, the awful truth was revealed. Sherman's victorious army was headed to the sea! One of the refugees, A. C. Cooper, exclaimed, "Then we learned the truth, the fateful truth! We were not threatened by a mere raiding party. It was Sherman—Sherman on his 'march to the sea,' and we lay in the course of his march. . . . We were. . .paralyzed. Had we not all heard of him?" she queried rhetorically? Cooper described Sherman as being "like a huge octopus" that had "stretched out his arms and gathered everything in." He left nothing behind except "ruin and desolation."[63]

Cooper went on to ask

> Had not the very heavens glowed with the reflection of the fires lit by his orders? Were there not among us, even then, those whose homes had been laid in ashes by his soldiers, and they themselves turned out without a second suit of clothing? There was not a place to which we could flee, for that army would spread for miles. . . .[64]

To the people of Georgia, Sherman had become a terrorist, and it was exactly the psychological effect he intended. For the blacks, the effect was just the opposite. They flocked to his columns by the thousands and greeted him as a messiah. Sherman, however, forbade his armies to take refugees unless they were able-bodied and could work.

---

[62] Official Report of William Sherman, January 1, 1865, *OR* 44, p. 13.

[63] A. C. Cooper, "Days That Are Dead," *Our Women in the War: The Lives They Lived: the Deaths They Died* (Charleston, SC. 1885), p. 435.

[64] Ibid.

Some freed slaves heeded his warnings and returned home, but many continued to attach themselves to the long blue columns. But Sherman was insistent, however, for he did not want them along because they would hamper his movement. On occasion, he would take up his bridges at river crossings, leaving the blacks on the opposite side. He could not care for them and his own men as well. As A. P. Austin, a Confederate cavalry officer in the 9th Kentucky Cavalry, observed:

> When the crowd became too burdensome the Federals would take up their bridges at the crossing of some river and leave the poor, deluded followers on the opposite bank, to ponder over the mutability of human plans and to cast a longing look at the receding of their supposed delivers.[65]

The success of Sherman's initial feinting maneuver was wryly noted by war correspondent Conyngham as one of his wings reached Milledgeville: "The fright of the honorable body of [Confederate] legislators must have been amusing," he mused. With different Union columns marching in such a manner as to create confusion for those in his path, the legislators "scarcely knew where to run or what to do." At first they heard Sherman was headed for Augusta, so "they felt secure." Then they received word that he was headed directly to Milledgeville, "and they shivered again," noted Conyngham. They also received reports that the destination was the industrial bastion of Macon "and [they] finally became valiant again and made their fiery speeches. . . ." News eventually reached the politicians that Sherman was moving "right on the capital, and [that] the cavalry were right in the city." This was too much, so "the Falstaff heroes. . .fled in such confusion that the railroad cars became crowded to an excess with furniture, private property, and goods, and fabulous sums were given for any kind of conveyances."[66]

While Sherman's strategy of splitting his army into wings and marching them in various directions stressed local politicians, it also

---

[65] J. P. Austin, *The Blue and the Gray* (Atlanta, 1889), p. 138.

[66] Conyngham, *Sherman's March Through the South*, p. 255.

played havoc with the authorities in Richmond, who were frantically attempting to arrest his progress through Georgia. Up until November 21, Confederate Lt. Gen. William J. Hardee, in command of the troops around Savannah, was convinced that Macon was the Federals' destination. A short time later, Hardee changed his mind and held out that Augusta was Sherman's primary target. As Hardee attempted to shift his forces to defend Augusta, he discovered that the railroad and telegraph had been destroyed and that Sherman had interposed between the two places. Georgia militia under the command of Brig. Gen. Pleasant J. Philips marched from Macon to Augusta, but unexpectedly ran into the rear guard of Sherman's right wing before falling back to Macon badly bloodied. Philips' force had been dealt a sharp repulse on November 22 at Griswoldville, where they had foolishly and unsuccessfully attacked a veteran Federal brigade. The bloodied militia eventually arrived in Savannah, where they reorganized and awaited Sherman's advancing forces.[67]

Major General Joseph Wheeler, by swimming his command over the Ocmulgee River, managed to get out of Macon and across Sherman's front, where he skirmished and harassed leading Federal elements. While the militia was suffering its stunning repulse near Griswoldville, and Wheeler's outnumbered troopers picked and clawed at the fringes of the Union columns, Gen. Braxton Bragg arrived in Augusta with a handful of reinforcements. Bragg, who had led the Army of Tennessee until its ignominious rout from atop Missionary Ridge in November of 1863, had traveled from his post at Richmond, Virginia, to take command of the motley Confederate forces assembling to stop Sherman's drive. Like Hardee and other Southern officers, he found himself cut off from the rest of the Confederate forces and for some days was in the dark as to what was transpiring in the Georgia countryside. Contradicting reports and misleading information caused Bragg and his assorted force of some 10,000 soldiers to remain idle and ineffective at Augusta while Sherman tranquilly pursued his path to the sea.[68]

---

[67] Liddell Hart, *Sherman*, p. 337.

[68] Ibid., pp. 337-338; For a good understanding of the routes of march and the various Confederate attempts to stop Sherman, see generally the correspondence, telegrams, and reports in

Sherman reached Milledgeville on November 23, just eight days after having vacated Atlanta. He had traveled almost one-third of the distance to Savannah and the waiting Union navy. Behind him was a sixty-mile-wide swath of destruction. Everything had gone according to plan. The weather had been near perfect and the enemy had thus far presented no serious threat. Roads, for the most part, had been good, food abundant, streams and rivers easy to cross, and his men exhilaratingly happy.

At Milledgeville, however, a number of events occurred that affected the rather carefree attitude of the troops. The first was direct evidence of the horrors of Andersonville Prison when a small band of escapees wandered into camp and told all in hearing distance of that dreadful place. The evidence gathered near Milledgeville was confirmed a few days later when Federal troops took over Camp Lawton, the abandoned Confederate prison near Millen, Georgia. The Millen facility was a log stockade approximately 300 yards square and provided no shelter from the elements or any visible source of water. Seven hundred unmarked graves were found, together with several dead and as yet unburied prisoners.[69]

In addition to the destitute conditions within Southern prisoner-of-war camps, rumors began to spread of atrocities committed by Joe Wheeler's cavalrymen. Wheeler, so the rumors went, had captured a number of Federals and had given them a choice: death or pledge an oath of allegiance to the Confederacy. The rumors were that some had remained loyal and, as a result of this loyalty, had their throats slashed.[70]

Federal soldiers read in newspapers that Confederate leaders, both military and civilian, were urging noncombatants to harass and attack the invading army at every chance available to them. They learned that Senator Benjamin Hill and six Georgia congressmen had urged the peo-

OR 44, pp. 856-970. The maps found throughout William R. Scaife, *The March to the Sea* (Atlanta, 1989), are the best available on the subject and should be consulted by any serious student of the campaign.

[69] Howe, Mark Antony DeWolfe, ed., *Marching With Sherman: Passages from the Letters and Campaign Diaries of Henry Hitchcock, Major and Assistant General of Volunteers, November 1864-May 1865* (New Haven, 1927), pp. 178, 150.

[70] Ibid., p. 98.

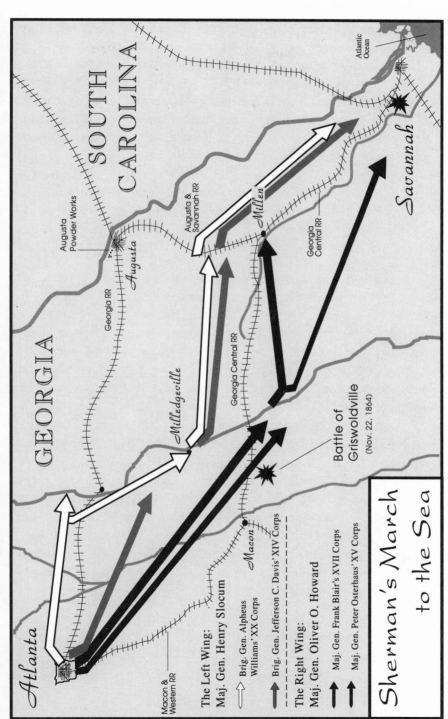

Atlantic
Ocean

SOUTH
CAROLINA

Augusta
Powder Works

Augusta &
Savannah RR

Millen

Georgia
Central RR

Georgia RR

Augusta

Savannah

GEORGIA

Milledgeville

Georgia Central RR

Battle of
Griswoldville
(Nov. 22, 1864)

Macon

Macon &
Western RR

Atlanta

The Left Wing:
Maj. Gen. Henry Slocum

Brig. Gen. Alpheus
Williams' XX Corps

Brig. Gen. Jefferson C. Davis' XIV Corps

The Right Wing:
Maj. Gen. Oliver O. Howard

Maj. Gen. Frank Blair's XVII Corps

Maj. Gen. Peter Osterhaus' XV Corps

*Sherman's March
to the Sea*

Theodore P. Savas

ple of Georgia to rebel. "Every citizen with his gun, and every negro with his spade and axe, can do the work of a soldier," Hill declared. "Remove your negroes, horses, cattle and provisions and burn what you cannot carry—Assail the invader. . . ."[71] While occupying the deserted mansion of Governor Joseph E. Brown (which had been hastily stripped of practically everything), Sherman received word that Gen. P. G. T. Beauregard at Corinth, Mississippi, had wired the people of Georgia the following impassioned plea:

> Arise for the defense of your native soil! Rally round your
> patriotic Governor and gallant soldiers! Obstruct and destroy
> all roads in Sherman's front, flank, and rear, and his army
> will soon starve in your midst![72]

These events brought Sherman's troops back to reality. This was not a holiday; the war was real and it hardened the soldiers' attitudes. To halt any noncombatant resistance that might arise as a result of the various patriotic appeals spreading throughout the state, Sherman simply reissued his order of November 9.[73] Harshness, as Sherman interpreted it, meant that if the enemy burned corn and other forage on his route, then houses, barns, and cotton gins must be destroyed in return. He could not and would not be hindered by mere civilians.

Despite the changing temper and mood of the troops, Milledgeville did not receive their full wrath. The burning of private structures was rare and only two plantation residences were destroyed—and these on the outskirts of the city. The only known fatality was Patrick Kane, a gardener and caretaker of a local plantation. Only two private homes were destroyed in the town itself, although a number of houses of state officials were severely damaged and looted. Surprisingly, the warehouses of the two richest cotton merchants of Milledgeville were spared, and a large flour mill was left standing. Two textile mills and an iron

---

[71] Sherman, *Memoirs*, vol. 2, pp. 191- 192.

[72] P. G. T. Beauregard to the People of Georgia, November 18, 1864, *OR* 44, p. 867.

[73] Sherman, *Memoirs*, 2, pp. 191-192.

and brass foundry also went undamaged. Despite the rumor that all public buildings in the city were to be torched, only two were destroyed—the arsenal and the magazine. The Central of Georgia Railroad station and the toll bridge over the Oconee River were also burned.

The most blatantly irresponsible act of vandalism occurred on the day Sherman's troops entered Milledgeville. Some of the younger officers staged a mock session of the Georgia legislature and matters quickly escalated out of control. The capital building, including the state library, was ransacked. Most of the books were thrown into the street and trampled by the soldiers, both on foot and horseback.[74] The scene was so disgusting that it led Major Connolly to label it ". . .a downright shame. Public libraries should be sacredly respected by all belligerents, and I am sure General Sherman will, some day, regret that he permitted this library to be destroyed and plundered."[75]

Major General Henry Slocum's two corps left Milledgeville for Millen and Savannah on November 24 under an Indian Summer sun, happy, healthy, and enthusiastic about what lay before them. Their approach to Sandersville, just twenty miles east and slightly south, was graphically captured by a seventeen-year-old girl who, peering from the front window of her home, was taken aback by what she saw.

> Looking out, I screamed in horror. It seemed to me the whole
> world was coming. Here came the woodcutters clearing the
> way before the army. Men with axes. . .men with spades. . . .
> Men driving herds of cattle—cows, goats, hogs, sheep. Men
> on horseback with bunches of turkeys, bunches of chickens,
> ducks and guineas swinging on both sides of the horses like
> saddle-bags. Then the wagons—oh, the wagons! In every
> direction, wagons, wagons! What do [sic] it mean? Have
> they stripped the whole country? I thought. Oh, we will

---

[74] James C. Bonner, "Sherman at Milledgeville in 1864," *Journal of Southern History* 22 (1956), pp. 280-284.

[75] Connolly, "Letters to his Wife," p. 408.

perish! Now came the soldiers—cavalry and infantry. . . .
Now the rush of Yankee ruffians![76]

Despite the best efforts of the authorities in Richmond and the plethora of general officers in Georgia, nothing hampered the movements of Sherman's columns as they tramped across Georgia. For all intents and purposes, the Federals were free to roam the land and take or destroy everything on it.

Sherman encountered another harsh aspect of mid-nineteenth century warfare outside Sandersville, where he came upon a group of men surrounding a young officer whose foot had been blown to pieces by a mine planted in the road. The shell had been loaded with a percussion primer so it would explode when stepped upon. An outraged Sherman, who later wrote that mine warfare ". . .was not war, but murder. . . ," immediately ordered a group of Confederate prisoners brought to the front. The captured Southerners were given spades and picks and made to "march in close order along the road, so as to explode their own torpedoes, or to discover and dig them up."[77] Six years after the incident, Sherman declared that ". . .prisoners should be protected, but mercy is not the legitimate attribute of war. Men go to war to kill and to get killed if necessary and should expect no tenderness. . . .But it was, I think a much better show of tenderness for me to have the enemy do this work than to subject my own soldiers to so frightful a risk. . ."[78]

By December 1, Sherman's march was two weeks old and according to one participant, had become "the most dramatic and suspenseful episode of the war."[79] What would be the outcome of this endeavor? Where would his army strike and reappear next? Would he be stopped and repulsed? Speculation was heard not only throughout America but in Europe as well. According to the *London Times*, "That it is a most

---

[76] Katharine M. Jones (ed), *When Sherman Came: Southern Women and the "Great March"* (New York, 1964), pp. 40-41.

[77] Sherman, *Memoirs*, 2, p. 194.

[78] Lewis, *Sherman, Fighting Prophet*, p. 462.

[79] George Ward Nichols, *The Story of the Great March From the Diary of a Staff Officer* (New York, 1865), p. 119.

momentous enterprise cannot be denied: but it is exactly one of those enterprises which are judged by the event. It may either make Sherman the most famous general of the North, or it may prove the ruin of his reputation, his army, and even his cause altogether."[80]

The British *Army and Navy Gazette* also had an opinion of Sherman's operation in Georgia: "It is clear that, so long as he roams about with his army inside the Confederate States, he is more deadly than twenty Grants, and that he must be destroyed if Richmond or *anything* is to be saved."[81] The *London Herald*, like its sister paper the *Times*, was confident that his campaign would result in either "the most tremendous disaster that ever befell an armed host. . .[or] the very consummation of the success of sublime audacity." If he failed, the *Herald* predicted, "he will become the scoff of mankind and the humiliation of the United States." But if he succeeded, the newspaper realistically noted, his name would "be written upon the tablet of fame side by side with that of Napoleon and Hannibal. He will either be a Xerxes or a Xenophon."[82]

Of course the North was apprehensive and seriously concerned about Sherman and his army, and newspapers wrote encouraging words about his successes and the glory still to come. On the streets, in the shops, at the dinner tables, and in government circles, the conversation was about where Sherman would emerge next. John Sherman anxiously awaited news of his brother and, on one occasion when a newspaper ran a Southern claim that Sherman had been stopped, he asked President Lincoln if it was true. Lincoln replied "Oh no, we have heard nothing from him. We know what hole he went in, but we don't know what hole he will come out of."[83]

---

[80] Quote from Richard Wheeler, *Sherman's March* (New York, 1978), p. 121.

[81] Ibid.

[82] Lewis, *Sherman, Fighting Prophet*, p. 457.

[83] Quoted from John Marszalek, *Sherman A Soldier's Passion for Order* (New York, 1993), p. 306. A similar statement by Lincoln is provided by Grant in his *Memoirs*: "Grant says they [Sherman's soldiers] are safe with such a general, and that if they cannot get out where they want to, they can crawl back by the hole they went in at." Ulysses S. Grant, *Personal Memoirs of U.S. Grant* (New York, 1952), pp. 495-496.

Southern papers were bitter and continued to label Sherman's movement the "retreat" of the Army of the West. The Richmond *Whig* exclaimed "Where is he now? We leave it to the Yankee papers to guess, supplying them only with the information that he has not found sweet potatoes very abundant in Georgia and hog and hominy have not been served up for the entertainment of his bedeviled troops."[84]

Reality, however, was quite different, for on December 9 Sherman's army was approaching the outskirts of Savannah, one of the last major seaports left open to the Confederacy. As his troops inched ahead, Sherman set his sites on Fort McAllister, a powerful earthwork fortification which stood guard on Genesis Point along the Ogeechee River, 14 miles below the city. The only way to open a secure line of communications with the Federal navy was to silence the fort, which proved to be easier than many expected. McAllister fell after a brief struggle on December 13, and Sherman promptly established contact with the nearby Federal fleet.[85]

Rejoicing filled the streets of Northern cities as news arrived by telegraph that Sherman has reached Savannah. In a matter of hours the news spread across the land, and people danced in the streets and sang victory songs amid the peals of church bells. At last, after more than three painful years of bloodshed, the foundations of the Confederacy were crumbling away.

On December 17, Sherman sent a dispatch to Lt. Gen. William J. Hardee, whose troops were defending Savannah, asking for unconditional surrender of the city. "Should you entertain the proposition I am prepared to grant liberal terms to the inhabitants and garrison," Sherman wrote, "but should I be forced to resort to assault, and the slower and surer process of starvation, I shall then feel justified in resorting to the harshest measures, and shall make little effort to restrain my army. . ." Sherman also informed Hardee that he would not hesitate to ". . .avenge a great national wrong" attached to Savannah by burning it.[86]

---

[84] Quote from Lewis, *Sherman, Fighting Prophet,* pp. 457-458.

[85] Sherman, *Memoirs,* 2, pp. 194-197.

[86] William Sherman to William J. Hardee, December 17, 1864, *OR* 44, p. 737.

Hardee, however, was not a soldier easily cowed into submission. He responded the same day by refusing to surrender the city, throwing in a threat of his own: ". . .I have hitherto conducted the military operations intrusted to my direction in strict accordance with the rules of civilized warfare, and I should deeply regret the adoption of any course by you that may force me to deviate from them in [the] future."[87]

Exactly what Hardee had in mind will never be known, for on the 19th and 20th of December, his 10,000 soldiers slipped out of the city around the Federal left flank leaving Savannah open for occupation by the Federal forces.[88] On the morning of December 21, Sherman entered the city and immediately dispatched his famous telegram to President Lincoln: "I beg to present you as a Christmas gift, the city of Savannah, with 150 heavy guns and plenty of ammunition, and also about 25,000 bales of cotton."[89]

The day after Christmas, Lincoln sent his letter of thanks to Sherman: "Many, many thanks for your Christmas gift, the capture of Savannah." The president proceeded to tell Sherman of the anxieties he had experienced concerning the march. "When you were about to leave Atlanta for the Atlantic coast, I was anxious, if not fearful; but feeling you the better judge, and remembering that 'nothing risked, nothing gained,' I did not interfere." Lincoln concluded with a small paragraph that must have pleased Sherman more than any compliment he had ever received:

> Not only does it afford the obvious and immediate military advantages, but in showing to the world that your army could be divided, putting the stronger part to an opposing forces of the whole—Hood's army—it brings those who sat in darkness to see a great light.[90]

---

[87] William J. Hardee to William Sherman, December 17, 1864, Ibid., pp. 737-738.

[88] Scaife, *The March to the Sea*, pp. 90-91. Although Scaife states that Hardee's response was written on December 18, the text is dated December 17. *OR* 44, pp. 737-738.

[89] William Sherman to President Lincoln, December 22, 1864, Ibid., p. 783.

[90] Abraham Lincoln to William Sherman, December 26, 1864, Ibid., p. 809.

Lincoln recognized what Sherman had done: he had broken up the enemy's army and gotten into the interior and done irreparable damage to Southern resources—just as he had discussed with Grant. Upon hearing of Thomas' defeat of Hood in Middle Tennessee at the Battle of Nashville, Sherman summed it up with these words of praise for Thomas: "His brilliant victory. . .was necessary to mine at Savannah to make a complete whole, and this fact was perfectly comprehended by Mr. Lincoln. . ."[91]

Sherman had taken possession of Savannah five weeks after leaving Atlanta. Journalist Conyngham wrote that with the capture of Savannah, Sherman had fulfilled his covenant with his troops by leading them to a new base. He summarized the march through Georgia by writing:

> The results of our campaign were more glorious than most sanguine could anticipate. We had passed through in our march over forty of the wealthiest counties of Central Georgia; occupied over two hundred depots, county seats, and villages; captured about fifteen thousand negroes. . .about ten thousand head of cattle, horses, and mules; destroyed nearly two hundred miles of railroad; burned all the gins, cotton mills, and government property throughout the country; also about fifty millions worth of cotton and Confederate bonds and currency, besides supporting our army. . .on the country.[92]

Sherman, in his official report of the Savannah Campaign, estimated the damage to the state of Georgia and its military resources at "$100,000,000 dollars, at least $20,000,000 of which has inured to our advantage, and the remainder is simple waste and destruction."[93]

The march was acclaimed by many to be the greatest movement of the entire war. Amid the words of praise, even Sherman revealed a hint of wonder and bewilderment. Writing to his wife Ellen on December 23,

[91] Sherman, *Memoirs*, 2, p. 219.

[92] Conyngham, *Sherman's March Through the South*, pp. 286, 288.

[93] Report of William T. Sherman, January 1, 1865, *OR* 44, pp. 7-14.

he mused that "Like one who has walked a narrow plank, I look back and wonder if I really did it."[94] His doubt, however, was only fleeting. In a dispatch to Maj. Gen. Halleck the next day, Sherman explained the consequences of his campaign. He proudly wrote that "We are not only fighting hostile armies, but a hostile people, and must make old and young, rich and poor, feel the hard hand of war, as well as their organized armies."[95] Sherman was convinced that his march through Georgia delivered the war to the doorsteps of the Confederacy's civilians. "Thousands who had been deceived by their lying papers into the belief that we were being whipped all the time realized the truth, and have no appetite for a repetition of the same experience, " he exclaimed. "To be sure Jeff. Davis has his people under a pretty good state of discipline, but I think faith in him is much shaken in Georgia. . ."[96]

The March to the Sea was over. What had it accomplished? First, the raid broke the stalemate that had settled in after the fall of Atlanta. The combined successes of Sherman in Georgia and Maj. Gen. Philip Sheridan in the Shenandoah Valley in Virginia pulled the war out of its standstill and sent it spiraling towards a conclusion. According to Grant, these victories left "the rebellion nothing to stand upon."[97] Many in the South either did not understand this fact or were unwilling to accept it. The Richmond *Whig* voiced the naive opinion of many in the South— except, of course, those who had experienced Sherman's march first-hand—by claiming that "Sherman is simply a great raider. His course is that of a bird in the air. He is conducting a novel military experiment and is testing the problem whether or not a great country can be conquered by raids."[98] No doubt the "experiment" was successful, the

---

[94] William Sherman to Ellen Sherman, December 23, 1864, Howe, *Home Letters of General Sherman*, pp. 318-319.

[95] William Sherman to Henry W. Halleck, December 24, 1864, *OR* 44, pp. 798-800.

[96] Ibid.

[97] U.S. Grant to Philip Sheridan, February 20, 1865, *OR* 46, pt. 2, pp. 605-606.

[98] Quoted in Lewis, *Sherman, Fighting Prophet,* p. 468.

"test" had been passed, and the country "conquered." The stalemate had indeed been broken.

The march through the Deep South also dealt a severe blow to the the Confederacy's logistical lifeline. Georgia was essentially removed from an ever-shortening list of states from which Robert E. Lee's army in Virginia could be supplied. By Sherman's estimates, the damage wrought in Georgia totalled $100,000,000. Almost 300 miles of track from Atlanta to Savannah were destroyed, along with bridges, trestles, and stations. Rolling stock was damaged beyond repair and locomotives dismantled and made immobile. Cotton was torched and mills and factories made useless. Individual soldiers also felt the sting of Sherman's march. In January 1865, a Maryland soldier in Lee's army noted in his journal that "There are a good many of us who believe that this shooting match has been carried on long enough. A government that has run out of rations can't expect to do much more fighting. . . ."[99]

According to one Confederate logistical historian, the destruction of Southern railroads and rolling stock resulted in "dissolving armies [that] wandered about the country while factories produced and storehouses held supplies that could not be moved to the troops. Shortages had hamstrung the [Confederate] armies."[100] The march also caused a dramatic decline in the morale of Confederate soldiers, especially those from Georgia. Douglas Southall Freeman, the preeminent historian of the Army of Northern Virginia, described the desperate situation confronting Confederate soldiers during the war's final months: "Desertion continued to sap the man-power of the army. After Christmas, when the winter chill entered into doubting hearts, and every mail told the Georgia and Carolina troops of the enemy's approach to their homes, more and more men slipped off in the darkness." Between February 15 and March 18, 1865, while Sherman was marching through the Carolinas, nearly eight percent of Lee's army simply left the ranks for home.[101] Confeder-

---

[99] W.W. Goldsborough, "Grant's Change of Base," *Southern Historical Society Papers*, 52 vols. (Richmond, 1901), vol. 29, p. 290.

[100] Richard D. Goff, *Confederate Supply* (Durham, NC. 1969), pp. 240-241.

[101] Douglas S. Freeman, *R.E. Lee, A Biography*, 4 vols. (New York, 1936), vol. 3, p. 541.

ate soldiers were rapidly becoming aware of the futility of continuing the war, and as each day passed more and more of them gave in to the inevitable. Sherman's indirect attack on them by bringing the war to their families, was successful.

The march, along with the fall of Atlanta and the re-election of Lincoln, severely crippled the Confederacy's will to win. The Southern civilian's morale was devastated; by the time Sherman reached Savannah, most of the citizens were ready to rejoin the Union. By marching almost unopposed through the heart of the South, thereby creating havoc and confusion, Sherman demonstrated to the world the growing weakness and vulnerability of the Confederacy.

One of the overlooked effects of Sherman's March was its contribution to the creation of a social revolution in the South, a drastic upheaval of its social, economic, and political systems. Of all the accounts that describe the results of the march as a social revolution, the most graphic and telling was penned by Charles Coffin, a correspondent for the *Boston Journal*. Coffin wrote that "the people of Savannah generally were ready to live once more in the Union. The fire of Secession had died out. Things were different now and would never be the same. Secession and the war had made it impossible to go back to the way things were. "Society in the South, and especially in Savannah," explained Coffin, "had undergone a great change." Prior to the war "the extremes of social life were very wide apart. . ." This gulf had been held in place up to "the night before Sherman marched into the city [Savannah]."

With the entrance of Sherman's army came the revolution. "[T]he morning after [Sherman entered Savannah], there was a convulsion, and upheaval, a shaking up and a settling down of all the discordant elements." Coffin continued almost with a touch of sadness: "The tread of that army of the West, as it moved in solid column through the streets, was like a mortal earthquake, overturning aristocratic pride, privilege, and power."[102]

Coffin's sociological perception was keen. He observed that

---

[102] Charles Carleton Coffin, *The Boys of '61* (Boston, 1884), p. 145.

Old houses, with foundations laid deep and strong in the
centuries, fortified by wealth, name, and influence, went
down beneath the shock. The general disruption of the former relations of master and slave, and forced submission to
the Union arms, produced a common level. . . .On the night
before Sherman entered the place, there were citizens who
could enumerate their wealth by millions; at sunrise the next
morning they were worth scarcely a dime.[103]

Everything was overturned. Wealth, according to Coffin, had been
measured in "cotton, Negroes, houses, land, Confederate bonds and currency, railroad and bank stocks." After Sherman's march, it was gone.
"Government had seized their cotton; Negroes had possession of their
lands. . ." and were no longer slaves. Troops occupied their houses.
"Confederate bonds were waste paper; their railroads destroyed, their
banks insolvent," Coffin expounded. Finally, he concluded, "They had
not only lost wealth, but they had lost their cause."[104]

Upon hearing of the fall of Savannah and the beginning of the
campaign to capture the forts protecting Wilmington, a clerk in the Confederate war office in Richmond recorded in his diary that "Men are
silent, and some dejected. It is unquestionably the darkest period we
have yet experienced."[105]

There are, of course, many issues entangled within Sherman's
March to the Sea that perhaps will never be resolved. The first is that of
violence. No doubt, violence can be psychological as well as physical.
Fear for one's life or fear for the lives of loved ones has lasting effects.
It cannot be argued that Sherman's march did not produce such violence.
But, *how much* violence is not known. It could have been worse had
Sherman's character been different. He could have been insensitive to
the wanton destruction of human life, but he was not. Instead, he pre-
ferred to take out his military wrath against property.

[103] Ibid.

[104] Ibid.

[105] John B. Jones, *A Rebel War Clerk's Diary at the Confederate States Capital*, 2 vols.
(Philadelphia, 1866), vol. 2, p. 368.

A second issue is that of abuses engaged in by the foraging parties of Sherman's troops. There is ample evidence supporting such activity. Looting and plundering of citizens' personal belongings clearly took place. Despite Sherman's orders that foraging must be limited to military needs, there were abuses. On this count, Sherman is responsible. He was lax in his discipline of violators, and his attitude even encouraged plundering. Many in the ranks believed that the commander approved of their actions. The perplexing question is: When does foraging end and plundering begin? The issue is even more complex in the context of Sherman's concept of total war. His intent was to subjugate the Southerner by bringing war to the front door of the noncombatant. Can that be interpreted to mean the parlor, dining room, and study as well? Sherman never provided any explanation to assist in the settling of this question.

Did Sherman's acts of terror plant seeds of future sectional hatred and postpone the development of unity after the war? This is obviously a subjective issue that will never be resolved. The main difficulty is the inability in this instance to measure the lasting effect of the March on subsequent events. However, Sherman's early ties to the South, his lenient treatment of Joseph Johnston at the surrender in North Carolina, and his opposition to a radical reconstruction policy, tend to tilt the scales against any "postponement of unity" argument.

Sherman was satisfied that he had accomplished more by attacking the South's economic, psychological, and sociological resources than by concentrating directly on its military power. Although his methods were unorthodox and even cruel, the fact remains that, whether he shortened the war or not, whether he postponed unity after the war or not, whether his foragers plundered or not, and whether there was tremendous violence or not, his methods saved lives on both sides.

William T. Sherman was not a naive man. He may not have appreciated the full revolutionary impact his march had on the South, and ultimately the United States, but he knew his actions would be misunderstood and long debated. It was inevitable that his contemporaries, as well as future generations all over the world, would most certainly regard him as a barbarian and a ruthless vandal, the leader of a mob of bummers and criminals.   But he never allowed such criticisms to deter him.

It has always remained a curiosity that a general who destroyed property rather than lives would be looked upon as more cruel and inhumane than one who led men into bloody, deadly combat.

The Unpublished Reports of Confederate Brig. Gen. James Holtzclaw's Brigade

edited by Zack Waters

A lthough the 18th, 36th, 38th, and 32nd and 58th (Consolidated) Alabama Regiments are generally referred to as "Holtzclaw's Brigade," the designation is, at least for the Atlanta Campaign, something of a misnomer. When Maj. Gen. Henry Clayton was given a division, James Thadeus Holtzclaw, colonel of the 18th Alabama, was promoted to the rank of brigadier general on July 8, 1864 and assigned to command the Alabama Brigade. Holtzclaw, a 31-year-old Montgomery attorney and pre-war militia officer, richly deserved the promotion. He was an experienced veteran, having seen action at Shiloh, the Tullahoma Campaign, Chickamauga, and Missionary Ridge. He gained experience as a brigade commander in the latter action, leading the Alabama regiments in Clayton's absence. Holtzclaw's health, however, failed during the 1864 fighting in northern Georgia. A shot through the right lung at Shiloh and a hard fall from his horse at Chickamauga had weakened his constitution. These injuries, coupled with a mysterious, recurrent illness, caused him to miss every battle in which his brigade took part during July and August except for the fighting at Ezra Church.[1]

Brig. Gen. James Thadeus Holtzclaw
(engraving from Ezra Warner, *Generals in Gray*)

Therein lies the misnomer of labeling the command "Holtzclaw's Brigade," for it was led by Bush Jones, the brigade's senior colonel, who assumed command of the Alabama veterans during Holtzclaw's convalescence. A 28-year-old native of Perry County, Alabama, Jones was

---

[1] Sources used for background information on Holtzclaw include: Authur W. Bergeron, Jr., "James Thadeus Holtzclaw," William C. Davis, ed., *The Confederate General*, 6 vols. (New York, 1991), vol. 3, pp. 118-119; Joseph Wheeler, "Alabama," *Confederate Military History*, 12 vols. (Atlanta, 1899), vol. 7, pp. 417-419; Ezra J. Warner, *Generals in Gray: Lives of the Confederate Commanders* (Baton Rouge, 1959), pp. 141-142.

educated at the State University (now known as the University of Alabama, Tuscaloosa) and at the law school at Lebanon, Tennessee. He opened a law office at Uniontown, Alabama in 1858, but abandoned his burgeoning practice in 1861 to enter a military company as a private. Jones saw action with the 4th Alabama Infantry at First Manassas before transferring to the Confederacy's western army. In this new venue he was elected lieutenant colonel of the 9th Alabama Battalion. When the unit was reorganized as the 58th Alabama Regiment, Jones was promoted to the rank of colonel.[2]

Jones rapidly built a reputation as both an excellent administrator and a bold combat officer. In describing Jones' composed conduct under fire, a soldier of the 18th Alabama recalled: "One of the most daring things I saw during the war was performed here [at the Battle of Jonesboro, August 31-September 1, 1864] by Col. Bush Jones. . . .[While on the firing line] I heard someone talking to the men, encouraging them. I looked back and Col. Jones was riding along the line on his horse talking as cooly and calmly as if there was no battle going on. I think he rode the entire length of the brigade and then back. There seemed to be a perfect hail of bullets about him. . .and he certainly showed no sign of fear."[3] Brigadier General Arthur M. Manigault confirmed the soldier's assessment, describing the Alabamian as "one of the coolest fellows I ever saw, handling his command with great ease and judgement."[4]

By the middle of the Atlanta Campaign, the regiments commanded by Colonel Jones were all tested, veteran units. The 58th Alabama began the war as the 9th Alabama Battalion, which was organized in New-

[2] Remarkably little has been written about either Jones or the units he led through the Atlanta Campaign, and much of what has been written is wrong. For example, a recent study of the Atlanta Campaign lists him as "Brig. Gen. Bushrod Jones." Both the name and rank are wrong. Albert Castel, *Decision in the West: The Atlanta Campaign of 1864* (Lawrence, 1992), p. 659. The highest rank attained by Jones was that of colonel, and following an old Southern tradition, he was named for his mother's family, which was Bush. Willis Brewer, *Alabama: Her History, Resources, War Record, and Public Men, From 1540 to 1872* (Montgomery, 1872), p. 496; "History of 18th Ala. Regiment," p. 18, newspaper clippings, 18th Alabama Regiment File, Alabama Department of History and Archives, hereafter cited as ADHA.

[3] "History of the 18th Ala. Regiment," ADHA, p. 18.

[4] R. Lockwood Tower, ed., *A Carolinian Goes to War: The Civil War Narrative of Arthur Middleton Manigault, Brigadier General, C.S.A.* (Columbia, 1983), p. 228.

bern, Alabama in November of 1861. The battalion fought at Shiloh, Farmington, Corinth, Hoover's Gap, and performed various garrison duties near Mobile, Alabama. With the addition of two companies in July 1863, the unit was redesignated the 58th Alabama Regiment and assigned to the division of Brig. Gen. William B. Bate. Several weeks later it participated in the Battle of Chickamauga, the unit's first and last engagement as a seperate entity. The fighting was severe and the unit suffered 63 percent casualties in two days. Because of its diminished size, the 58th was transferred to Henry Clayton's Division in November and consolidated with the 32nd Alabama. Perhaps as an omen of future engagements, the consolidation order was, according to one member of the 58th, "executed under fire of the enemy in front of Fort Wood at Chattanooga, on the Rossville Public Road and so united were in the Battle of Lookout Mountain on the evening."[5]

The 32nd Alabama was the brigade's hard luck regiment. Raised at Mobile in early 1862, the unit was transferred to General Braxton Bragg's army in Middle Tennessee during the Kentucky Campaign. In its first action near LaVergne, Tennessee, the 32nd attempted to stand toe-to-toe with a larger Federal force, despite having been abandoned by its infantry support, an untrained band of Tennessee conscripts. The Unionists routed the obstinate Alabamians, taking 35 of their number prisoner, including Lt. Col. Harry Maury, the regimental commander. Maury was exchanged in time to lead the 32nd at Murfreesboro, where he was wounded and the regiment lost more than 100 killed and wounded in Brig. Gen. Daniel W. Adams' December 31 attack on the Round Forest. Subsequent actions at Jackson, Mississippi, and in the Chickamauga Campaign, added to the butcher's bill and provided the unfortunate Maury with two additional wounds. At the time of its consolidation with the 58th Alabama, the 32nd Alabama numbered less than 150 men and was commanded by a captain.[6]

---

[5] John W. Inzer Letter, dated June 24, 1909, 58th Ala. Regiment File, ADHA. General information regarding the units in Holtzclaw's Brigade is taken from Brewer, *Alabama*; and, Wheeler, "Alabama," *Confederate Military History*.

[6] After Chickamauga, Maury became colonel of the hard-riding 15th Confederate Cavalry. He served ably around Mobile, Alabama, where, in his last battle of the war in April 1865, he was again wounded. A memorial to Maury is housed in the 15th Confederate Cavalry File, ADHA.

Organized at Auburn in September 1861, the 18th Alabama received its baptism of fire at Shiloh as part of Brig. Gen. John K. Jackson's Brigade. After more than a year of garrison duty near Mobile, the regiment returned to the Army of Tennessee, where 322 of the 536 officers and men carried into the Battle of Chickamauga were killed or wounded. Among the wounded was the 18th's colonel, James Holtzclaw. Command of the 18th devolved upon Maj. Shep Ruffin, a pre-war attorney from Pike County and one of the most colorful figures in the brigade. One soldier later noted that "Major Ruffin was one of the bravest men I think I ever came in contact with during the four years I was in service. His bravery amounted to recklessness. . . .Major Ruffin would have fought the whole yankee army if allowed to do so. Some officer was required on picket at all times, and Major Ruffin would often ask permission to take the place of some field officer. . . . He was not a popular officer. He was too crabbid to be loved, but no man ever doubted his courage."[7] When Ruffin was transferred to command the 38th Alabama, Maj. Peter Forney Hunley, a former captain of Company I and pre-war planter and horticulturalist from Lowndes County, replaced him.

The history of the 38th Alabama Regiment was similar to its sister units in Holtzclaw's Brigade. Organized at Mobile in May, 1862, its first significant action was at Chickamauga, where it suffered 37 percent casualties. It went on to lose 214 men, killed, wounded, and captured at Lookout Mountain and Missionary Ridge. After the capture of Col. A. R. Lankford at Resaca early in the campaign for Atlanta, Major Ruffin took command of the battered 38th.[8]

The brigade's final unit under consideration in this essay is Lt. Col. Thomas Hoard Herndon's 36th Alabama Infantry. Mustered into Confederate service May 12, 1862, at the Mount Vernon Arsenal, the 36th Alabama spent its first year constructing defenses around Mobile before being transferred to Braxton Bragg's Army of Tennessee. Like the bri-

---

See also, Dabney H. Maury, *Recollections of a Virginian* (New York, 1894), pp. 197-203.

[7] "History of the 18th Ala. Regiment," ADHA, p. 17.

[8] U.S. War Department, *The War of the Rebellion: The Official Records of the Union and Confederate Armies*, 128 vols.(Washington, D.C., 1890-1901), series I, vol. 38, pt. 3, pp. 838-840. Hereinafter cited as *OR*. All references are to series I; Brewer, *Alabama*, p. 649.

gade's other regiments, it was cut to pieces at both Chickamauga and in the battles around Chattanooga later that fall. One historian estimated that the regiment entered the Atlanta Campaign with 450 effectives, which would have made it the brigade's largest regiment.[9]

Lieutenant Colonel Herndon commanded the 36th Alabama through much of the fighting across north Georgia. Herndon was a cool character. He was an aristocratic pre-war lawyer and politician from Mobile, born in 1828 and educated at Tuscaloosa and Harvard. As did many officers, he pursued a career in law and represented Mobile County in the state legislature for a single term. Herndon was also a representative to the Secession Convention of 1861. After secession became a reality he helped to raise the 36th Alabama Regiment, rising from the rank of major to lieutenant colonel. Herndon was promoted to colonel after the 36th's commander, Col. Lewis T. Woodruff, was wounded at the Battle of New Hope Church on May 25, 1864. He retained this position until the regiment surrender near Mobile in 1865. In one of its final acts as an organized force, the regiment drew up a tribute to Herndon, noting his faithful attention to duties, constant presence in every place of danger, and his gallantry and skill.[10]

During the opening stages of the Atlanta Campaign, Holtzclaw's Brigade was extremely active. It skirmished at both Crow Valley and Rocky Face near Dalton, and participated in the futile, late-afternoon charge on May 14 at Resaca. The Alabamians also held the line near New Hope Church as Lt. Gen. A. P. Stewart's Division withstood the bruising assault delivered by Maj. Gen. Joseph Hooker's XX Corps. This hard fighting, coupled with daily skirmishing and an embarrassing rash of desertions, further reduced the numbers of Henry Clayton's (later Holtzclaw's) already depleted brigade.

* * *

[9] Ibid., p. 645. Brewer's estimate of available muskets at the outset of the Atlanta Campaign may be exaggerated.

[10] "Col. Thomas H. Herndon," *Confederate Veteran,* 40 vols. (1900), vol. 8, No. 12, p. 542; Brewer, *Alabama,* p. 428.

Historical Overview of the Battle of Atlanta, July 22, 1864

In order to place the following reports in context, a brief overview of the fighting on July 22 is necessary. General John B. Hood's plan for the attack east of Atlanta was basically sound. Apprised by his cavalry that Maj. Gen. James McPherson's Army of the Tennessee was six miles east of Atlanta near Decatur with his "flank in the air," the Southern chieftain moved quickly to capitalize on what he perceived to be a Federal blunder. Hood's desire to combine the elements of surprise and speed led him to ignore or at least overlook the human factor in the equation. Hood directed Lt. Gen. William J. Hardee to move his corps through the streets of Atlanta to a position east of the city, where he would be in a position to strike McPherson's Federals at dawn. This order required a grueling 15-mile night march. Hardee's men— who had participated in the attack and were bloodily repulsed at Peachtree Creek on July 20— were simply exhausted, and the Confederates straggled badly. It was past noon before the divisions of Maj. Gens. William B. Bate and William H. T. Walker, much reduced in size, were ready to begin the assault.[11]

Although the disorganized attacks launched by Bate and Walker, made without any reconnaissance, were rather easily repulsed, Maj. Gen. Patrick Cleburne's Division attacking further to the left, met with some initial success. Brigadier General Daniel C. Govan's hard-charging Arkansans drove a wedge-like opening in the Union lines, and Brig. Gen. James A. Smith's Texans pushed into the gap, only to be driven back by artillery and the timely arrival of Union reinforcements. Piecemeal Confederate attacks continued along the line, but they accomplished little except to inflate the casualty lists. Govan's men, however, regrouped and rested, drove east around 4:00 p.m. They were joined by

---

[11] Several sources were used in preparing the background report on the Battle of Atlanta, including the five Atlanta volumes of the *OR*; Castel, *Decision in the West*; Stanley F. Horn, *The Army of Tennessee: A Military History* (Indianapolis, 1941); Stephen Davis, "The Battles of Atlanta: Events from July 10 to September 2, 1864," *Blue & Gray Magazine*, August, 1989, pp. 9-62; and William R. Scaife, *The Campaign for Atlanta* (Atlanta, 1985). Tower, *A Carolinian Goes to War*, was particularly helpful in providing information on Manigualt and Jones.

Brig. Gen. Alfred Vaughan's Tennessee Brigade, which charged the Union position from the southwest. This double pressure cracked but did not collapse the patchwork Federal line.

When news of Hardee's progress (or lack thereof) on the right was relayed to Hood, he ordered the corps of Maj. Gen. Benjamin F. Cheatham to attack on the left. Hood hoped that, at best, the assault by Cheatham would lead to the destruction of McPherson's army, and at worst, would prevent the Federals from moving reinforcements from that sector to shore up the battered left flank.

At first, it appeared that Cheatham's men would fare no better than had those of Bate or Walker. Major General Carter L. Stevenson's Division, which made up Cheatham's right wing, sallied forth against the Union breastworks and was quickly repelled, in some cases without even managing to drive in the enemy skirmishers. The terrain traversed by Brig. Gen. John C. Brown's Division, which held the center of Cheatham's Corps, was densely wooded and hilly, broken by small patches of cleared ground and bisected by the tracks of the Georgia Railroad line and a wagon road. A gap existed in the Union defenses where the rail line and wagon road crossed the breastworks. Inexplicably, Union Brig. Gen. Morgan L. Smith guarded this critical location with only four guns of Company A, 1st Illinois Light Artillery and a handful of skirmishers. Just west of the defenses stood a two-story white house.[12]

John Brown's brigades attacked on both sides of the Georgia Railroad in two columns of two brigades each. The two brigades south of the railroad were both commanded by colonels. John G. Coltart, who was leading Zachariah C. Deas' regiments, advanced in tandem with Col. William Brantly, who was commanding Edward Walthall's Mississippians. Their combined assault moved forward several hundred yards south of the rail line and thus separated, eventually managed to take and briefly hold a part of the Federal breastworks. They were in no position

---

[12] Brown took command of Thomas Hindman's Division after that general suffered a severe eye injury on July 3, 1864, near Smyrna. The breastworks which the Federals occupied were those which Cheatham's Corps had constructed and manned until the morning of July 22. The Federals strengthened and reversed the works during the morning and early afternoon. *OR* 38, pt. 3, p. 179.

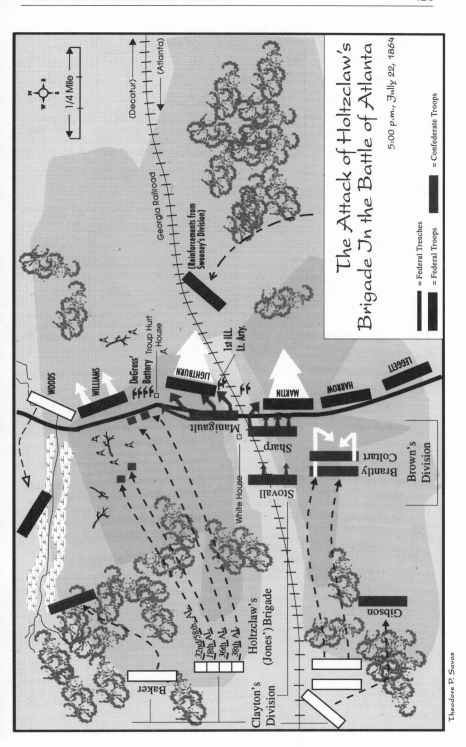

The Attack of Holtzclaw's
Brigade In the Battle of Atlanta

5:00 p.m., July 22, 1864

Theodore P. Savas

to support Brown's other two brigades led by Brig. Gen. Arthur Manigault and Col. Jacob Sharp, however, which were throwing themselves
against the Union lines north of the railroad.

At first the assault by Manigault and Sharp seemed doomed to failure. After driving back the Ohio and Illinois pickets, their attack ground
to a halt just short of the Union breastworks, where the South Carolina,
Alabama, and Mississippi troops took refuge around the white house,
seeking shelter from the hail of rifle and artillery fire. The tide turned,
however, when some quick-thinking South Carolinians climbed to the
second story of the structure and began to pour a deadly fire into the
hapless Union cannoneers. Taking advantage of the enemy's confusion
and diminished firepower, Manigault's and Sharp's troops surged forward, routing the Federal defenders and capturing Company A's four
12-pounders. Upon entering the breastworks, Manigault's men fanned
out to the left and Sharp's contingent drove to the right, taking possession of perhaps one-half mile of the fortifications. Manigault's surge
took his men as far as the large, unfinished brick residence of George M.
Troup Hurt, where the Confederates also captured the spiked guns of
DeGress' battery (Company H, 1st Illinois Light Artillery). After falling
back to regroup, Brown addressed Manigault's and Sharp's men and
ordered them to reoccupy the defenses. The Confederates rushed back
into the lightly defended fortifications, and Lt. R. M. Gill, of the 41st
Mississippi, noted that he "had the pleasure of shooting at Yankees as
they ran without being shot at much."[13] Subjected to a galling artillery
bombardment and sensing that a counterattack was imminent, Manigault
urgently requested reinforcements.

General Sherman, who observed Manigault's breakthrough from his
headquarters at the Howard house approximately a thousand yards to the
north, hurriedly assembled twenty pieces of artillery which opened a
terrific, raking fire upon Manigault's and Sharp's Confederates. Sherman also ordered Maj. Gen. John A. ("Black Jack") Logan to bring
reinforcements from the right. More importantly, Brig. Gen. Charles
Woods, whose hardy XV Corps veterans were stationed to the left of the

---

[13] Bell I. Wiley, "A Story of Three Southern Officers," *Civil War Times, Illustrated* (April,
1964), p. 33; *OR* 38, pt. 3, pp. 781, 819-820; Tower, *A Carolinian Goes to War*, pp. 225-230.

Troup Hurt house, swung his troops around until they faced south, to meet any further advance by the Rebels.[14]

Meanwhile, Henry Clayton, whose troops formed the left of Cheatham's Corps line, sent his troops forward to support the center. In a performance similar to Brown's advance, Clayton's brigades became separated from one another near the railroad and went into battle in a piecemeal and rather haphazard fashion. Colonel Abda Johnson, commanding Brig. Gen. Marcellus Stovall's Brigade, crossed to the south of the rail line and briefly drove the enemy from the ditches in his front. Unsupported and subjected to an enfilading fire, however, his men could not hold their position for long and were eventually forced to fall back toward Atlanta. Although Johnson formed his survivors with Brig. Gen. Randall L. Gibson's Louisiana Brigade, the combined Confederates were unable to mount a second offensive, and fighting in that sector soon petered out altogether.[15]

Bush Jones led his brigade along the north side of the Georgia Railroad. Because of dense woods, they lost sight of Johnson's [Stovall's] Brigade and continued forward until coming upon Manigault and Sharp, who were hanging on to the lodgment they had earlier gained. Thereafter, the reports of Holtzclaw's Brigade tell the story.

* * *

[14] William T. Sherman, *Memoirs of Gen, William T. Sherman by Himself,* 2 vols. (New York, 1875), vol. 2, pp. 79-84.

[15] *OR* 38, pt. 3, pp. 819-820.

Report of Col. Bush Jones, 58th Alabama Infantry,
commanding the 32nd and 58th Alabama Infantry,
Battle of Atlanta, July 22, 1864

Head Quarters Holtzclaw's Brigade
July 27th, 1864

Major: I respectfully submit the following report of the action of
Holtzclaw's Brigade in the engagement of the 22nd instant. About four
P.M. the Brigade being in the trenches that had been occupied by [Maj.
Gen. Thomas C.] Hindman's Division and about a mile west of the battle
field. I received orders from Major General [Henry D.] Clayton to move
in support of [Brig. Gen. Marcellus A.] Stovall's Brigade keeping 400
yards in the rear, and as a general direction to advance with the sun to
my back. I was directed to support Stovall's Brigade if necessary, and if
they should succeed in driving the enemy from his works, I was to
continue the attack, prolonging the left of Stovall; and was notified that
the other two brigades of Clayton's Division, would follow my left with
similar orders.

In accordance to these orders I moved the Brigade by the front as
rapidly as practicable. On account of the dense woods I could not see
the movement of Stovall's Brigade but I moved steadily forward as
directed and came in sight of the breastworks of the enemy at a white
dwelling where the left of [Brig. Gen. Arthur M.] Manigault's Brigade
was holding the works taken from the enemy. I halted the Brigade at this
point and several officers, amongst whom I recognized Genl Manigault
and Col. [Jacob H.] Sharpe [sic] Comdg. [Brig. Gen. William F.]
Tucker's Brigade, told me that the enemy were massed in heavy force on
my left flank, and moving on me, and that it was necessary to execute a
rapid change of front. At the same time the officers on the left of the
Brigade called to me that the enemy were advancing on the left flank.
Holtzclaw's Brigade then formed a nearly right angle with Manigault's.
The Brigade was under a very heavy fire of shells that nearly raked the
line. I executed the movement of change front to rear on first company

with rapidity, the regiments preserving very good order though under a very galling artillery fire.

The Regiments were posted in the following order from right to left, 38th Ala. Maj. Shep Ruffin Comdg, 36th Ala. Lt. Col. Thos. H. Herndon Comdg, the 18th Ala. Regt. Col. P. F. Hunley Comdg. and 32nd & 58th Ala. Capt. John A. Avirett, Comdg. The Brigade numbered for action 678 muskets—the remainder being on the picket line. Having indicated to Maj. Ruffin the direction in which I wished the new line formed, I rode on down the line superintending the formation of the new line and whilst I was on the left of the Brigade and before the two regiments on the left were formed in line, the 38th Ala. Regt. was moved to the front and without my knowledge.

The regiment was under heavy fire of artillery and I have since learned that Col Sharpe, Genl Manigault & others urged the importance of a charge at once, saying they could not hold the position much longer. The 38th Ala., led by Maj. Ruffin, charged in a run through an open field about two hundred yards, and occupied the enemy's works, they fleeing before the assaults. The movement was followed almost immediately by the 36th Ala. with similar results. As soon as I discovered that the right was moving to the charge, I ordered forward the other two regiments, but the ground over which they passed being more difficult for movement, the right of the 18th Ala. did not connect with the left of the 36th Ala.

The enemy advanced in our front four pieces of artillery and two caissons, and one team of horses. But just as the two Regiments were advanced to the enemy's works, the forces on the right [Manigault and Sharp] were withdrawn thus exposing the right of Holtzclaw's Brigade to an enfilading fire—and was the cause of the loss of many prisoners in attempting to retire. The two right Regiments held the works they had taken about five minutes, and poured several volleys into the enemy's ranks.

I ordered the Brigade to retire as soon as I learned of the withdrawal of the forces on my right.

I take pleasure in commending generally the good conduct of the Brigade. But I think the dashing and conspicuous gallantry of Col. Herndon and Major Ruffin require at my hands a special commendation.

They inspired their commands with their own enthusiasm, and led them gallantly in the charge. I regret to announce that Maj. Ruffin fell, it is believed mortally wounded, whilst endeavoring to bring off his command in order, but under such a heavy fire that his body fell into the hands of the enemy. He was one of the most zealous, gallant and efficient officers in the Confederate army.

Shortly after withdrawing the Brigade from under fire, their movements were under the immediate supervision of Maj. Genl. Clayton.

I have the honor to be very respectfully, your obedient servant,

BUSH JONES
Colonel, Commanding Brigade

Maj. R. A. Hatcher
Assistant Adjutant-General

Casualties: There were four killed, 47 wounded, 77 missing, for a total of 128 casualties.

[*Cheatham Papers, Tennessee State Library and Archives*]

* * *

Report of Lt. Col. Thomas H. Herndon,
36th Alabama Regiment, Holtzclaw's Brigade,
Battle of Atlanta, July 22, 1864

Headquarters 36th Alabama Infantry
In line in front of Atlanta
July 24, 1864

Captain: I have the honor to make the following report of the part taken by my regiment in the action of the 22d inst. About 4 oclock P.M. I moved out of the breastworks on the east part of Atlanta to a road a few

Lt. Col. Thomas Hoard Herndon

hundred yards in rear and there formed with the 38th Regt on my right and the 18th and 32 & 58 Regt on my left; moved thence by right flank to a point opposite a fort on the second line of entrenchments and then by front to the outer entrenchments. Pausing in them a few minutes under orders from Colonel Jones, commanding the Brigade, my regiment was moved to the front with instructions to keep the sun to my back. Keeping in this direction about 5 o'clock p.m. it entered an open field in sight of a line of breastworks occupied by Manigault's Brigade, from which they had driven the enemy, and halted in an hundred yards of them. Colonel Jones gave the command to change front to east on first battalion. This change was made, throwing the line a few paces [   ] of a thin strip of undergrowth skirting that side of the field fronting toward the north: the whole line was again advanced a few yards & halted my regiment occupying the field with its right resting near a large mansion house. This movement was executed under a galling fire of. . .cannister, & shrapnel which raked the entire field & which continued during the time my regiment remained in that position (about 15 minutes). The men were protected only by laying [   ] to the ground and but one casualty occurred.

Brig Gen. Manigault, or some officer whom I presume represented him, came to the line & saying "there was more danger in remaining in that position than in going forward," ordered an advance. I did not at once order my regiment forward; but seeing the 38th Regt on my right about to move, I gave the order. The men promptly sprang to their feet and went forward with alacrity, passing through the field in the face of a raking fire of. . .canister from six & perhaps more pieces of artillery and not halting or faltering until they reached the works of the enemy. The enemy did not wait to receive them, but fled hastily & in confusion leaving in my front four pieces of artillery and two limbers with one team of four horses. My men poured repeated volleys into them as they fled.

The line occupied by Manigault ran north & south; a short distance to his left it made an angle and ran in a northwesterly course about 300 or 400 yards; with an interval of perhaps an hundred & fifty it took again a northerly course. The 36th & 38th Regts occupied that part of the line which ran in a northwesterly course leaving an interval of 150 or 200 yards between the right of the 38th and the left of Manigault. Upon the approach of the 36 & 38th the enemy abandoned the line on the left, leaving on it two pieces of artillery; but soon discovering that the left of the 36th was unsupported (the 18th & 32 & 58th Regts failing for some cause to connect) they returned to this line and running down a piece of artillery opened upon my left an enfilade fire of. . .canister and a rapid fire of musketry. They at the same time advanced with a line of battle in my front & moving another around to my right occupied the line held by Manigault's Brigade at the time my regiment was ordered in but from which it had withdrawn almost as soon as the 38th Regt had passed its flank.[16]

Thus were the works held by the 36th & 38th Regt flanked on the right & left, compelled by an advancing line of battle subject to a partial cross fire from the [   ]. My regiment, however, remained until the enemy approached within 20 paces of the works when it was withdrawn under orders under a heavy triangular fire, but left in disorder and rallied only at the breastworks. I had no notice or knowledge of Manigault's withdrawal.

My loss was heavy. Lieut. W. H. Gladden, a brave officer was wounded & left in the hands of the enemy. Lieuts. Hutchinson, Britton, Marshall, & Owen are missing. Killed 2; wounded 17; & missing 42. I regret to say that most of the severely wounded fell into the hands of the enemy. I carried into the engagement about 150 guns.

I am satisfied with the conduct of my regiment; and I mention with pride the conduct of Ensign Jos. W. Tillinghast. He bore the colors far to the front, and mounting the breastworks defiantly flaunted them in the faces of the enemy amidst a shower of missiles & did not withdraw until the enemy were within 30 paces & only then upon compulsion. A more gallant & chivalrous man never lifted a Confederate banner to the breeze.

---

[16] Manigault and Sharp withdrew after receiving orders from John C. Brown to abandon the breastworks. Manigault later maintained that he could have held his lodgment. Tower, ed. *A Carolinian Goes to War,* p. 229.

Respectfully, your obedient servant,

THOMAS H. HERNDON
Lt. Col. Commanding

Capt J. H. Dickens
Acting Assistant Adjutant-General, Holtzclaw's Brigade

[*Cheatham Papers, Tennessee State Library and Archives*]

*   *   *

Report of 1st. Lt. John C. Dumas, 38th Alabama Infantry,
Battle of Atlanta, July 22, 1864

Headquarters, 38th Regiment Alabama Infantry
July 25, 1864

Captain, I have the honor respectfully to make the following report of the part taken by the 38th Reg in the action of the 22d inst. The Regiment was commanded by Maj Shep Ruffin and carried 108 guns. Its movements up to the time it went into the action were under your eyes and are known to you.[17] As [the regiment] passed through the edge of an old field it found itself confronting a line of heavy breastworks with a dwelling house directly in front and advanced on the works and Manigault's Brigade occupying the works on the right. At this point a very heavy fire of. . .canister, and shrapnel opened upon us and the regiment was ordered to lie down for protection. In this position Lieut James P. Agee of Co B was severely wounded and several men. Remaining here a few minutes the regiment as directed formed & making a half wheel to

---

[17] Part of Dumas' report is cross-written (written on top of an old letter or report in the opposite direction from the first writing) and is very hard to read. This was commonly done by the Confederates to conserve paper.

the right charged the works driving the enemy from them and from a Battery of four guns. It held the works until flanked on the right by the enemy and ordered to fall back when the men finding that they were fired on from both flanks broke & retreated in disorder. Previously to leaving the works Maj Ruffin finding that the works could not be held and ordered the men to kill the horses of the Battery which was done.

In leaving the works Maj. Ruffin was shot down having displayed throughout great gallantry and heroic courage & coolness. Acting Sergt Major Chas R. Wilson having acted with distinguished gallantry in the action was also shot down. Acting Ensign John Raiford carried the colors to the front and planted them in the enemy works.

The Regiment acted well until almost cut off when it became necessary for each man to take care of himself or be captured. For the casualties of the regiment [smudged word] refer to the official report already sent to Headquarters. [18] Respectfully,

JOHN C. DUMAS
Ist Lt., Company K, 38th Alabama Regiment

Captain J. H. Pickens
Acting Assistant Adjutant-General, Holtzclaw's Brigade

Memorandum
[There were] 108 muskets in action; no officers killed, enlisted men: killed, one; wounded, 11; missing, 33 [Total: 45]

[*Cheatham Papers, Tennessee State Library and Archives*]

*   *   *

[18] Whether Dumas refers to the report of Colonel Jones or to a another report, now lost, is unclear. It is possible that he refers to the memorandum included herein.

Report of Lt. Col. Peter F. Hunley, 18th Alabama Infantry,
Battle of Atlanta, July 22, 1864

Headquarters 18th Alabama Volunteers
July 26, 1864

Captain: I have the honor to make the following report of the part taken by the 18th Ala. Regt in the engagement of the 22nd. The Regiment went into action with two hundred and fifty five guns and nine line officers. The Regiment was under fire for nearly an hour and lost two (2) officers wounded, one man killed; thirteen wounded and 1 man thought captured and two missing.

I am, Captain, very respectfully your obedient servant,

P.[ETER] F. HUNLEY
Colonel, 18th Alabama Regiment

Captain [J. H.] Pickens
Acting Assistant Adjutant-General, Holtzclaw's Brigade

[*Cheatham Papers, Tennessee State Library and Archives*]

* * *

Volume One

A Reassessment of Confederate Command Options During the Winter of 1863-1864, by Steven E. Woodworth

...The Heavens and Earth had Suddenly Come Together":
The Battle of Peachtree Creek, by Albert Castel

A Reappraisal of the Generalship of John Bell Hood in the Battles for Atlanta, by Stephen Davis

*Feeding Sherman's Army: Union Logistics in the Campaign
for Atlanta,* by James J. Cooke

*Is it Surrender or Fight? The Battle of Allatoona
October 5, 1864,* by Phil Gottschalk

*The Flash of Their Guns was a Sure Guide: The 19th Michigan
Infantry in the Atlanta Campaign,* by Terry L. Jones

Lines of Battle: Major General William B. Bate's Partial Reports of the Atlanta Campaign, by Zack C. Waters

Volume Two

A Policy So Disastrous: Joseph E. Johnston's Atlanta Campaign, by Richard M. McMurry

Sherman's Pioneers in
the Campaign to Atlanta, by Philip Shiman

Waltz Between the Rivers: An Overview of the Atlanta Campaign
from the Oostanaula to the Etowah, by William R. Scaife

Windows in Time: Dalton to Cartersville,
A Photographic Essay, by William E. Erquitt

*The Western & Atlantic Railroad in
the Campaign for Atlanta*, by James G. Bogle

*The Forgotten "Hell Hole": The Battle
of Pickett's Mill, May 27, 1864*, Jeffrey Dean

*Atlanta to Savannah: A Sociological Perspective of
William T. Sherman's March Through Georgia*, by Charles E. Vetter

Lines of Battle: The Unpublished Reports of Confederate Brig. Gen. James Holtzclaw's Brigade, by Zack C. Waters

ADDITIONAL NOTES

INDEX

CONTRIBUTORS

RICHARD M. McMURRY

A Policy So Disastrous:
Joseph E. Johnston's Atlanta Campaign

Noted author Richard McMurry has written widely on the Civil War in the West, and is a favorite on the Civil War speaking circuit. McMurry is the author of *John Bell Hood and the War for Southern Independence* (Lexington, 1982), the winner of the 1982 Mrs. Simon Baruch University Award of the United Daughters of the Confederacy, and *Two Great Rebel Armies: An Essay in Confederate Military History* (Chapel Hill, 1989). He currently makes his home in Decatur, Georgia.

PHILIP SHIMAN

Sherman's Pioneers in the Campaign to Atlanta

Mr. Shiman earned his B.A. degree at Yale University and recently received his Ph.D in military history from Duke University. His disertation, *Engineering Sherman's March: Army Engineers and the Management of Modern War, 1862-1865*, won the American Blue and Gray Association's 1992 Evelyn and Lee Combs dissertation prize, and will be published by Louisiana State University Press. In addition to an ongoing investigation of the role of Civil War engineers, Mr. Shiman is currently conducting research into the history of computing.

WILLIAM R. SCAIFE

Waltz Between the Rivers: An Overview of the
Atlanta Campaign from the Oostanaula to the Etowah

Bill Scaife is an Atlanta architect and engineer, a graduate of Georgia Tech, and a veteran of the 82nd Airborne Division. Scaife is a past president of the Atlanta Civil War Round Table, a director of the Kennesaw Mountain Historical Association, and the author of several books on various Civil War topics, including *The Campaign for Atlanta* (Atlanta, 1985) and *March to the Sea* (Atlanta, 1989).

Scaife is a leading proponent of the premise that an intelligent understanding and interpretation of the *Official Records* and other firsthand sources requires a thorough knowledge of the battlefields, wartime landmarks, and military ground evidence available only in the field. He utilizes his experience as a civil engineer and cartographer to prepare composite maps on which critical wartime landmarks are superimposed over U.S. Geological Survey topograhical maps for use both in interpreting primary source material and as a basis for preparing the detailed maps which appear in his publications and which, indeed, have become his trademark.

WILLIAM E. ERQUITT

Windows in Time:
Dalton to Cartersville, A Photographic Essay

Bill Erquitt, a native of Atlanta, Georgia, is the current president of the Atlanta Civil War Round Table. He is the author of several articles on the 1864 war in Georgia. Erquitt co-authored, with William R. Scaife, *The Chattahoochee River Line: An American Maginot* (Atlanta, 1992).

JAMES G. BOGLE

The Western & Atlantic Railroad
in the Campaign for Atlanta

Colonel Bogle, a retired U.S. Army career officer, is a native of Tennessee and longtime resident of Atlanta. His interest in the Civil War and railroad history began at an early age. He has focused these dual interests within Georgia and Tennessee, with special attention to the Western & Atlantic Railroad. The "Great Locomotive Chase," or Andrews' Raid, has been the subject of study by Colonel Bogle for more than sixty years. His is the author of "The Great Locomotive Chase," which appeared in the July, 1987 issue of *Blue & Gray Magazine*, and has also written for *Atlanta History Bulletin*, *Railroad Magazine*, *Railroad History*, *Georgia Magazine*, and *The Landmarker* (Cobb County, GA).

———

JEFFREY DEAN

The Forgotten "Hell Hole":
The Battle of Pickett's Mill, May 27, 1864

Mr. Dean earned his B.A. degree in history from Emory University in Atlanta. From 1984-1992 he served as manager of the Pickett's Mill State Historic Site. In the six years prior to the site's opening to the general public, Mr. Dean was responsible for the development and creation of the trail network and trail guides, and his extensive on-site surveys and research laid the groundwork for base maps, exhibit plans, and all other aspects of site interpretation. Jeff is presently conducting research on the Battle of New Hope Church and other aspects of the Dallas Line for future volumes in this series.

———

CHARLES EDMUND VETTER

Atlanta to Savannah: A Sociological Perspective of
William T. Sherman's March Through Georgia

Eddie Vetter is a sociology professor at Centenary College in Shreveport, Louisiana. He is president of the North Louisiana Civil War Round Table, and the author of numerous articles, including the feature article in Volume Four, No. 1 of *Civil War Regiments*, a special Spring 1994 Red River Campaign issue. Vetter's first full-length work on a Civil War title, *Sherman: Merchant of Terror, Advocate of Peace,* was released in 1992 by Pelican Press.

―――――――

ZACK C. WATERS

Lines of Battle: Confederate Brig. Gen. James Holtzclaw's
Unpublished Battle of Atlanta Reports

Mr. Waters, a fifth generation native of Florida, holds a Juris Doctorate from Memphis State University and is now an English teacher at Rome Middle School in Rome, Georgia. He has published several articles on various aspects of the Civil War and is currently conducting research for a book that will examine the role of Florida's contingent in the Army of Tennessee. Mr. Waters' article *The Florida Brigade at the Battle of Cold Harbor* appeared in Volume Three, No. 4 of *Civil War Regiments*.

―――――――